CO

The
Software Business
in Canada

GEORGE TAKACH

The
Software Business
in Canada

GEORGE TAKACH

Foreword by

MICHAEL COWPLAND
President and CEO of Corel Corporation

McGraw-Hill Ryerson Limited
Toronto, Montréal, New York, Auckland, Bogotá,
Caracas, Lisbon, London, Madrid, Mexico, Milan,
New Delhi, San Juan, Singapore, Sydney, Tokyo

The Software Business in Canada:
Financing, Protecting, and Marketing Software

Copyright © 1992, 1997 by George S. Takach.

"Income tax and GST Considerations for Software Companies"
© 1992, 1997 Karen Wensley and Irene J. David

"Raising Money for Growing Software Companies" © 1989, 1992, 1997 Software Ontario. This chapter, an earlier version of which first appeared in *Business for Software Developers* (published by Software Ontario), is reprinted with the kind permission of Software Ontario.

"Protecting Intellectual Property Rights in Computer Products and Related Technology" © 1992, 1997 Barry B. Sookman

Care has been taken to trace ownership of copyright material contained in this text. However, the publishers welcome any information that will enable them to rectify any reference or credit in subsequent editions.

McGraw-Hill Ryerson Limited
300 Water Street
Whitby, Ontario L1N 9B6

1 2 3 4 5 6 7 8 9 0 TRI 6 5 4 3 2 1 0 9 8 7

Canadian Cataloguing in Publication Data
Takach, George S. (George Steven)

   The software business in Canada: financing, protecting, and marketing software
2nd ed.

Previous ed. published under title: The software business: funding, protecting, and marketing software.
Includes index.
ISBN 0-07-552605-0 (bound)   ISBN 0-07-552770-7 (pbk.)

1. Computer software industry - Law and legislation - Canada. 2. Computer software - Law and legislation - Canada. I. Title. II. Title: The software business

HD9696.C63C38344 1996   343.71'0780053   C96-931069-2

Publisher: **Joan Homewood**
Editor: **Erin Moore**
Production Coordinator: **Sharon Hudson**
Cover Design: **Orpin Graphic Services Inc.**
Interior Design/Composition: **Pages Design**
Editorial Services: **Allyson May**

This book was composed in Palatino and Helvetica fonts using QuarkXPress 3.31.

Printed and bound in Canada by Tri-Graphic Printing (Ottawa) Ltd. using acid-free and recycled paper.

CONTENTS

ACRONYMS

ACL	Area Control List
BDBC	Business Development Bank of Canada
CAAST	Canadian Alliance Against Software Theft
CBCA	Canadian Business Corporations Act
CICA	Canadian Institute of Chartered Accountants
COBOL	Common Business-Oriented Language
COIN	Computerized Ontario Investment Network
CRS	Computerized Reservation System
DND	Department of National Defence
DSS	Department of Supply and Services
ECL	Export Control List
EDL	Event Driven Language
EIPA	Export and Import Permits Act
FAITC	Foreign Affairs and International Trade Canada
GATT	General Agreement on Trade and Tariffs
GST	Goods and Services Tax
IPO	Initial Public Offering
IRAP	Industrial Research Assistance Program
MSDP	Microelectronics and Systems Development Program
NAFTA	North American Free Trade Agreement
NATO	North Atlantic Treaty Organization
OBCA	Business Corporations Act (Ontario)
OECD	Organization for Economic Co-operation and Development
OTC	Over-the-Counter
PEMD	Program for Export Market Development
PRC	Procurement Review Committee
RAM	Random Access Memory
R&D	Research and Development
RCMP	Royal Canadian Mounted Police
ROM	Read Only Memory
RRSP	Registered Retirement Savings Plan
SBDC	Small Business Development Corporation
SSO	Structure, Sequence, and Organization
UCC	Universal Copyright Convention
WIPO	World Intellectual Property Organization

FOREWORD

By Michael C.J. Cowpland, Founder, President and CEO of Corel Corporation

This book is a lot like Corel's software — easy to use, great for first time users but also valuable for seasoned veterans. And by addressing tax, financing and legal issues, this book resembles a Corel suite of products — it covers a range of topics in a coordinated, organized manner. The result is exceptional value to the user, a powerful tool for people involved with software companies.

The range of people who will benefit from the clear-headed, common sense advice in this book — like the user community of Corel products — is wide indeed. The start-up entrepreneur. The owner-manager of a growing technology company. Officers, directors and employees of small and large software companies alike. Investors and lenders to these businesses. And their professional advisors, the lawyers, accountants, tax advisors, consultants and others who provide valuable support to these businesses.

George Takach and the other contributors to this book understand the software business. They have witnessed the challenges, problems and pitfalls facing growing and more mature software companies through their work with literally scores of these businesses. They have distilled this experience and communicated it in this book as very helpful practical advice and in a style that is clear, concise and easy to understand.

Corel is a Canadian success story. We have grown to become the world's second largest pc-applications software company. We see a bright future for Canadian software entrepreneurship. This book will help many of Canada's new, as well as more established, software players succeed in the Canadian and global marketplace.

Michael C.J. Cowpland
Ottawa
September, 1996

x

PREFACE TO THE SECOND EDITION

Like good software, a reference book needs to be updated periodically. This is particularly true in the case of a book on the software business. Since the first edition of this work appeared four years ago, there have been a number of legal developments affecting software companies, as well as changes in the areas of tax and financing. These changes are reflected in this second edition of *The Software Business.*

There have also been several important new developments in the software industry. The increasing importance of multimedia titles, currently marketed primarily in a CD-ROM format, represents the fusion of the software and entertainment industries. And of course we have recently witnessed the meteoric rise in importance of the INTERNET and other network-related systems. A discussion of multimedia and INTERNET issues has therefore been added.

This edition of *The Software Business* will probably not be the last. The updating process for a text, like the upgrading exercise for superior software, should strive to reflect the particular concerns and issues relevant to its users, namely, the readers of the book. Accordingly, I would be obliged if those of you with thoughts for new topics or other comments or suggestions would jot these down and mail or fax them to me, or send them to me over the INTERNET. You can reach me at the following:

McCarthy Tétrault
Suite 4700
Toronto Dominion Bank Tower
Toronto-Dominion Centre
Toronto, Ontario M5K 1E6
Tel: (416) 601-7662/362-1812
Fax: (416) 868-1891/868-0673
INTERNET: gtakach@mccarthy.ca

I look forward to hearing from you.

George S. Takach
Toronto, June, 1996

INTRODUCTION

This book is intended to serve as a practical guide to the key legal, contracting, tax, and financing issues facing software companies. The primary readers of the book will be owners and managers of companies that develop, distribute, and support software products, as well as entrepreneurs who wish to enter the software business. Bankers, venture capitalists, and other lenders to and investors in computer companies, and government officials charged with helping this sector of the economy, will find the book useful as well. It will also be of interest to the vast number of users of software, particularly those companies and other organizations whose information systems groups, in addition to operating computers, are developing software programs that could be marketed to other companies or organizations.

While the focus of the book is the software business, readers involved in the production and distribution of multimedia products, as well as providers of INTERNET-related and other on-line information services, will also find the book relevant. In essence, "software" can be said to include a wide range of content and information-based assets. What the software and these other businesses have in common is that their primary assets are intangible, giving rise to unique and often difficult challenges. The objective of the book is to help people in these knowledge-based industries understand and successfully meet these challenges.

The book is divided into three parts, each dealing with an important aspect of software companies. Part I, Financing the Software Business, begins with a discussion of certain significant legal issues relevant to the operation of a software company, including general corporate matters, such as the personal liabilities of the directors of a software company, as well as questions unique to the software business, such as how to guard against some common risks when buying a software company. Karen Wensley and Irene J. David, tax practitioners at Ernst & Young, then provide a concise but effective overview of the principal income tax and Goods and Services Tax considerations relevant to software businesses.

Finding adequate capital is an on-going challenge — some would say an obsession — for software businesses. In Chapter 3 Linda Willis of Allelix Pharmaceuticals Inc. (and formerly of Yorkton Securities) sheds extremely helpful light on this area by analyzing the various sources of funds available and the costs and benefits associated with each. Part I concludes with a brief discussion of some legal aspects of strategic partnering, a practice heralded as an important mechanism for software companies to fund their research and development and to attain other critical objectives.

Barry Sookman, a lawyer specializing in high-technology matters at the law firm of McCarthy Tétrault, leads off Part II, Protecting Software, by discussing in Chapter 5 how software and related assets can be the subject of protection under the intellectual property laws relating to trade secrets, copyrights, and patents.

Chapter 6 reviews briefly those provisions in Canada's criminal law that may be used by software companies and users of software to safeguard their critical computer software and other information-based resources. How a software company might implement a number of different protection policies and procedures is the subject of Chapter 7. Completing Part II is a discussion of the types of contractual measures that software companies should have in place with their employees and independent contractors (such as consultants and contract programmers) in order to best protect the interests of the software firm.

When marketing, promoting, and selling software products, care must be taken not to run afoul of Canada's *Competition Act*; the first chapter of Part III, Marketing Software, is intended to help software company personnel succeed in this objective. Then Chapter 10 explains some key aspects of dealing with the federal government on export control matters and government procurement tenders for high technology products. The book ends with three chapters on agreements that software companies regularly enter into with customers and distributors.

These are all important subjects for the software company. They can present numerous pitfalls for the unwary; falling into any one such trap can cost the software company dearly. It is extremely unfortunate when a software company makes one of the expensive mistakes described in this book, in part because, with a little advance planning and the institution of some basic protective measures, the error (and subsequent loss) can likely be avoided altogether, or at least the extent of the damage may be reduced significantly.

The book is not, of course, a substitute for professional legal, tax, or similar advice. Readers who have particular legal, tax, or other questions, or who require appropriate language for inclusion in a specific contract, or who are in need of tax advice for a particular situation, should consult a lawyer, accountant, or some other relevant professional. It is only through such personal contact with a professional advisor that specific circumstances can be addressed. As well, the law itself, particularly in the tax area, but in other areas also, is continually evolving, and many if not most of the legal and tax rules discussed in this book will change over time. It is therefore only through live professional advice that the reader can be sure of being informed of the most current legal rules affecting his or her particular case. Accordingly, this book does not aim at replacing live professional assistance; rather, its objective is to provide general information which can then be applied to particular circumstances with the help of competent legal counsel or others.

The software industry represents Canada's best hope for participating in a meaningful way in, and reaping part of the economic benefits of, the global information-technology revolution. Canada has all the factors that make for a successful software community: several first-rank universities involved with computer science and related fields, a high quality of life, and a large group of bright people interested in software, multimedia, INTERNET and related technologies. It is hoped that this book can help software suppliers in Canada to achieve the greatest possible success, both domestically and abroad, by highlighting the important legal, contracting, tax, and financing issues that participants in the software business must be aware of if their technological assets are to become successful and lucrative products.

Contributors

Irene J. David, a partner with Ernst & Young, directs Ernst & Young's Toronto Commodity Tax Practice. A 1976 graduate of Queen's University, she worked for Revenue Canada, Customs and Excise, before joining Ernst & Young in 1980. Since then, she has advised clients on all areas of commodity taxes including federal and provincial sales taxes and customs duty. More recently, she has been actively involved in assisting clients with issues related to the GST. Ms David has given many presentations and speeches, both on the current commodity tax rules and on sales-tax reform, to a variety of audiences from all sectors of business. She is a co-editor of *The Complete Guide to the GST*, published by the Canadian Institute of Chartered Accountants (CICA) and is a contributing editor to a number of sectoral guides on GST. She can be reached at "davidi@ey.geis.com".

Barry B. Sookman, a partner in the law firm McCarthy Tétrault, practices computer/technology law in Toronto. He is one of Canada's foremost authorities in the area of computer law and is the author of *Sookman Computer Law: Acquiring and Protecting Information Technology*, published and updated by Carswell (1989-1996). Mr. Sookman's experience extends to the commercial, intellectual property, and litigation aspects of computer and high technology law, including licensing transactions, financings, distribution agreements and high-technology procurements. He can be reached at "bsookman@mccarthy.ca".

George S. Takach, a partner at McCarthy Tétrault in Toronto, is the author of *Contracting for Computers*, published by McGraw-Hill Ryerson (1989), now in its second edition (1992). He practices corporate/commercial law with an emphasis on technology, computers, and related matters. Mr. Takach regularly represents software developers and hardware vendors, assisting them with licensing, distribution, and related intellectual property issues, as well as with general corporate matters such as equity and bank financings. He also assists suppliers and purchasers of computing resources with the negotiation and drafting of various computer contracts. Mr. Takach teaches computer law at Osgoode Hall Law School, York University. He can be reached at "gtakach@mccarthy.ca".

Karen Wensley is a tax partner at Ernst & Young in Toronto. She specializes in providing taxation and other business advice to entrepreneurs, with a particular focus on high-technology companies. Ms Wensley is a director of the Information Technology Association of Canada (ITAC) and is a frequent speaker at software industry association meetings on tax and financing issues. Her practice includes structuring and financing software companies as well as preparing and defending their research and development tax credit claims. She can be reached at "wensleyk@ey.geis.com".

Linda L. Willis is chief financial officer at Allelix Pharmaceuticals Inc., a leading Canadian bio-technology company. Before joining Allelix, Ms. Willis was a vice-president at Yorkton Securities and, earlier, a vice-president of Canadian Pension Equity Corporation, the equity investment arm of Canadian Corporate Funding Limited. Before joining CCFL, Ms Willis was a partner in the National High Technology Services Group of Ernst & Young, where she specialized in financing advice to high-technology and other entrepreneurial growth businesses.

PART

I

Financing the Software Business

1

Some Legal Aspects of Operating the Software Business

There are several legal arrangements that may be used to carry on a software business. The most common is the corporation, but other vehicles include sole proprietorship, partnership, limited partnership, and joint venture. This chapter discusses the major legal aspects of each of these arrangements. It should be noted that the general income tax rules related to each of these vehicles, which can often be critical in determining which one to choose for a particular objective, are discussed in Chapter 2, and therefore these two chapters should be read in conjunction. Also addressed here are the more important legal questions raised by the agreements entered into between a software business and its lenders and investors, be they banks, venture capitalists or other providers of funds. The chapter concludes with a discussion of several significant legal matters germane to the purchase and sale of a software business, and of specific software assets, such as the intellectual property rights in a computer program and the business related to such program.

THE CORPORATION

The corporation with share capital is the entity most often used to carry on a software business, as well as most other commercial activities in Canada. This type of corporation (as distinct from the "nonshare capital corporation," which has members and is typically used as the legal vehicle for nonprofit organizations) can be established in Canada under federal law (the *Canada Business Corporations Act*) or under one of the provincial business corporations statutes. Whichever jurisdiction is chosen, the major characteristics of such a corporation are roughly the same, though there can be some reasons for choosing to incorporate a company under a particular business corporations statute, as noted below.

The essential legal structure of the corporation is as follows. The corporation issues shares, or ownership interests, to individuals or corporations or other entities, who thus become shareholders. The shareholders then elect the directors, who are responsible for supervising the general management of the corporation. The directors in turn appoint the officers, such as the president, one or more vice-presidents, and a secretary (and possibly others), who are responsible for the day-to-day operation of the corporation. The number of shareholders, directors, and officers will vary from company to company; a start-up software company may begin with a single founder who is the sole shareholder, director, and officer, while a mature software business may have a large number of shareholders, a board of five to ten (or more) directors, and perhaps six to eight or more officers.

The corporation, unlike a sole proprietorship or a partnership, is a legal entity separate from its owners, the shareholders. The shareholders do not directly own the property of the corporation (though this property can be distributed to the shareholders under certain conditions), and the rights and liabilities of the corporation are not those of the shareholders. For example, if a shareholder invests $100,000 in a software company by buying shares totalling this price, and if the company incurs debts in excess of $100,000 and then goes bankrupt, the shareholder would, generally speaking, have at risk only the $100,000 invested in the company; the creditors of the corporation would not, in most circumstances, be able to recover additional monies from the shareholder. This principle of limited liability is subject to certain important qualifications (such as the personal liabilities of directors and officers discussed immediately below and the personal guarantees often required by lenders from the principals of the company discussed below under "Agreements with Lenders"), which are extremely relevant to the persons operating or owning a software company. In certain limited circumstances a court will also "pierce the corporate veil" by allowing creditors or others to reach behind the corporate entity in order to visit liability on the directors and officers or shareholders of the corporation.

Notwithstanding these qualifications, the principle of limited liability makes the corporation very attractive as the mechanism by which a software business is operated. A software company, even a small one, can accumulate significant financial, contractual, legal, and other liabilities, and the owners of such a business should do whatever possible to shield themselves from directly incurring such risks. Thus, the corporate vehicle is usually chosen over the sole proprietorship and partnership options (both of which make the owners of the business directly responsible for the liabilities of the business), even if there may be some tax advantages to these latter two arrangements in certain circumstances. Indeed, many individuals who operate consulting businesses in the software sector as sole proprietorships or partnerships should seriously consider incorporating their businesses in order to take advantage of the principle of limited liability.

PERSONAL LIABILITY OF DIRECTORS AND OFFICERS

One significant exception to the rule of limited liability is the personal liability that directors and officers (but not shareholders) have under certain laws. There are two important laws providing for personal liability for directors and officers of software (and other) companies:

- Under Ontario's *Business Corporations Act* (and under similar statutes in the other provinces, and under the federal business corporations law as well), directors are personally liable for up to six months' unpaid wages of employees, including vacation pay, if the corporation becomes bankrupt or insolvent and cannot satisfy such wage and vacation pay claims.

- Under the federal *Income Tax Act*, directors are personally responsible for ensuring the proper remittance of source deductions for employee income taxes, and failure of a corporation to remit such deductions would make the directors liable to Revenue Canada for such amounts. Similar rules apply for the Canada Pension Plan and unemployment insurance and under provincial tax statutes, as well as under several other federal and provincial tax and related laws.

Certain other laws quite relevant to software companies, such as Canada's competition law (discussed in Chapter 9) and the *Copyright Act* (discussed in Chapter 5), also make directors and officers personally liable for certain matters or wrongdoings of the corporation. For example, in the *Prism* case, a software copyright infringement case discussed in Chapter 5, a company *and one of its employees* were found liable for copyright infringement. Accordingly, an individual who is about to become a director or officer of a company should review with a lawyer what types of personal liabilities the individual will be exposed to, given the actual or planned activities of the company in question.

Rules regarding the personal liabilities of directors and officers for wages and source deductions make it imperative that individuals who serve as directors and officers of a software company monitor the operations of the company to ensure that all employee wages are paid promptly and that the precise amount of source deductions for income tax, pension, and similar amounts are in fact deducted and remitted regularly to the relevant government authority. This is particularly important for the outside director, such as a nominee of a bank or a venture capital investor, who sits on a company's board of directors in order to monitor the particular loan or investment. This individual is not usually aware of the day-to-day management decisions of the officers of the company. If the software company hits a difficult period — and most do at some point, given the volatility of the industry — with the result that its cash flow is severely squeezed, there may be a temptation not to remit required source deductions for employees, but rather to use these funds for other purposes (such as paying a supplier of goods that is threatening legal action over an unpaid bill). Similarly, if the company also sells hardware items or other products for which it collects sales tax, it may be tempted to fail to remit this tax during a cash flow crunch. Such action is quite illegal and could expose the company and the employee to serious legal liability. In sum, the outside director (and the other directors and officers) have to ensure that the software company does not succumb to these temptations.

It should be noted that the corporation can indemnify a director and officer in respect of certain personal liabilities, but this indemnity may not be worth much if the corporation, at the time the director or officer claims under the indemnity, is bankrupt or insolvent. Accordingly, if the software company is a Canadian subsidiary of a foreign corporation, or if one or more shareholders of the company are wealthy individuals or solvent corporations, it is quite common for the directors and officers of the software company to request an indemnity from such individual or corporation. It is also worth exploring, especially if no such indemnity is available, whether directors' and officers' liability insurance is available for the particular software company on reasonable terms. It should also be noted that the potential of personal liability for directors and officers often leads investors in a software company, who would otherwise be entitled to appoint a director to the board of the software company, to have an arrangement whereby the investor can merely have a nonvoting observer attend all meetings of the board of directors.

CHOICE OF JURISDICTION

As noted above, a corporation may be incorporated under federal law or under a business corporations statute of one of the provinces. This means, in effect, that an individual contemplating starting up a software company usually has to choose between using a federal corporation or one incorporated under the law of the province in which the individual resides. For instance, someone in one of the high-technology regions in and around Toronto, Kitchener-Waterloo or Ottawa can opt for incorporating under the *Canada Business Corporations Act* (CBCA) or Ontario's *Business Corporations Act* (OBCA).

While the CBCA and the OBCA are substantially similar, there are certain differences between the two as well as certain other considerations that may be relevant in determining in which jurisdiction to incorporate. For example, there are significant differences in disclosure requirements. Under the CBCA, a corporation is required to submit to the government its annual financial statements, whereupon the statements are available to the public, if the corporation and its affiliates, including foreign corporations, have revenues or assets in excess of stated thresholds. Exemptions from this filing requirement are available in certain circumstances, but they are granted only for limited periods and must be reapplied for on an on-going basis. By contrast, under the OBCA, a corporation need only file public financial statements if its securities are offered to the public (such as when they are listed on a stock exchange or otherwise freely tradeable by investors). It is for this reason that most individuals in Ontario who hope their new software companies will grow to be sizeable businesses (and which entrepreneur doesn't hope for this!) incorporate under the OBCA rather than the CBCA.

Another advantage of the OBCA is that while both the OBCA and CBCA require that a majority of a corporation's directors be "resident Canadians," under the OBCA there is an exception to this rule when the corporation has only two directors. In this case only one of them need be a resident of Canada. This is an attractive feature for foreign software companies establishing subsidiaries in Canada. It means that the OBCA subsidiary can have one director from outside Canada (typically the officer of the parent company responsible for international operations) and one director (instead of two, as would be required under the CBCA) from Canada (typically the president of the Canadian operation — assuming this person is a "resident Canadian" as defined in the OBCA, which is not always the case). The Canadian entrepreneur also can find this feature of the OBCA useful if the board of the new company will consist of only two members, and the Canadian entrepreneur wants, for example, an American or a European to join the board.

Where the software company has offices or otherwise carries on business in more than one province, it is often thought that a CBCA incorporation provides some advantage, because it does not require the additional effort or expense of registering in each province. If only this were true. In fact, a company with its existing office in Ontario, for example, would have to register locally in British Columbia regardless of whether it was incorporated under the OBCA or the CBCA if it opened an office in Vancouver.

It should be noted that, generally speaking, a corporation can change jurisdictions within Canada with relative ease. Thus, if a software company finds that the law under which it was incorporated is no longer sufficiently attractive or flexible, then it is likely able to transfer itself to another, more accommodating jurisdiction. This can usually be done without the company experiencing any adverse tax consequences.

CHOOSING A CORPORATE NAME

Under both the CBCA and the OBCA each corporation is given a corporation number upon incorporation. This number may be used as the name of the corporation, such as "923733 Ontario Limited," in which case the corporation is said to have a "number name." Most shareholders, however, prefer to give their companies corporate names which, by law, must end with one of the following legal designations, or contractions thereof: Limited (Ltd.), Incorporated (Inc.), or Corporation (Corp.). Many Canadian software companies planning on making sales into the U.S. use the "Inc." legal designation because it is considered to be more common in the U.S. than "Limited" or "Corporation."

As for the words chosen to precede the legal designation, some thought should be given to using words, or at least one of several words, that are as distinctive as possible. "Canadian Software Sales Inc." is not a very strong corporate name, and it would be more difficult to build up substantial goodwill in such a name than if a name like "Xyxix Software Inc." were used. The more coined, and the less descriptive, the name is, the better. Moreover, each proposed corporate name is compared by the government with all other existing corporate names on a large corporate name database. If the proposed name is identical to or too closely resembles an existing name, the government will not permit the new name to be used. This is an important threshold reason for choosing a unique name.

Once a corporation is incorporated, it must put its full corporate name (including the legal designation) on its contracts, invoices, and other official documents. It can, however, in its marketing material and advertisements, call itself by a name other than its full corporate name (such as "Xyxix" alone, to use the above example), provided it registers this trading name with the government (this allows someone to look up the trading name in a government registry to determine which company is behind it, a useful thing to be able to do if, for example, somebody was run over by a delivery truck and all that the injured party could see on the side of the truck was the trading style of the company). It should be noted that sole proprietors and partnerships also have to register their business names with the government.

SHAREHOLDERS' AGREEMENTS

Most Canadian software companies have more than one shareholder but the shares of the company are not usually traded on a stock exchange or otherwise publicly tradeable. A typical medium-sized software company might have five or so individual shareholders, each of whom is also a director and officer of the company. Depending on how the company is financed, it may also have one or two shareholders who are venture capitalists or other investors. All of these shareholders should enter into an agreement among themselves that would stipulate, among other things, what rules would apply if one or more shareholders should desire to sell its shares in the company. These are important issues that, if not dealt with in a shareholders' agreement, could lead to serious problems or misunderstandings, or even a paralyzing deadlock, among the shareholders.

As a result, shareholders' agreements are very common among the shareholders of software (and other) companies while they are still private companies (that is, their shares are not offered to the public). Set out below are the kinds of provisions typically found in a shareholders' agreement of a software company:

- *Board of directors.* The agreement sets out which shareholders (perhaps all of them) are entitled to appoint nominees to the board of directors. If one shareholder owns 50% plus one (or some other significant percentage) of the shares, the provision may also allow this shareholder to appoint a majority of the board, at least for as long as this shareholder continues to hold such large percentage of the shares.

- *Shareholder approval of certain matters.* One or more shareholders, typically those owning a significant percentage of the shares, or perhaps a venture capitalist investor, may require that, regardless of the composition of the board of directors, certain actions of the company (such as paying a dividend or selling the intellectual property rights in a particular software product) will require the approval of one or two key shareholders or at least those shareholders who hold, in the aggregate, a certain (usually high) percentage of the shares.

- *Preemptive rights/anti-dilution.* All shareholders are entitled to buy, on a pro-rata basis, additional shares proposed to be issued by the company before outside investors are offered such shares. This permits the shareholders to avoid being "diluted" by allowing them to maintain their same percentage ownership interest in the company. Such a provision may be made not to apply to the issuance of a specific number of shares to certain employees of the software company under an employee stock-option plan; as discussed in greater detail below, such a program is often useful to provide an incentive structure for key employees.

- *Additional funding.* The agreement might contain a provision that requires one or more shareholders, such as a venture capital firm, to invest additional funds in the company, particularly if certain performance targets, measured in terms of sales, profits, shipment of a new release of software, etc., are met by the company. On the other hand, the agreement may grant an option to such an investor that allows it to purchase additional shares without the company having to offer shares to any other shareholder, in order that the investor can increase its percentage ownership of the company. A word of caution for such options. If the option allows the investor to acquire a number of shares that, when added to its existing shares, results in the investor holding more than 50% of all the shares, then the company will lose its CCPC (Canadian-controlled private company) tax status if the investor is a public company or a nonresident of Canada (or is owned, ultimately, by a public company or a foreign company, whether public or private). Losing CCPC tax status can have significant adverse consequences for a Canadian software company, as explained in Chapter 2.

- *Right of first refusal.* A shareholder who receives an offer for the purchase of his or her shares must first offer such shares to the other shareholders at the same price as contained in the offer. This allows existing shareholders to keep out new investors, as long as they are willing to buy out the shareholder who wishes to leave.

- *Piggyback rights.* Where a shareholder proposes to sell shares, the other shareholders may participate in such sale on a pro-rata basis, even if this means the shareholder who secured the initial offer does not sell as many of his shares as originally anticipated.

- *Drag-along rights.* If an offer is received for 100% of the shares, and if those shareholders who hold, in the aggregate, a certain percentage of shares (say 66%, but it can be higher or lower) accept such offer, the remaining shareholders must also accept such offer to sell their shares, or they can buy out the majority at the same price as is provided in the initial offer. This is an important provision because many potential buyers of a software company will be interested in purchasing it only if they can buy 100% of its shares; they do not want to buy a minority interest, nor do they wish to buy a majority of the shares and have an on-going minority shareholding that they cannot control. Thus, the shareholders should have some fair mechanism whereby all the shares can be sold, and a drag-along provision usually serves this purpose.

- *Demand registration rights.* This provision would give a holder of a large percentage of the shares, typically a venture capital or other investor, the ability to require the company to go through the process of having its shares become publicly tradeable, typically by obtaining a listing on a stock exchange (more on this process, called an "IPO" (initial public offering) in Chapter 3). Moreover, the provision would also permit the shareholder to sell a certain percentage of its shares upon the closing of the IPO. Other shareholders might be permitted to participate in such a right as well, thereby providing an avenue for shareholders to achieve some liquidity for their shares.

- *Put/call.* Any shareholder may make an offer to all other shareholders to purchase all their shares, which offer must also include a simultaneous offer to sell all of the first shareholder's shares to the other shareholders, and the price for both offers must be the same. The other shareholders can either sell, or are given an opportunity to participate, pro-rata, as buyer in such a provision. This is sometimes referred to as a "shotgun" or "divorce" clause, because it allows a single shareholder to end up owning all the shares if the shareholders have come to an irreconcilable impasse about the direction or management of the software company.

- *Death/disability/termination.* The shareholders' agreement will often contain mandatory sale provisions that come into effect upon the death, disability, or termination of employment of a shareholder who is an employee of the software company. These provisions may also require that, provided such insurance can be obtained at reasonable rates, the corporation maintain life insurance on certain employee shareholders, and that if they die while employed by the company the proceeds of the life insurance will be used to fund the purchase, from their estate or legal representatives, of the shares previously held by them. Some shareholders' agreements also make a distinction, in terms of the purchase price paid for an employee shareholder's shares, between employees that were terminated without cause and those that resigned (the latter normally receiving a lower price for their shares).

- *Proprietary rights issues.* The shareholders' agreement should include provisions regarding nondisclosure of proprietary information, noncompetition, nonsolicitation of clients and employees, and ownership of work product. These issues, discussed in the context of employees, are canvassed in Chapter 8. If, however, all the shareholders are also employees of the company, and if each shareholder is also party to a proprietary rights agreement that covers these issues, as recommended in Chapter 8, then it may not be necessary to include similar provisions in the shareholders' agreement.

- *Amendment to agreement.* That holders of a certain percentage of shares (say 80%, but it can be higher or lower), can change the terms of the shareholders' agreement, and that such a change would be binding on all the shareholders, even those that did not vote for it. Such a provision allows for some flexibility;

without it, all changes to the shareholders' agreement would require the unanimous consent of all the parties to the agreement.

Whichever of these provisions ultimately appears in a shareholders' agreement, it is certain that each shareholder will be affected differently by these provisions. Accordingly, it is necessary that each shareholder obtain independent legal advice regarding the proposed shareholders' agreement.

EMPLOYEE SHARE PLANS

Most software companies whose shares are publicly traded on stock exchanges have long permitted employees to acquire shares of the company, or options to acquire shares, at favourable prices, as a means of encouraging employees to exert their best efforts on behalf of the company. If this in turn causes the company to succeed, the company's share price will increase, thereby making the employees' shares more valuable. Increasingly, even private software companies are turning to share plans as a means of motivating employees. Particularly for the smaller software company, remunerating employees partially in shares instead of scarce cash can allow the company to pour every extra penny into R&D and sales/marketing. As well, given that the shares of a private software company will only become liquid if the company is sold or does an IPO, an employee share plan can be a useful way to retain the allegiance of an increasingly mobile high tech work force, provided the plan is well structured and carefully considers the following issues.

An important threshold question is which employees should be permitted to participate in the plan: all of them, right down to the company receptionist, just key, senior managers, or some number in between? And how many shares should be allocated to employees? Ten to 15% of the total is quite standard, but amounts as high as 25 to 30% are not uncommon. In answering these sorts of questions, the owners of the company should be careful to plan ahead three to five years, and make sure the shares are distributed to each employee over time, in a manner that matches the performance of the company and that of the particular employee.

An employee, such as the vice-president of sales, who is to be issued a large number of shares/options may be invited to sign the company's main shareholders' agreement (the one discussed above). It may not be appropriate, however, to have employees with much smaller shareholdings sign this main shareholders' agreement, as it contains a number of rights and privileges (such as the right to purchase additional shares, etc.) that are not really intended for smaller shareholders. On the other hand, it is not wise to issue shares to employees without having them sign some document governing what they can do with them; otherwise they might, for example, sell them to people unrelated to the company, which would allow such "strangers" to receive the financial statements of the company at the shareholders' annual meeting.

What is required, therefore, is a short agreement for each employee shareholder to sign in respect of his or her shares. The agreement should include all or some of the following provisions: that the employee shareholder will vote her shares to elect the board of directors appointed under the main shareholders' agreement; that the employee shareholder will sell his shares as required by the "drag-along" or "shotgun" provisions of the main shareholders' agreement; and that the employee will resell the shares to the company for the same price she paid if, prior to a general sale of the company or an IPO, she resigns from the company or if she is terminated for cause. If she is terminated involuntarily without cause, the agreement might require a reasonable (but still relatively low) price to be paid for the shares. And most importantly to the employee, the agreement would provide that upon any sale of the company, the employee will receive the same price per share for his shares as is received by the controlling shareholders.

The point of such an agreement is to try to ensure that the employee does not leave the company until an "exit strategy" is exercised for all of its shareholders, either by way of a sale or an IPO. In order to achieve this end, the proposed plan should also be reviewed from a tax perspective, as there are numerous specific tax rules relating to employee share plans. Some of these are touched on briefly in the next chapter. In sum, with proper legal and tax advice, and an employee shareholders' agreement that reflects properly the intention of the plan — as well as the company's corporate culture — the employee share ownership program can be extremely effective in contributing to the company's success.

SOLE PROPRIETORSHIP

A sole proprietor is a person who carries on a business alone, personally, and not through a corporate entity. A common example of the sole proprietor in the software business is the individual consultant or contract software programmer who provides his or her services to others as an independent contractor. In Ontario any individual can carry on business this way by merely registering with the appropriate government ministry the name under which the person carries on business.

While a sole proprietor, in certain circumstances, may stand to gain certain tax advantages, as noted in the discussion in the next chapter, as a sole proprietor you often will be well advised to incorporate your business in order to take advantage of the limited liability principle applicable to corporations and discussed above. For example, if as a contract programmer, operating your business as a sole proprietor, you fail to deliver on time a certain module of software as required under a contract with a purchaser, you yourself will be exposed to litigation over the matter and, if the purchaser is successful in obtaining a judgment for money damages, your assets (including bank accounts, RRSPs, house, car, and certain other personal possessions) could be used to satisfy the judgment if you do not satisfy it through an immediate cash payment. By contrast, if the business is operated through a company, it is the company, except in unusual circumstances, that is solely responsible for any such liability. It is for this reason that all consultants, contract programmers, and others in similar positions should seriously consider the option of incorporation if they are not already conducting business through a company.

The same is true for an individual who starts a software business merely as a sole proprietor. You might not have incorporated a company for various reasons, including the fact that you might have wanted to see whether your software product will be well received in the marketplace before you set up a company. Once you are satisfied that your software product is viable, and before you begin to license it to customers, you should seriously consider incorporating your business. And when you do, you should consider transferring to the corporation, in writing, all your ownership and other rights to the software, so that it is in all respects the company that owns the software and carries on the business related to the software.

PARTNERSHIP

A partnership is two or more people, organizations, companies, or other entities carrying on business together with a view to making a profit. It is similar to a sole proprietorship in that the business, when carried on by two or more individuals, for example, is not separate from the people carrying on the business. Accordingly, the point made above about why a person operating a business as a sole proprietorship should consider incorporation applies to partnerships as well. Where, for instance, several consultants or software programmers operate a partnership, they expose themselves personally to liability if their business incurs debts or is the subject of lawsuits.

Indeed, each partner is in law jointly and severally responsible for the liabilities of the partnership. This means that if there are four partners, each partner may be responsible for more than a quarter of the firm's liabilities. If, for example, three of these partners did not have any assets to cover liabilities, and the fourth partner was quite well-to-do, then the creditors of the partnership could recover all their amounts owing from this fourth partner. Thus, consultants or software programmers operating as a partnership should seriously consider the merits of incorporation (unless they are prohibited from carrying on business through a corporate vehicle, as is the case with certain professions).

If, however, for tax or other reasons the partnership option is chosen, the partners should enter into a partnership agreement which addresses the various issues relevant to the operation, funding, management, and dissolution of the partnership. In the absence of such an agreement, the relevant provincial law governing partnerships will apply to the partners, and while this law is quite useful, it is far better for the partners to have their own agreement drawn up so that all issues are dealt with exactly as they wish. The statutes governing partnerships tend to be drafted so that their provisions apply only if the partners have not provided otherwise in a partnership agreement. A partnership agreement, therefore, will override most of the provisions contained in the statute, thereby establishing for the partners their own, customized set of rules.

The following items are often covered in a partnership agreement: the name of the partnership, and whether a partner can use the name if he leaves the partnership; how much capital each partner will contribute to the partnership; how much income each partner will receive from the partnership (the agreement may establish a committee of partners that determines income on a periodic basis); a management structure for the partnership, often including an executive committee, or managing partner, charged with overseeing the day-to-day affairs of the partnership; rules for admitting new partners; and a process for dissolving the partnership.

Related to the standard partnership described above is the "limited partnership." In the limited partnership there are two types of partners: a general partner (or more than one, though usually only one) and one or more limited partners. The general partner's liability is not limited, just as in the typical partnership described above. (In order to limit the liability of the individuals involved as the general partner, the general partner can itself be a corporation with liability limited to the extent of its own corporate assets.) The limited partner, by contrast, resembles somewhat the shareholder of a corporation in that if the limited partner does not take part in the management of the limited partnership (this task is left up to the general partner alone), then the limited partner's liability for the obligations of the limited partnership is restricted to the amount of money the limited partner has invested in the limited partnership.

Limited partnerships are sometimes used to raise capital for specific software development projects. The limited partners would invest the funds required for the project, and would be able to claim directly a certain amount of the expenses (but not R&D tax incentives — see Chapter 2) incurred by the limited partnership, which is quite advantageous compared to the treatment that would be received by an equity investment in a corporation undertaking the same software development. The general partner would manage the development project. The limited partnership would then license to the general partner, or perhaps others, the resulting software technology in order to have it commercially exploited. The royalties received by the limited partnership would be distributed among its limited partners.

Another variation on the partnership arrangement is the joint venture, which in the software business is typically established by two software companies who wish to develop jointly a certain product or technology. Or the joint venture might be a mutual effort to develop and exploit a CD-ROM product undertaken by a software company and a company that creates or owns multimedia content, including text, pictures, graphics and music. The joint venturers enter into a joint venture agreement that addresses the following issues: what each party will contribute to the joint venture, either in cash or in kind, such as access to and a licence of previous R&D, personnel, or a certain amount of their time; a management plan for the joint venture, usually implemented through some form of committee structure; rights to the technology developed by the joint venture, such as whether they will be conferred by outright assignment of ownership for one or more specified countries, or by licence, be it exclusive or nonexclusive; resolution of disputes by arbitration, particularly if the joint venturers are located in different countries; and a mechanism for termination of the joint venture, possibly including the provision that one party can buy out the other party at a certain price.

AGREEMENTS WITH LENDERS

As Willis notes in Chapter 3, software companies spend a great deal of time and effort raising money to fund their R&D efforts and to finance marketing and other costs. One source of financing will likely be a bank or other lender who loans money pursuant to a loan agreement, under which the company grants certain security to the lender. Various other documents may also be required by the lender, such as a personal guarantee from each shareholder of the company.

All of these documents — the loan agreement, the documents granting security to the lender, and the personal guarantees — must be read and understood by the relevant managers of the company, typically at least the president and the officer in charge of finance. Of course, anyone asked to give a personal guarantee must also be fully aware of what it means and how it works before signing it. These agreements must always, always be reviewed by the lawyers for the company and the individuals giving the personal guarantees. It is surprising how often these agreements are signed by software companies and individual guarantors without first being reviewed by a lawyer. This is a dangerous practice. These documents tend to contain a good deal of hard to understand legal terminology and they can have serious consequences for the company or persons signing them. These consequences invariably will come to light if the company is having difficulty meeting its loan payments. At that point, however, it is usually too late to do anything about the documents and the sometimes onerous provisions they contain.

For example, loan agreements often contain numerous obligations on the part of the software company to do such things as maintain certain debt-to-equity or other financial ratios. The agreement may prohibit the company from obtaining other types of financing, or they may permit the company to assume additional debt but prohibit it from granting to any other lender any security in the company's assets. As security for the loan, the lender will usually require the company to pledge to the lender, as collateral, all the receivables, inventory, equipment, and other assets (such as critical software programs, or CD titles in the case of a multimedia products developer) of the company, which, if the company defaults on payment of its loan or violates some condition in its loan agreement, can be seized by the lender and sold to satisfy outstanding debts. It should also be noted that in Canada it is somewhat unclear how to register a security interest in a copyright work like a computer program or a CD title, because the *Copyright Act* does not include a security interest registration system. Accordingly, some lenders will require an absolute assignment of the copyright, but will provide elsewhere in the loan documentation that the assignment is provided only as collateral security, and that until a default occurs under the loan, the borrower company can use the copyright asset exclusively and without any interference from the bank. Other lenders will merely record the security document in the Copyright Office in the copyright registration file of the particular copyright work. In any event, the security interest in the copyright asset should also be registered under the relevant provincial personal property security registry system. Similarly, assignments of copyrights, and other interests in a copyright, such as an exclusive distributorship for a software program, should also be registered in the Copyright Office.

Most importantly perhaps, a personal guarantee given by a shareholder to back up a loan advanced by a lender to a software company means, practically, that if the assets of the company are insufficient to satisfy the amount of indebtedness, then the lender can look to the net worth of the shareholder (represented by items such as the cash balance in a bank account, the equity that the shareholder has in his house, and certain other assets) to satisfy any deficiency. This makes the personal guarantee a very critical document that should be signed only after the utmost consideration and reflection. It negates, effectively, at least as between the shareholder and the company's lender, the principle of limited liability for corporations that stipulates, as noted above, that a shareholder's responsibility for the liabilities of a company is limited to the money invested by the shareholder in the company. The personal guarantee means that all the other assets of the shareholder who gives it are also at risk in the event that the company being guaranteed falls on financial hard times.

Some software company executives take the view that these documents are simply part of the exercise of borrowing money from a bank or other lender, and accordingly they do not bother reading and understanding them, let alone trying to negotiate changes to them. The law is clear that failure to read and understand the contents of a document is no defence to strict enforcement of its terms. Moreover, this is not a sensible approach to a relationship with a lender. In many cases lenders can be convinced to agree to certain important changes to all these documents. For example, less onerous restrictions on the operations of the business might be negotiated in the loan agreement. Or perhaps it can be agreed that not all assets of the company be pledged as collateral, but rather that, for example, security be limited to receivables only (leaving, perhaps, the software assets to be pledged to another lender if additional funds are required). And it may be possible to limit the liability under the personal guarantee to a certain dollar amount. Moreover, depending on the size of the credit being advanced, on the amount and quality of the assets of the company being pledged as collateral for the loan, and on other factors, it may be possible to convince the lender to forego the personal guarantee altogether. Or perhaps the lender will agree that once the business attains certain financial or other targets, the personal guarantee will be terminated. Lenders seldom suggest such limitations and are happy to take as security anything that is available. Borrowers who are well advised can at least test the limits of lenders' sensitivity to changes in these provisions.

To attain some or most of these concessions, it is usually necessary to approach more than a single lender when searching for debt financing. There is increasing competition among lenders. Some are more comfortable with software companies than others. Perhaps none will meet a particular software company half-way on the issues noted above. The company will never know, however, until it engages in a competitive review of various lending alternatives. It is only by approaching several possible sources of funds that a company can reasonably determine what scope there is for negotiating a more favourable business and legal relationship with a lender. Moreover, given that Canadian banks are promoting lending groups that are devoting substantial resources to understanding software, multimedia, INTERNET and related high tech and knowledge-based companies, the prospects for borrowing from Canada's financial institutions on more advantageous financial and contractual terms have never been better.

AGREEMENTS WITH INVESTORS

As Willis notes in Chapter 3, a second major means of financing all or at least some of the cash requirements of a software business is through selling equity in the company, that is, permitting investors to purchase a portion of the ownership of the company. This can be done by selling common shares, or by selling special shares, also called preferred shares, tailored to meet the requirements of the new investor. Preferred shares rank ahead of common shares in respect of one or more of the key attributes of shares — the right to receive dividends, the right to receive the property of the corporation if it is dissolved, and the right to vote. Preferred shares may provide for payment of a guaranteed quarterly dividend, for instance, making the investment look somewhat like debt. Whatever the particular equity instrument, several important considerations must be kept in mind.

The first is to be careful not to run afoul of the law that governs the issuance and resale of shares of companies, typically called the *Securities Act* in each province. This statute sets out a series of complex rules that, in essence, provide that shares of a company may not be sold to anyone unless the purchaser first is given a lengthy document, called a prospectus. The prospectus describes the company in great detail so that the potential purchaser of the shares can make an informed investment decision. There are, however, a number of exceptions under this type of rule, and indeed an important legal exercise that must be carried out before shares of a software company are issued to a venture capitalist or most other investors (except when a public offering of shares by a prospectus is contemplated) is to review the availability of just such an exemption.

One commonly used exemption is the provision that makes a prospectus unnecessary when the value of the shares bought by the purchaser exceeds a certain amount, currently $150,000 under Ontario's and Quebec's securities laws and $100,000 in most other provinces. The rationale behind this exemption is that a purchaser buying shares worth this much likely knows how to evaluate the company issuing the shares without the assistance of the information contained in a prospectus. Depending on the particular buyer of the shares, and other factors, other exemptions may be available as well. A second important one is the "seed capital" exemption, which involves submitting a disclosure document, called an offering memorandum, to no more than 50 potential investors, and having no more than 20 of these investors buy shares. The third important exemption is for the issuance of shares of a "private company" as defined by the securities laws, where the shares are not being offered for sale to the public. This exemption is very commonly used, but its availability is very technical and should be reviewed with legal counsel experienced in securities law before shares are issued in reliance on it. Indeed, it should be noted that these exemptions and other securities laws are very complex, and therefore the individuals within the software company responsible for raising investment funds should seek expert legal counsel regarding them at the earliest possible phase of the financing process.

The second important issue, or cluster of issues to be precise, raised by an equity investment is not dissimilar to the key point made above in respect of debt financing. An equity investment will typically involve two documents, a share purchase agreement and a shareholders' agreement (or an amendment to the latter if one is already in place for the particular software company). The share purchase agreement prepared by the investor, like the loan agreement prepared by a lender, together with the shareholders' agreement, will invariably contain a number of provisions intended to restrict the management latitude of the executives of the software company. Certain of these will be reasonable, and indeed necessary, in order for the investor to ensure that its investment is adequately protected. For example, the share purchase agreement will likely contain some "anti-leakage" provisions intended to help ensure that the money paid for the shares is used as working capital of the company and is not merely siphoned off by the executives of the company through bonuses or other payments.

Some of the provisions asked for by an investor in the share purchase agreement, however, may be quite unreasonable, particularly if the investment is of a relatively modest size. This raises two important points. First, as with loan documentation, the principals of the software company must read and understand the paperwork related to an equity investment, and they must have it reviewed by a lawyer. The second point is that owners of a software company should consider seriously whether, in respect of any particular investment, too much control of the company is being given up in relation to the money being invested in the company. A similar question should also be asked in respect of each debt financing contemplated by a software company: is the price of the debt, when all the restrictions imposed by the loan documents are considered, too high?

These questions are often asked in hindsight, only after a company runs into trouble with a lender, or after a company has been sold and the founder of the company realizes that the relatively recent investor, courtesy of a rather small investment, realized a better return than the founder. These questions, however, need to be asked before the company takes on the debt or issues shares to the investor. It may be that the particular software company will not have the luxury of asking these sorts of questions prior to a financing because it is desperate for the cash (perhaps it is going to have trouble meeting payroll the following week without it), and hence it is willing to sign just about any piece of paper to get the funds. This is, however, an unfortunate and dangerous situation to be in, and all software companies should strive to avoid ever having to experience it.

A final word on debt and equity financing is that the professional advice that software companies will need for such transactions, provided by lawyers, accountants and others, will not be inexpensive. But rather than avoiding using professionals (which practice can cost the company dearly in the long run), the better response to this requirement is to increase the number of dollars being raised by the particular financing so that, proportionately speaking, less of the funds are spent covering the "transactions costs" of the deal. Indeed, some venture capitalists will not even consider making investments that have a value of less than, say, $500,000 (or, in some cases, as high as $1 million), because below that amount the accounting, legal, and other professional fees, as a proportion of the money raised, are prohibitively high.

BUYING A SOFTWARE BUSINESS
OR A SOFTWARE PROGRAM

The purchase and sale of a software business presents many of the legal issues germane to the purchase and sale of most other businesses generally. For example, assuming the purchaser wishes to buy the whole business of a particular software company, the purchaser must decide whether to buy the shares of this company from its shareholders or to acquire the assets of the business, as a going concern, from the company. A key consideration in making this decision is whether the company has material liabilities, and if so, whether the purchaser is willing to assume them. If the shares of the company were purchased, the purchaser would then acquire everything related to the company, including any lawsuits (or potential lawsuits), all contracts (including those that may be on unfavourable terms), all employees, and all liabilities (including previously incurred tax liabilities, which might come to light only after the purchase of the company).

A purchaser not wishing to assume all the liabilities of a software company would buy its assets instead, such as the relevant software products and the related intellectual property rights as well as certain receivables and any acceptable contracts, and it might hire a number of the employees who were previously involved with the software as well. It should be noted, as explained in Chapter 2, that tax considerations will likely also play a role in deciding whether the shares of a company, or merely its assets, are purchased. Of course, if a purchaser is interested in buying the intellectual property rights for only one of several computer programs owned by a software company, then it will merely buy the asset itself. This is happening with increasing frequency in the software industry as companies buy and sell specific programs to realign themselves in the marketplace or to complement their existing product offerings. It should be noted that the term "intellectual property rights" denotes the trade secrets, patent rights, copyrights, and trade-marks associated with the computer program, rather than merely the physical copies of the program (intellectual property rights are discussed in Chapter 5).

One unusual aspect of buying a software business, or a software program, is that the purchaser may well require some technical assistance for some time from one or more of the individuals selling the company (if they were, say, the primary developers of the key software product of the company), or from the company selling the software program. Accordingly, it is not unusual for the purchaser of the company, or of the software program, to enter into a consulting agreement with such individuals, or with the company selling the software, for such purposes. Similarly, there may also be a need for the new owner of a software program to license the use of the program back to the seller of the program so that the seller can continue to provide software support services to its customers. This type of arrangement would be necessary where the new purchaser does not wish to assume all the software support agreements entered into by the seller, because, for instance, they are not attractive from a financial point of view.

In addition to the usual legal issues relevant to the purchase and sale of a business, buying and selling software and related assets (or a whole software business) raises a number of important, unique problems, most of which stem from the intangible nature of software. Indeed, the first exercise to conduct during the "due diligence" review of the software company being purchased, or when buying all the intellectual property rights to a computer program through an asset purchase, is to determine and define exactly what software is being bought. The buyer will want to ensure that what it is purchasing comprises all the software necessary to achieve a particular result, and that there are, for example, no other programs belonging to the seller (or to third parties) that are needed to operate a particular program but that are not being sold. For example, it may be the case that the particular software program being purchased incorporates a base product that the selling company needs for use in its other programs. In such a case it may be necessary for the purchaser to buy these other programs as well, and then to license them back to the seller for use in its other software products.

A similar issue involves determining exactly what elements, if any, of the software being purchased are owned by third parties. A good deal of software today incorporates portions of programs licensed for such purposes by other computer software suppliers. It is increasingly rare for one company to build a computer program from scratch, using only software developed by it. Accordingly, it is crucial to set out in the purchase agreement precisely what portions of the software are owned by the seller (as the purchaser will come to own only these portions) and what elements are merely licensed to the seller (as the purchaser will have to obtain similar licences, perhaps at significant cost, in respect of these portions). And if these portions of the software owned by third parties represent important — perhaps even indispensable — parts of the program, then the purchaser will wish to negotiate suitable rights for such portions, including perhaps entering into escrow agreements for the source code for these elements (see Chapter 12 for a discussion of source-code escrow agreements).

After determining precisely what portions of the software are owned by the seller, it is then necessary to ensure that the purchaser will take ownership of these portions free of any interests of others. Thus the purchaser should conduct searches in the Copyright Office and other relevant government offices to ensure that no other interests, except those of the prospective vendor of the software, are registered in respect of the software (and, of course, immediately after the sale the new owner should register its own interest in the software in the Copyright Office and other offices if appropriate). Various patent searches should also be undertaken in certain situations. As well, the purchaser will want to ascertain what end-user or distribution licences the seller may have granted for the software, and whether under any of these arrangements the source code for the program — the really critical version of the program that contains its trade secrets — has been disclosed. This latter point is very important because many purchasers take the view that once the source code is made widely available, even under stringent licence agreements, the program has lost some of its value. Existing distribution agreements are also an important factor because they may, particularly if they grant exclusive rights to a particular territory, restrict the purchaser of the program from licensing or selling the program in such territory. Indeed, the existence of an unfavourable distribution agreement, perhaps a long-term one that gives too many rights to the distributor for too small a royalty paid to the owner of the software, usually results in a significant reduction in the purchase price for the software, much to the dismay of the software's owner.

Another question that the purchaser should explore thoroughly during its due diligence review of the software being purchased, and through the numerous representations and warranties to be given by the seller in the agreement governing the sale of the company or the particular asset, is whether the seller has good ownership rights in the intellectual property rights in such software. For example, as is explained below in Chapters 5, 7, and 8, a software company should have all the individuals who work on the production of a program transfer to the company their ownership rights to, and waive their moral rights in, the program by means of a written document. Failure to do so, particularly in the case of nonemployee contract programmers or consultants, may mean that the seller does not have good title in all of the software (and that parts of it, perhaps large parts, are in fact owned by these third-party programmers or consultants). Such a revelation can also cause a significant reduction in the purchase price willing to be paid for the program, and in some cases it may cause the prospective purchaser to walk away from the deal altogether.

In addition to conducting a thorough due diligence review of the software assets being acquired, here are a few more considerations if you are contemplating buying a software company (referred to below as the "Target"):

- *Phased disclosure of confidential information.* Prior to being allowed access to confidential information about the Target, you will probably be asked to sign a nondisclosure agreement. Under this agreement you will undertake to keep confidential the information you learn about the Target. Even in the absence of such an agreement, you will likely have a legal obligation not to disclose or use any confidential information learned from the Target. As a result, sound advice to purchasers — as well as Targets — is to be very careful about how information on the Target is disclosed to the potential purchaser. If, for example, the purchaser was interested in acquiring the intellectual property ("IP") in a particular software program, the purchaser should initially review no more than the software in operation on a computer screen; that is, the purchaser should not be in a hurry to see the source code for the software. If, after a review of the operation of the product, the parties are still interested in pursuing negotiations, they should turn to the business parameters of the deal, such as negotiation of the purchase price.

  Only after the parties have more or less settled on the business terms should the purchaser's detailed review of the software begin. Even then the potential purchaser should look at the material in stages, and should go no further in each stage than is necessary to determine that it may not want to go to a further stage. By following such a phased disclosure procedure the purchaser can attempt to minimize the risk of becoming contaminated with the trade secrets or other proprietary information of the Target. The danger to guard against is that the deal does not go forward, but the purchaser has learned a great deal from the Target's technology. This would lead to a suspicion that any competitive product of the purchaser which is released after the purchaser's review of the Target's product may be considered to incorporate secret elements developed by the Target. It is therefore in both parties' best interest to control very carefully the exposure of the purchaser to the confidential crown jewels of the Target.

- *Understand what you are buying.* This sounds trite, but you must understand what you are buying, and why. This does not mean you have to know the difference between purchasing shares or assets, though of course, as noted above, it is important to understand this distinction. Rather, you have to decide if, for example, you are buying a balance sheet, or merely some IP assets and people. Many smaller software companies are in fact little more than some valuable technological assets, a handful of key and even more valuable people, and access to some important distribution channels. Thus, you will have to understand thoroughly the nature of the key software product(s). Are they stable, do they need a lot of support, are they in a market that demands constant upgrades, etc.? You must know the answers to these sorts of questions before you embark on negotiating and documenting the purchase of a software business.

- *Agree on valuation early on.* Once you have decided what you are buying, it is necessary to determine what you will pay for it. This sounds like a rather straightforward exercise, but valuing knowledge-based companies, or certain of their assets, is fiendishly difficult. Asset-based valuation tests are usually not relevant because, for example, the value of the software carried on the books rarely indicates its true value. Earnings-based valuations can also be difficult to apply, given that many software companies will have a spotty earnings history. Invariably, some amalgam of these and other valuation approaches is adopted by the parties. The key is to agree upon the approach early on, and to have an understanding that it will be adhered to even if the various numbers driving the formula(s) change as the due diligence exercise reveals increasingly accurate data. There are lots of deals where valuation questions plague the participants throughout the acquisition process, and a lot of angst can be avoided if the valuation rules of the road are firmly established early in the process.

- *Do tax homework early.* The tax regime applicable to all acquisition scenarios is complex and often times unruly. With technology-based deals, the tax issues can become even more complicated. How does one keep alive a technology company's status as a Canadian controlled private company after the acquisition, for example, in order to maintain significant R&D tax credit benefits, as well as the capital gains exemption for the shareholders? How do the capital cost allowance rules work for software, and how is software valued for tax purposes? These are just some of the intriguing tax questions that can arise on the sale of a technology-based business. The answers to the tax questions can affect the very structure of the deal, as noted in Chapter 2. Accordingly, get your tax advice early. And make sure relevant personal tax advice is provided to actual or prospective shareholders at the same time. It is very important to get the whole tax picture so that the structure ultimately chosen best suits the interests of all concerned.

- *Understand the transitioning employees.* Given that people are the source of intellectual property — as opposed to real estate and tangible goods that are the products of land and natural resources — it's not surprising that employees are critical to the knowledge-based business. Thus, it is very common for a large percentage of the staff at a software company to be participants in an employee stock option plan at the Target. Before you buy the Target, you must know precisely what share incentive (and other similar) programs are in place, particularly if you are buying shares. If you are buying assets, what about the employees? Are they to come with the purchased assets? If so, you should have them all — or at least the key ones — sign employment agreements with you as a condition of closing. This employment agreement should also include non-competition covenants in case the employee wishes to leave you prematurely (as discussed in Chapter 8). As well, if you are buying shares from key employees of the Target, you should also receive a non-competition covenant incident upon the sale of the shares. As a general rule, these latter "non-competes" are more favourably looked upon by courts than the non-competes in employment agreements. In any event, you may decide — and need — to offer them a stock option plan in the new company in order to attract and retain them. These are all critical items which should be settled early on in the acquisition process.

- *Proper due diligence takes time.* From the brief discussion above, it should be clear that proper "due diligence" — the term used for the process of learning all about the Target — takes time. So begin as soon as possible. There are lots of questions to ask, and invariably lots of answers will require follow-up investigation before you are satisfied with the Target's state of affairs. For example, in one asset purchase involving a software program, the Target announced at the eleventh hour that the program being sold actually required all sorts of utilities and other software of the Target in order for the purchased software to operate fully, and that these utilities were also used in other products of the Target that were not being sold to the purchaser. The solution finally agreed upon was to have the purchaser acquire the utilities as well, and then license them back to the Target for use in conjunction with its other programs. This was all done at the last minute in a state of frenzy. It would have been preferable to learn about the issue earlier.

You should also commence your searches in the relevant trade-marks, copyright and patent offices as early as possible. If the Target has registered any of its IP, you will want to satisfy yourself that the registrations are valid and in good standing. More importantly, whether or not the Target has registrations, you will likely also want to conduct infringement or registrability searches in the trade-marks and patent offices in order to try to understand whether the Target's IP infringes, or potentially infringes, any existing third party rights. These infringement opinions, if done properly, take time. For example, in a recent technology cross-licensing deal between two public companies, where a minority share swap between the companies was to occur upon the commencement of the licence agreement, one company had several patents and the other company had none. The deal was held up for some time beyond the scheduled closing date as the patentability and infringement opinions on the one party's technology were prepared. Share prices gyrated, putting unwelcome pressure on the parties, as the prior art searches were conducted and the results analyzed. Again, an earlier start to the technical due diligence would have been much preferable.

- *Anticipate problems.* A sound approach to due diligence is to actively anticipate problems. This methodology uncovers the problems earlier, and therefore affords more time to fix them. For example, anticipate that a software company Target will have used a number of non-employee programmers to develop some portions of its product's source code, and that these independent contractors will not have assigned, in writing, their copyright in the custom code to the Target. Or, anticipate that the Target has not had staff waive their moral rights in the code and other material created by them. Or, that the Target does not have access — even on an escrow basis — to the source code of a third-party software development tool that is critical for the ongoing evolution of the Target's flagship product. And the list of potential problems goes on. If you anticipate these problems, do not merely ask the Target to tell you about its products and people. Rather, ask very specific questions. This can be done effectively through the representations and warranties in the acquisition document.

- *Customizing and understanding representations and warranties.* The document that should serve as the focal point for the due diligence exercise is the share purchase or asset purchase document, and specifically the various representations and warranties given by the Target relating to the assets, business and people being acquired. Two problems tend to arise with this document. First, the "standard" acquisition documents used to acquire businesses with no or very little IP are simply not good enough. These documents will invariably have a short representation and warranty as to the Target having good title to any IP, and that's it. This is woefully inadequate. The IP representations and warranties should cover specific issues related to ownership (i.e., the Target should list all people who worked on the software and what agreements they signed), exploitation and encumbrances, all licences and other rights granted to use the software, all other interests in the software such as bank security interests, as well as the quality of the software. Customizing and expanding the acquisition document to reflect IP issues comprehensively is only the first step. The second step is ensuring that the Target understands what the specific representations and warranties are all about. Accordingly, the purchaser should have at least one intensive session with the principals of the Target and their counsel, where each representation and warranty is discussed in detail in order to acquire a firm understanding of the Target's IP and other assets (and liabilities). The key objective of the acquisition document is to allow you to learn as much as you can about the nature of the Target's business. Without a thorough due diligence session focused on answers to detailed IP-sensitive representations and warranties, this objective can be difficult to attain. You can also raise your "anticipated problems" (discussed above) in this session .

- *Run the acquired business as if you will soon sell it.* One last point for the purchaser of a knowledge-based business. Having just been through the time consuming and probing exercise of conducting intensive due diligence on the Target, you have learned a lot of practical lessons about protecting and exploiting software assets. You now know, for example, that all agreements with independent contractors should be in writing, and that the written agreement should clearly provide that the contractor assigns copyright to — and waives moral rights in favour of — the software company. Always keep these lessons in the forefront of your mind and run your day-to-day operational affairs as if you were going to sell the company in the not-too-distant future. It is often when selling a particular software program that the mistakes made by its developer in respect of the program's protection and distribution come home to roost. Parts II and III of this book are intended to help software companies avoid such mistakes, which can severely reduce the price paid for the software when it, or the company, is sold. It is a good idea, therefore, as the company conducts its various day-to-day affairs, to keep in mind the question, "How will this transaction or matter affect my ability to sell the software one day?" By continually asking this question, and by taking to heart the points raised in Parts II and III of this book, software companies should be able to avoid the costly mistakes that so often come to light upon sale of their business or a particular software asset.

CHAPTER

2

Income Tax and GST Considerations for Software Companies

By Karen Wensley
(wensleyk@ey.geis.com)

and Irene J. David
(davidi@ey.geis.com)

This chapter discusses, selectively, several key Canadian income tax issues, as well as the primary issues related to the Goods and Services Tax (GST), that are likely to be important to software developers. Space limitations dictate that many more tax matters will not be covered, and that even those topics covered will be addressed on an introductory level. Readers will, of course, have to consult their own tax advisors to apply the general principles discussed here to their own specific circumstances. Readers should also keep in mind that tax legislation, as well as its interpretation, is always subject to change, which may significantly affect the comments made in this chapter.

INCOME TAX ISSUES

Four key income tax topics have been selected for this chapter. A discussion of how to structure a new business is important for young companies, particularly since selecting the wrong structure can be a costly mistake to correct later. The R&D tax credit incentives warrant a lot of discussion, since they can put cash into the hands of software entrepreneurs who are invariably short of money. Selling a software business is also included, in part because software businesses seem to be sold almost as frequently as they are created. Structuring the sale appropriately can result in significantly more after-tax cash in the vendor's pocket. Finally, this chapter will touch on international tax issues such as non-resident tax that may be imposed on software licence payments from abroad and that can surprise the entrepreneur and create an unexpected cash shortfall.

All of these topics raise some issues that are unique to the software developer. They require not only tax knowledge, but also an understanding of software development and how software businesses work. It is hoped that this chapter will make the reader aware of the issues and knowledgeable enough about them to seek professional help when it is required.

SELECTING THE FORM OF BUSINESS

Many new businesses are immediately incorporated. This may or may not be the best choice of business structure from a tax perspective. A software developer starting a business should consider the alternative forms under which the business can be carried on, and the pros and cons of each, from both a tax and a legal perspective, before making a decision. In that regard, this chapter should be read in conjunction with Chapter 1, which discusses the legal implications of the various business structures available.

The biggest tax difference between a corporation and the other types of entities, such as a sole proprietorship, a partnership, or a joint venture, is that the corporation is an entity that is taxed separately from the individuals who own it. As a result, income, losses, tax credits, and other tax balances remain with the corporation and do not automatically flow out to the owners. In the other forms of business, income or losses incurred by the business are automatically recognized as income or losses of the owner or owners. These differences in tax treatment should be kept in mind when considering how best to structure a start-up business.

Sole Proprietorship

The term sole proprietorship is used to refer to an individual carrying on a business without any specific legal structure, as opposed to a corporation or a partnership. In a sole proprietorship, there is no tax difference between the owner, or proprietor, and the business. For tax purposes, the proprietor is considered to own the assets of the business, and any income or losses generated by the business are income or losses of the individual.

This business structure can be an advantage in the early years of a business if losses are being generated. If the proprietor has other sources of income, such as salary or interest, losses from the software business can be deducted from the other sources of income, thus reducing overall tax payable.

In order for the software business losses to be deductible, however, the activities must constitute a genuine business and not merely a hobby. The software activities must be undertaken with a reasonable chance of eventually making a profit from the business. If the business is still in the development stage, and is not yet earning revenue, Revenue Canada will look for evidence that the activities are being carried on in a businesslike manner and that the proprietor has a well-thought-out business plan for marketing the software or otherwise making the business profitable.

Provided that the software activities constitute a business with a reasonable expectation of profit, expenditures incurred in the course of that business are generally deductible for tax purposes. The types of expenditures that can be deducted in computing the income or loss from the business would include the following:

- Salaries or wages paid to an assistant (but not "salary" paid to the proprietor)

- Materials, such as computer paper

- Travel

- Expenses of maintaining an office

- Interest expense on funds borrowed to carry on the business

- Depreciation (capital cost allowance) of assets purchased for use in the business

The proprietor's spouse can also be paid a reasonable salary for work performed for the business. The spouse would, of course, have to declare the salary as income on his/her tax return. Many specific limitations apply to particular expenditures. For example, if the business is incurring losses and is located in the proprietor's home, expenses of maintaining the home office are not deductible and must be carried forward and claimed once the business is profitable. If the proprietor has no other sources of income, the losses from the software business may be carried forward for up to seven years (or carried back for up to three years) against other sources of income in those years.

If the software development activities constitute "Scientific Research and Experimental Development" for tax purposes, as discussed later in this chapter, such expenditures would not only be deductible in computing the income or loss from the business, but would also generate 20% investment tax credits. The credits are used by the individual to directly offset federal taxes payable. If there are no taxes payable, any investment tax credits earned on the software development activities are generally refundable to the extent of 40% of those tax credits. In other words, the individual will receive a tax refund from the government of 40% of the tax credits earned.

A sole proprietor must generally choose December 31 as the tax year end of an unincorporated business. Businesses in existence prior to 1995 that had a different year end are subject to transitional rules under which income deferred due to a non-calendar year end is taxed over a ten-year period.

It should be noted that where the individual's income comes from activities such as the software business that are not subject to employee source deductions, the individual will be required to pay quarterly instalments in respect of the individual's income tax if the tax owing (after subtracting any tax deducted at source) is over $2000. As a self-employed individual, Canada Pension Plan contributions are also required on income from the business.

Partnership

A partnership is similar to a proprietorship for tax purposes, except that more than one party is involved. It is not necessary that the partners in a partnership be individuals. They can also be corporations or even other partnerships. The partnership computes its income or loss and then allocates it to the partners in the proportion determined by them under the partnership agreement. For example, two equal partners would each recognize 50% of the income or loss of the partnership in their own tax returns. Similarly to a proprietorship, the partnership, other than a partnership all of the partners of which are corporations, must have a December 31 year end, starting in 1995. A partnership, like a proprietorship, is most beneficial from a tax perspective if the partnership is losing money and the partners have other sources of income against which to offset the losses. The partners would also generally receive the R&D investment tax credits on qualifying software development activities, provided the partners are active in the business.

Partnerships are often used as financing vehicles. An individual with money to invest may agree to finance a new software business. The cash expenditures may not, early on, produce any offsetting revenue. By structuring the relationship as a partnership, the investor-partner can receive the tax benefits of the losses arising from the business. This reduces the investor's after-tax cost of making the investment.

In investment-type partnerships, the investor often requires limited liability. As discussed in Chapter 1, the partners in a partnership are jointly and severally liable for the debts of the partnership. By structuring the business as a limited partnership, however, a limited partner can limit his liability to the amount he initially invested. There must be at least one general (unlimited) partner.

A limited partnership brings several more tax rules into play. First, a limited partner can generally deduct losses allocated to him by the partnership, but only up to the amount the limited partner has invested in the partnership. A limited partnership is also subject to limitations if the software business is undertaking development work that qualifies as "Scientific Research and Experimental Development" for tax purposes. Neither the deductions nor the tax credits arising from such research and development expenditures can be deducted by a limited partner. Accordingly, a partnership, other than a general partnership of parties active in the business, should not generally be used to carry on a business that would otherwise be eligible for R&D tax incentives on software development.

Joint Venture

A joint venture is similar to a partnership, except that rather than the venturers jointly owning the business or partnership, each owns certain assets or undertakes certain activities and they agree to work together. For example, two parties may agree to work together to develop new operating system software. One party may be a hardware company that wants to embed the operating system in its hardware. The other party may wish to adapt the system to use as a base for certain applications software. The two parties could agree to undertake a joint venture to develop the operating system, but each would own certain aspects of the final result. They would have no intention of carrying on business in common.

For tax purposes, each venturer is considered to make his own expenditures and own his own assets, whereas in a partnership the expenditures and assets are the joint property of the partnership. Each party would claim, for tax purposes, the costs incurred by that party, would depreciate its own assets, and so on. If one party was contributing the R&D work and the other party was doing some routine development, or perhaps incurring marketing expenditures, only the party undertaking the R&D would be able to claim the R&D tax incentives.

It is often difficult to determine whether a particular relationship is in fact a partnership or a joint venture, and the terms are often used interchangeably. If the parties want the income tax consequences of the particular form of a joint venture discussed above, they should take all possible steps to ensure that it is not a partnership and that they are not carrying on business in common.

Corporation

As discussed earlier, a corporation is a structure entirely separate, for income tax purposes, from the owners. A shareholder cannot claim the tax deductions or credits of the corporation and can withdraw cash from the corporation only by taking a specific action such as drawing a salary or dividend or perhaps causing the corporation to repay loans that the shareholder had earlier made to the corporation.

If the corporation is a Canadian-controlled private corporation, there can be a number of significant tax advantages for software developers. (A Canadian-controlled private corporation is a corporation not listed on a public stock exchange and not controlled by any combination of nonresidents and/or public companies.) First, provided that the corporation, together with any associated corporations, maintains its taxable income below $200,000 per year (if the taxation year is, for whatever reason, less than 365 days, the $200,000 must be reduced accordingly) and has taxable capital (generally, debt, equity capital and retained earnings) below $10 million, it is eligible for a higher rate of tax credits earned on scientific research and experimental development expenditures (35% vs. 20% for other entities, on up to $2 million of R&D per year). Furthermore, these tax credits can result in cash refunds, if the corporation has no tax payable. The tax credits will be discussed in more detail later in this chapter.

Another advantage of a Canadian-controlled private corporation comes into play when the software business is being sold. Individuals resident in Canada currently have available to them a capital gains exemption which exempts the first $500,000 of certain capital gains from tax. This includes the capital gain on the sale of shares of a qualifying small business corporation (which must be, among other things, a Canadian-controlled private corporation). The definition of a qualifying small business corporation is discussed later in this chapter.

Canadian-controlled private corporations with taxable capital below $10 million are also entitled to a low rate of tax on the first $200,000 of taxable income each year. Depending on the province, this tax rate is approximately 23% compared with approximately 45% for other corporations (or for income above $200,000) and a top marginal individual tax rate above 50%. The low corporate tax rate is advantageous if the income generated is being retained in the corporation to finance further development or expansion.

Once the income is paid out as dividends to shareholders, the total combined corporate and personal tax will approximate the tax that would have been paid if the income had been earned by the individual directly (see Table 2:1).

Table 2:1

TAXATION OF A CANADIAN-CONTROLLED PRIVATE CORPORATION VS. AN INDIVIDUAL

	INCOME EARNED BY CORPORATION	INCOME EARNED BY INDIVIDUAL
Net income	$100,000	$100,000
Less: Corporate tax @ 23%	(23,000)	—
Less: Personal tax @ 50%[1]	—	(50,000)
Income after tax	77,000	$ 50,000
Dividend paid to shareholder	77,000	
Less: Personal tax on dividend [2]	(27,000)	
Income after tax to shareholder [3]	$ 50,000	

1. Assuming the individual has other income such that the $100,000 is all taxed at a top marginal tax rate of 50%.

2. Tax rates are approximate and will vary by province of residence.

3. Note that, while the total tax is the same, there is a deferral of $27,000 of tax until dividends are paid.

The biggest disadvantage of a corporation, from a tax perspective, is that if the business is incurring losses, the shareholders can obtain no immediate tax advantage from the losses. Instead, the losses will reduce tax payable on income earned by the corporation in the three prior years or the following seven years.

A corporation also introduces additional complexity. A separate corporate tax return is required. Tax planning is also more complicated, since it involves tax planning both for the corporation and for the shareholders. A common planning issue relates to the decision to remunerate shareholders by means of salary or dividends. Generally, salaries or bonuses paid would be sufficient to keep taxable income below $200,000. If taxable income exceeds $200,000, the combined tax rate, including both the corporate tax and the personal tax on dividends paid to the individual shareholder, can exceed 60%.

As a business grows, it is often beneficial to create more than one corporation. For example, if the business begins to operate in another location outside Canada, it can be advantageous to operate through a new corporation rather than as a branch of the Canadian company. There can also be business advantages to having more than one corporation in Canada, each carrying out a different function.

Incorporating a Sole Proprietorship or Partnership

While a complete discussion of the tax rules involved in changing the type of legal structure used to carry on the business is beyond the scope of this chapter, certain basic points should be made. First, a proprietorship, a partnership, or a joint venture can be moved into a corporation if the appropriate tax elections and filings are made. In effect, all assets are deemed sold to the corporation at their tax cost and the individual or partner receives shares of the corporation as consideration for transferring the assets. If the appropriate tax elections are not made, all assets of the software business, including the intangible assets such as the software under development, knowhow, and goodwill are considered to be disposed of at their fair market value. This can create a significant tax burden to the proprietor or partner making the transfer. Such transfers should therefore be done only with the assistance of a tax advisor. For tax purposes, the transfer of a business from a corporation into an unincorporated proprietorship is much more difficult, and generally cannot be done on a tax-free basis.

Case Study: Part 1

The following case study, which is divided into several parts throughout this chapter, illustrates some of the tax considerations and planning steps that might apply to a software business through several stages of its growth. The appropriate tax planning for a particular business will depend, of course, on the facts and circumstances of that business.

Robert and Susan are interested in starting a software business. Robert, an experienced programmer, has an idea for an innovative new applications package. Susan is not much of a programmer, but she understands the software business and knows how to find markets for the software. She also has $20,000 to invest in the venture.

Robert and Susan decide to form a general partnership (they have concluded that the risks posed by their business will be quite low for a few years, and therefore they are willing to forego the benefit of limited liability that they would have if they incorporated their business). They have drawn up for them a partnership agreement that provides, among other things, that Susan will be allocated the initial losses of the partnership up to the amount of her $20,000 investment. She will also be entitled to the first $20,000 of income generated by the partnership. After that, Susan and Robert will share income and losses of the partnership fifty-fifty.

In the first year of the partnership, they spend the entire $20,000 investment on renting a computer, buying paper and supplies, renting a small office, paying travel expenses, and other similar expenditures. The loss for the year, $20,000, is all allocated to Susan and she deducts the $20,000 from her other income on her personal tax return.

In the second year, Susan finds a customer who is so excited by the product, that he buys 50 copies of the first version of the software. As a result, the partnership has a profit for the year of $30,000. In accordance with their partnership agreement, the first $20,000 of the profit is allocated to Susan. The balance of profit, $10,000, is split equally between Robert and Susan. Robert and Susan decide that they will not, in fact, draw any cash out of the partnership, but will instead use the cash to hire another programmer to produce a second version of the software. For tax purposes, Robert and Susan must include in their income, and pay tax on, the income allocated to them by the partnership, even though they do not receive the amount in cash. When they actually do withdraw the cash, it will not be taxable to them, since they have already paid tax on the income.

In the third year, the partnership is doing very well in terms of finding customers but needs to bring in outside investors to fund the growing marketing expenses. Robert and Susan decide to incorporate their partnership to allow them to bring in new investors as shareholders. They consult their tax advisor and discover that the partnership assets can be transferred to a new corporation on a tax-free basis by making the appropriate tax filings. They also learn that the corporation will be eligible for a special low rate of tax on its first $200,000 of income each year. This is a pleasant surprise to them, as they need to conserve their cash as much as possible to move into new premises and to buy some needed computer hardware.

R&D TAX INCENTIVES

One of the most important tax issues for software developers is the tax incentives available for expenditures on scientific research and experimental development. For simplicity, this chapter will use the term "R&D" to mean expenditures that qualify as scientific research and experimental development for tax purposes.

The tax incentives for R&D are of two types. First, the cost of both current and capital expenditures on R&D carried out in Canada can be deducted in full for tax purposes. This contrasts to other capital expenditures, the deductions for which are limited to the depreciation (capital cost allowance) as allowed by regulations under the *Income Tax Act*. To be deductible in the year, current R&D expenditures must generally relate to activities in the year (as opposed to prepaid amounts) and capital assets must generally be put into use. Both types of expenditures must be related to the business of the taxpayer. Unlike ordinary loss carryforwards, which expire after seven years, R&D expenditures that are not claimed in the year incurred can be carried forward indefinitely.

In addition to the tax deduction, there is a tax credit on R&D expenditures. For corporations other than Canadian-controlled private corporations with taxable income less than $400,000 in the prior year, or for individuals, the tax credit is 20% of expenditures. The credit can be used to reduce federal tax payable in the year, carried back for three years, or forward for ten years. Note that the tax credit does not reduce provincial corporate tax. The tax credit reduces the R&D expenditures that can be deducted in the year following the year in which the tax credit is claimed.

For a Canadian-controlled private corporation whose income, together with all associated corporations, was less than the small business limit in the prior taxation year, the tax credit is 35% on up to $2,000,000 per year of R&D expenditures. The small business limit is generally $200,000; however, if the corporation, together with associated corporations, has taxable capital over $15 million, starting in 1996 the small business limit is zero. Between $10 million and $15 million of taxable capital, the $200,000 is gradually reduced to zero. For corporations eligible for the 35% tax credit, the tax credit is refundable in cash even if no federal tax is payable. The percentage of the credit that is refundable is 100% on current expenditures and 40% on capital expenditures. In other words, for $100 of R&D expenditures, a 35% tax credit would be earned. If the $100 of expenditures were current expenditures (e.g., salaries, materials), and there were no federal tax payable, the corporation would receive a cheque for $35 as a tax refund. If the $100 of expenditures were on capital equipment, such as computer hardware, the refund would be 40% of $35, or $14. The corporation would also be able to deduct its expenditures in computing its income (although if it had no income, the deduction would generally be deferred until a subsequent year). The deduction in the year would be $100, with the following year's deduction reduced by the current year's tax credit of $35 (or $14, depending on whether the expenditures were current or capital). Looking at the two years together, the net deduction of $65 would result in a tax saving of approximately $15. Including the tax credits, there would be total tax savings of about $50 on the $100 of expenditures, as shown on the next page.

Table 2:2

R&D TAX INCENTIVES FOR A CANADIAN-CONTROLLED PRIVATE CORPORATION

R&D current expenditures	$100
Less: Tax Credit[1]	(35)
Tax Deduction[2]	65
Tax Savings from Deduction[3]	15
Tax Savings from Tax Credit	35
Total Tax Savings[4]	$ 50

1. This credit is based on the assumption that the corporation, together with all associated corporations, had taxable income of less than $200,000 in the prior year and taxable capital below $10 million.

2. In fact, the $35 credit does not reduce the amount that can be deducted until the following year.

3. A corporate tax rate of 23% is assumed.

4. An expenditure of $100 on a non-R&D activity would generate a tax deduction but no tax credit, for a total tax savings of $23.

Corporations with taxable income between $200,000 and $400,000 may be eligible for the 35% refundable tax credit on all or part of their R&D expenditures, depending on the magnitude of their total R&D expenditures. In some of the provinces, a provincial tax credit is also provided for certain R&D expenditures.

Qualifying Activities

Software development may qualify as R&D for tax purposes, depending on the nature of the activities. The income tax regulations define "experimental development" as "use of the results of basic or applied research for the purpose of creating new, or improving existing, materials, devices, products or processes." Further, the R&D must be carried out "by means of experiment or analysis" and must constitute "a systematic investigation." The development cannot constitute a mere "style change." Up to now, the courts have been of limited assistance in helping taxpayers understand what these regulations mean. Revenue Canada has set out its interpretation in *Information Circular IC-86-4R3*. It should be noted that Revenue Canada's position does not have the force of law and may not be considered correct by the courts. However, if one wishes to obtain tax credits without the necessity of going to court, IC-86-4R3 is important reading.

The Information Circular sets out three key criteria that must be met for the software development to qualify as R&D. The first, referring to "scientific or technological advancement," requires that the new or enhanced software being developed is new in a technological sense, that it has required more than routine programming, and that the company has learned something new about software as a result. It is not necessary to write a fifth-generation language in order to qualify as R&D. On the other hand, routine porting of the software to a new platform would likely not be R&D, unless technological problems arose in the course of the porting that had to be overcome.

The second criterion refers to "scientific or technological uncertainty." Uncertainty in this sense means technological uncertainty rather than uncertainty as to whether the market will respond to the new software. Technological uncertainty need not mean that there is uncertainty as to whether the program can be made to work (most programs can probably be made to work, given an infinite amount of resources and no constraints on the final selling price). Instead, it means that, at the start of the programming process, there is uncertainty about how the anticipated technical problems will be overcome and about what configurations or approaches will be required to make the software work successfully.

The third criterion refers to "scientific or technological content." This in turn refers to the requirement in the regulations that there be a systematic investigation. The key element here is to keep proper documentation of the software development process as it is carried out.

If the software development qualifies as R&D for tax purposes, a number of ancillary activities may also qualify for the tax incentives, to the extent that they are necessary to the R&D process. They include the initial technical feasibility study for the software, a review of competing technology from a technical standpoint (as distinct from market research to see if there is room in the market for another competing product), training of the development team, design of the program, testing the program, and technical documentation of the program necessary for the testing. One of the activities excluded from the R&D tax incentives is research in the social sciences or humanities. Thus it is necessary to ensure that the innovative aspects of the software development do not relate to an application in social sciences or humanities but rather to an advancement in the field of computer science. For example, a program that analyzed Shakespeare's plays in a totally new way would not qualify unless the program itself was technically innovative within the field of computer science.

At the time of writing, Revenue Canada was in the process of finalizing an Application Paper dealing specifically with the qualifications of software development activities as R&D for tax purposes. Readers should request a copy from Revenue Canada.

Qualifying Expenditures

Once the R&D activities have been identified, it is necessary to capture the costs related to those activities which qualify for the R&D tax incentives. Certain expenditures are specifically excluded under the *Income Tax Act*. They include rent of premises (other than payments under the terms of a lease entered into prior to June 18, 1987), expenditures to purchase or construct a building, and leasehold improvements. Also excluded are general and administrative expenses, such as legal and accounting fees, interest expense, convention expenses, dues for membership in scientific bodies, and so on, and any expenditures for R&D carried on outside Canada.

Most other current expenditures qualify for the R&D tax credits provided they are "directly attributable" to R&D. This would include the salaries of individuals who spend all their time on R&D; an allocation of salaries of individuals who spend part of their time on or supervising R&D; an appropriate allocation of occupancy costs such as heat, light, and property taxes; direct materials used such as paper; and other expenses that would not have been incurred had the R&D; activities not taken place. In lieu of claiming occupancy and other overhead-type costs, taxpayers can use the "proxy" rule, which allows a mark-up of 65% of salary costs to cover those other expenses. The proxy election, which must be made in the tax return, is subject to a number of complex rules that are beyond the scope of this chapter.

Capital expenditures, such as computer hardware, must be used "all or substantially all" for R&D in order to be eligible for tax credits on the full expenditures. This is defined to mean that the computer will be used at least 90% of the time for R&D over its useful life. Capital assets must be new in order to qualify for tax credits. Costs to acquire rights to R&D are not considered R&D expenditures by the taxpayer.

Different rules apply to certain capital assets that are used at least 50% but less than 90% for R&D. Generally, newly acquired equipment used at least 50% of the time for R&D in the period ending at the second year end after purchase will be entitled to one-quarter of the normal tax credit (e.g. an 8.75% credit for a taxpayer otherwise entitled to the 35% R&D credit). A further one-quarter of the credit is available if the use is still 50% for R&D at the end of the subsequent year, thus resulting in a total of half the tax credit that would be available if the equipment met the 90% R&D criterion.

Nonqualifying Development Expenditures

Expenditures to develop software that do not qualify as R&D may be treated in different ways for tax purposes, depending on the circumstances. Certain expenditures would be considered current operating costs of the business and would be deductible in the year incurred. These would include programming costs, such as programmers' salaries, if the software produced was not likely to be of enduring value to the taxpayer. For example, the cost of updating a payroll package to incorporate annual tax changes would be deductible in the year.

If the software is of enduring benefit to the taxpayer, the programming costs may be capital in nature. Costs to develop applications software that is a capital asset would be included in capital cost allowance class 12, with a depreciation rate of 100% (limited to one-half in the year the cost is incurred). Systems software would be included in class 10, with a 30% depreciation rate. In many cases, however, revision to and updating of software is virtually continuous, with each year's version differing significantly from the last. In these circumstances, it can be argued that the programming costs are a current expenditure since no single year's costs result in an enduring benefit.

In some cases, custom software is developed under contract for a third party. If the expenditures qualify as R&D, they can be deducted (and give rise to tax credits) as they are incurred. If they are not R&D, the costs would generally be inventoried and deducted in the same period as the related revenue was recognized. Revenue Canada's comments on these issues are set out in *Interpretation Bulletin IT-283R2*.

Case Study: Part 2

Susan and Robert are now the majority shareholders of ABC Software Limited. They sold 25% of the new corporation to an outside investor for $500,000. This money will be spent to gear up the corporation's marketing effort and to start the development of a second software product.

The company has budgeted approximately $200,000 per year for the direct costs of software development, most of which are the salaries of the programmers. They have read (and discussed with their professional tax advisor) *Information Circular IC-86-4R3*, and they are convinced that they are breaking new ground and making technological advances in their software development. They are particularly interested in the cash refunds of the investment tax credits on their R&D expenditures, because although the revenue of the company continues to increase, the expenses are increasing even faster.

Accordingly, Susan and Robert put in place procedures to document their spending on R&D. In addition to the direct expenses on programmers' salaries and benefits, they realize they can allocate a number of other costs:

- An allocation of Robert's salary, based on the time he spends supervising the R&D effort

- An allocation of premises' costs other than rent, such as electricity and office cleaning, based on the proportion of the total office space used by the R&D staff

- Secretarial time and supplies used by the R&D department.

Then they compare the proxy mark-up (65% of salaries) to the indirect costs they could otherwise allocate, and decide to elect to use the proxy.

In addition, they will earn tax credits on the cost of buying computer hardware, since it will be used at least 90% by the R&D staff.

All R&D staff are asked to fill in weekly timesheets showing the time spent on various R&D projects each week.

At the end of the year, Susan and Robert have assembled the following schedule of R&D costs and tax credits (Table 2:3):

Table 2:3

ABC SOFTWARE LIMITED: YEAR-END SCHEDULE OF R&D COSTS AND TAX CREDITS

R&D salary costs plus 65% proxy	$310,000
Less: government grant received	(10,000)
Net: R&D expenditures	300,000
Tax credit — 35%	105,000
Tax credit refund — 100%	105,000
Computer hardware purchases	$ 60,000
Tax credit — 35%	21,000
Tax credit refund — 40%	8,400
Total refund	$113,400

The total refund being claimed of $113,400 will make a significant contribution to next year's budget. Their tax advisor warns them, however, that because of the pre-audit and possible audit procedures required by Revenue Canada, it will probably be at least four months from the time they file their tax return until they receive their refund.

Documentation and Reporting

The claim for the R&D tax credits is made on form T661, which must be submitted with the taxpayer's tax return. Some leeway is allowed for late filing; however, a claim for R&D tax credits that is made after the due date for the *following* year's tax return is automatically disallowed. Form T661 requires details of expenditures by category as well as a description of each R&D project that explains the technical advances and uncertainties involved. Taxpayers eligible for an R&D tax credit refund are also generally subject to an audit. Before the taxpayer receives a cheque, the project description will be reviewed by a Revenue Canada science advisor, who may also wish to visit the taxpayer, and by a Revenue Canada auditor, who will check that the expenditures were made as reported. Once a taxpayer has successfully received an R&D investment tax credit refund, a full or partial refund of the subsequent year's tax credits may be forthcoming upon request without or in advance of the audit for the subsequent year.

Even if the taxpayer is not claiming a tax credit refund, an audit by Revenue Canada is likely from time to time. Because of the likelihood of audit, it is essential that the software developer carefully document the R&D activity. It is much more difficult to try to recall, after the fact, the technical problems that arose in the course of the software development. Software developers should keep weekly time reports of the hours spent on various projects. Documentation should also be kept regarding the basis of any cost allocations that are made and the purpose of third-party expenditures such as consultants. Most important, descriptions of the projects should be drafted before software development begins, and deviations from or difficulties arising during the development process should then be noted in the final version submitted with the T661.

Contract R&D

Payments to most third parties to do software development on the taxpayer's behalf will count as R&D expenditures provided the activities themselves are technically innovative and are related to the taxpayer's business. Note that the third party must carry out the R&D in Canada in order for the payment to be eligible for tax credits. Conversely, if a taxpayer does R&D under contract for someone else, the R&D tax credits would generally not be available except to the extent that expenditures on the contract exceeded the contract revenue received. For example, if a company agreed to carry out certain R&D services for a fee of $200,000, but it actually cost them $230,000 to provide those services, they would only be entitled to R&D tax credits on the $30,000 "overrun." There is an exception to this rule, however, which generally applies to contracts with persons who are not resident in or carrying on business in Canada. In other words, a Canadian software developer could undertake a contract for a United States resident to do technically innovative software development that qualified as R&D for Canadian tax purposes and be paid in full for the work by the U.S. resident. Nonetheless, the Canadian developer would be entitled to tax credits on the software development expenditures. This can be a key factor in deciding which contracts to bid on and how to price them.

Even if work is being done for a Canadian customer, it is important to distinguish between a contract to do software development on behalf of the customer and the licence of the software end product. If the customer is buying the development services, the fee would be considered a contract fee and would be subtracted from the software developer's expenses for purposes of computing the R&D investment tax credit. However, if the customer is licensing a completed software system and the software developer will continue to own the rights to the software and be entitled to license the software or versions of the software to other customers, the payment would not be considered a contract fee and the software developer would be entitled to the R&D tax credits on his expenditures. Effective for taxation years starting in 1996, new rules apply to R&D contracts between related parties in Canada. Readers with such contracts should consult with their tax advisors.

R&D Tax Planning

Given the magnitude of the potential R&D tax incentives, careful planning should be done to maximize the benefit. This involves more than just keeping good documentation and allocating all reasonable costs to R&D. One key planning point is for Canadian-controlled private corporations to attempt, if at all possible, to keep the taxable income of the associated group of corporations below the small business limit (provided the taxable capital limit is not exceeded). This can be done by accruing bonuses to owner/managers that will bring income below the limit (generally $200,000). (The bonuses must be paid within 180 days of the year end.) This is good tax planning in any case, as discussed earlier; for corporations eligible for R&D tax incentives, it is crucial. This is because corporations with taxable incomes below $200,000 are eligible for the 35%, fully refundable tax credit. As noted earlier, taxable incomes between $200,000 and $400,000 gradually reduce the amount of R&D expenditures on which the 35% tax credit can be claimed.

Decisions on contracts should also be made with the R&D tax incentives in mind. As discussed above, R&D contract work for nonresidents generally makes the company eligible for tax credits that it would not receive if the contracts were carried out for residents of Canada. Corporations should also consider where the R&D carried out on their behalf takes place. Because the R&D tax incentives apply to R&D carried out *in Canada*, by another Canadian taxpayer, hiring someone else to do software development on the taxpayer's behalf is best done in Canada, from a tax perspective.

Many other smaller planning details should be kept in mind. For example, salaries expenses are eligible for the 65% proxy mark-up, whereas fees paid to a consultant under contract are not. Also, before purchasing previously used capital assets, taxpayers should take into account the fact that such assets are not eligible for R&D tax credits. In general, the R&D tax credits involve a complex set of rules. It requires considerable time and effort to document the R&D, go through the Revenue Canada audit, and stay abreast of the changing rules. Some taxpayers decide the effort is not worth it. However, if the software developer is making significant R&D expenditures, the returns can be substantial.

SALE OF THE SOFTWARE BUSINESS

Another crucial tax-planning point for a software developer arises when the business is being sold. In particular, an analysis should be done of the tax impact of selling the shares of the corporation (or incorporating a proprietorship and then selling the shares) as opposed to selling the assets of the business. In many cases, the purchaser will dictate which of the two alternatives is acceptable to him or her. However, where the purchaser is willing to be more flexible, significant tax advantages for the vendor may result in a lower negotiated sales price, making both parties happy.

Share Sale

The vendor will generally prefer to sell shares. The proceeds received on the share sale minus the tax cost of the shares will result in a capital gain (or loss). Three-quarters of the capital gain is subject to tax at the shareholder's regular tax rate. If the vendor is an individual, he or she may have access to the capital gains exemption. This exemption provides that the first $500,000 of capital gains realized over the individual's lifetime on certain assets, including shares of a small business corporation, is exempt from tax. The exemption may be reduced in certain circumstances, such as when the individual has, since 1987, deducted investment expenses and certain tax shelter deductions in excess of investment income. To the extent the individual claimed the $100,000 capital gains exemption (now repealed) that previously was available on all capital assets, the $500,000 is reduced by the amount previously claimed. Generally, however, if the exemption is available, it will reduce the tax payable on the sale.

Whether the shares are qualified small-business corporation shares is subject to a number of detailed and complex rules; in general, the vendor must be an individual who has held his shares for at least 24 months. A key exception is that a proprietorship can be incorporated and then immediately sold, and the vendor may be able to make use of the $500,000 capital gains exemption without being required to meet the 24-month test. The corporation must, at the time of sale, be using at least 90% of its assets, measured by reference to fair market value, in an active business carried out primarily in Canada, and for the prior 24 months, at least 50% of the assets must have been used in this way. "Assets" include all assets of the business, including intangibles such as goodwill and knowhow, even if they are not recorded on the balance sheet. If more than one corporation is involved, such as a holding company and an operating subsidiary, the rules are even more complex and require detailed analysis.

Asset Sale

In many cases, the purchaser will prefer to buy assets of the software business from the corporation rather than to buy its shares from the shareholders. In this way, the purchaser can try to ensure that no unexpected liabilities are being assumed. In addition, the purchaser will receive a tax cost equal to the full amount paid for all the assets, which will generally result in higher tax deductions for the purchaser in subsequent years. In contrast, in a share purchase, the purchaser will generally step into the depreciated cost of the assets owned by the corporation being purchased.

On an asset sale, each asset is disposed of by the corporation, with tax consequences to the vendor depending on the type of asset. Software developed by the vendor will generally be a capital asset, and its sale will give rise to a capital gain, 75% of which is subject to tax. Some of the proceeds may be allocated to knowhow or goodwill. This would include the value the purchaser gets from taking over the customers of the company or inheriting the assembled group of knowledgeable employees. Proceeds of this type are known as eligible capital, which are also 75% taxable. The taxable portion of eligible capital is considered business income, eligible for the low tax rate (about 23%) on the first $200,000 of income discussed earlier in the chapter. Other inventory and fixed asset items will give rise to income, capital gains, and/or terminal losses, as appropriate.

In an asset sale by a corporation, the corporation receives the proceeds and calculates its taxable income. Following payment of the corporate tax, the corporation may be wound up, with the proceeds distributed to the shareholders. Depending on the capitalization of the corporation, the proceeds received on winding up are generally taxed as a dividend. This winding-up dividend would not be eligible for the capital gains exemption. In some cases, the corporation may not be wound up and the shareholders may keep the proceeds in the corporation to begin another business venture. If the purchaser is willing to be flexible, the vendor should compare the after-tax proceeds arising from both a share sale and an asset sale to determine the most advantageous offer. Careful structuring can minimize or defer the tax cost on the sale.

Sale For Noncash Consideration

Different tax consequences can arise when cash payment of the selling price is deferred to another year or when the consideration received includes shares of another Canadian corporation. If payment of the sale proceeds extends beyond the year of sale, the vendor can generally stagger the recognition of the capital gain to coincide with the payments, provided that at least 20% of the capital gain is recognized in each year. Often, the continuing value of the corporation's goodwill needs to be proven to the purchaser and the total amount to be paid for the shares is based on future earnings of the corporation. In this case, Revenue Canada will administratively allow the capital gain to be recognized and taxed as the amounts become known, provided guidelines set out in *Interpretation Bulletin IT-426* are met.

Many software businesses are sold to larger software or hardware companies for consideration that includes shares of the purchaser. To the extent that consideration is received in the form of shares of a Canadian corporation, the vendor can choose to defer tax on the shares received as part of the purchase price, provided generally that the appropriate joint elections are filed by the purchaser and the vendor. Although the gain can be deferred, the vendor may want to recognize up to $500,000 of the gain and immediately use the balance of any capital gains exemption, especially if the purchaser corporation will not qualify as a small business corporation after the sale. Tax on the capital gain generally cannot be deferred if the shares of the purchaser received as consideration are shares of a non-Canadian corporation.

Case Study: Part 3

ABC Software Limited is now in its fifth year of operation. It has started to produce profits; in its most recent taxation year, it earned $750,000 on $4 million of revenue, before bonuses and taxes. The company then declared and paid bonuses of $550,000 to Susan and Robert, the net amount of which, after employee withholding tax was deducted, they loaned back to the company.

Susan and Robert have now received an offer for the business, which they are seriously considering. The potential purchaser is a computer hardware company that wants to incorporate the software of ABC Software Limited into its product line. The purchaser makes three alternative offers:

1. It will purchase all rights to the software application package that it is most interested in for $2.8 million. It would also make job offers to certain key employees and acquire all the on-going licences to existing customers for that software.

2. It will purchase 100% of the shares of the company for $4.5 million. Susan and Robert, who now each own one-third of the shares, would receive $1.5 million each.

3. It will invest $1.5 million for treasury shares equal to 25% of the company.

Susan and Robert analyze the three offers carefully. The first offer is attractive, since they can continue to sell and develop computer software other than the specific rights sold to the purchaser. They consider how the proceeds would be allocated to various assets sold (primarily software and goodwill) and the after-tax cash left in the company. They consider new business opportunities that they could take up with this cash, compared to the ongoing income they would have expected to earn from the software technology being sold. They are concerned that some of their new software development is based on underlying technology in the rights to be sold.

The second offer is attractive in that each can use their $500,000 capital gains exemption and walk away from the deal with over $1,000,000 of after-tax cash.

However, they enjoy running ABC Software and are not sure they want to "cash out." The third alternative is rejected. If they are going to take on a new shareholder, they want to realize some of the cash personally. In addition, ABC Software is now generating a good cash flow, and does not need an additional $1.5 million of cash to continue its existing business.

Ultimately, an alternative deal is worked out whereby instead of subscribing for treasury shares, the purchaser buys half of the shares currently owned by each of Robert and Susan for $750,000 each, reducing their combined interest in the company to one-third. They each use their $500,000 capital gains exemption and each has $650,000 after-tax cash for personal use. The purchaser becomes a shareholder of ABC Software and a separate deal is put into place allowing the purchaser to incorporate the technology into its hardware in exchange for payment of an ongoing royalty. Ultimately, Susan and Robert's decision is based on the needs of the business and their personal preferences for continued involvement in it. The deal is structured to minimize the tax cost, but is not driven by tax considerations.

INTERNATIONAL ISSUES

Even young software companies frequently have markets outside Canada. The software market for a Canadian company is at least North American and may be worldwide; although the software entrepreneur may not consider international borders very important, they can have significant tax consequences.

The first issue in which the taxing authorities may become concerned is transfer pricing with a related party. This would generally arise where a Canadian software developer establishes an American or other foreign subsidiary corporation to reproduce or market the software in the foreign jurisdiction. For tax purposes, the Canadian company cannot allow the foreign subsidiary to sell the software without receiving some kind of compensation in return. Compensation may be a royalty or licence fee paid to the Canadian company for each copy of the software licensed in the foreign jurisdiction. Alternatively, the Canadian company may use the foreign subsidiary as its sales agent, paying a sales commission. In some cases, the various entities jointly develop the software by sharing the R&D costs.

It is tempting to set the amount of the licence fee or other intercompany charge to maximize tax advantages, such as lower tax rates in another jurisdiction or unused losses in that jurisdiction or in Canada. However, the taxing authorities of both countries will look at the pricing to make sure it is reasonable. The first test of reasonableness would generally be to look at comparable arm's-length pricing, especially if the Canadian company is licensing the software to a third-party distributor in another jurisdiction at a very different price. Revenue Canada's approach to the topic is found in *Information Circular IC-87-2*. In the U.S. the IRS has very rigorous documentation requirements that should be followed to avoid possible penalties.

Even if the transfer price is acceptable to the taxing authorities, the payments may be subject to nonresident withholding tax. Many countries tax a royalty, which would generally include a licence fee, paid to a nonresident. Importantly, a new protocol to the Canada-United States tax treaty eliminated withholding tax on software license payments between these two countries effective January 1, 1996. Between countries where the tax continues, the rate varies from 0% to 30% or more. Depending on how the licence agreement is written, there may be ways, which vary from jurisdiction to jurisdiction, to avoid this withholding tax. The tax withheld is generally available as a foreign tax credit in Canada. However the foreign tax credit can be used only to offset taxes otherwise payable. Accordingly, particularly if the foreign tax credit is not of immediate use in Canada, inquiries should be made in the taxpayer's jurisdiction to see whether steps can be taken to legally avoid the tax.

Software companies doing business outside Canada, whether through a foreign subsidiary, a branch of the Canadian company, or an independent sales agent, should get tax advice in the foreign jurisdiction, where the tax laws may be very different from those in Canada. The U.S., in particular, has extensive filing requirements imposed on entities carrying on business in the U.S., even if they may not be subject to U.S. tax. Canadian parent corporations of foreign subsidiaries can also, in some circumstances, be taxable in Canada on certain income, including software license fees, of the foreign entity.

CONCLUSIONS REGARDING INCOME TAX

Two income tax mistakes are commonly made by entrepreneurs. The first is to ignore income tax considerations in the hope that ignorance will protect the taxpayer. The opposite tactic is to carry on the business with the primary objective of achieving the best tax result. Both mistakes can be fatal. Ignoring tax considerations can lead to paying much higher tax than would otherwise have been applicable, and/or being subject to interest and penalties. Focussing on tax to the exclusion of other considerations can result in missed business opportunities or complex, unwieldy corporate structures designed solely for some hypothetical tax advantage. The middle ground is to keep one's mind on the business but to be aware of tax considerations, especially at crucial stages in the business. These stages include the initial structuring of the business, licensing arrangements and sales of rights, especially internationally, and selling the business.

One matter that warrants significant time and effort spent on tax issues is R&D tax incentives. The returns can be very significant for a relatively modest investment of time. Above all, it is important to have a trusted tax advisor who knows the software industry and who is prepared to be attentive to the business on an ongoing basis in order to raise tax issues when the entrepreneur may not otherwise think of them. Just as tax practitioners hire qualified programmers to produce software versions of personal and corporate tax returns, software developers should learn to trust tax specialists with their tax affairs.

GOODS AND SERVICES TAX ISSUES

The remainder of this chapter provides an overview of the Goods and Services Tax (GST) with some explanation of the specific application of the rules to the software industry. As a general rule, the GST applies to the software industry in the same way as it does to other goods and services. There are, however, some unique features of the software industry that require particular attention when addressing GST issues.

GENERAL INTRODUCTION TO THE GST

The GST became effective on January 1, 1991. It is imposed on the consumption of goods and services in Canada and is designed to be paid by the ultimate consumer. It is collected by businesses or vendors, referred to as registrants, throughout the production and distribution chain. The tax is calculated at the rate of 7% on sales of goods or the provision of services (collectively referred to as supplies) made in Canada, and is generally paid by the recipient of the supply at the time the consideration is paid or becomes payable.

The vast majority of supplies made in Canada are taxable. However, a number of supplies are zero-rated under the GST. These supplies are still taxable supplies; however, the rate of tax that applies is 0%. As a result, no GST applies on the sale of these goods. Since they are still taxable supplies, a full input tax credit is available for GST paid on inputs used in making the supplies. Exports are an example of a zero-rated supply under the GST legislation.

Supplies made in Canada can also be exempt. A person making exempt supplies is not entitled to claim input tax credits in respect of GST paid on purchases attributable to those supplies. However, for certain persons, such as public sector bodies, a rebate of a portion of the tax may be available. Some examples of exempt supplies are health-care services, educational services, legal-aid services, and financial services.

As agents of the federal government, registrants collect tax on the value of supplies but are entitled to input tax credits for the tax paid on their purchases. Registrants periodically remit the net amount (i.e., amounts collected less input tax credits) to the government or claim a refund if the input tax credits exceed the amounts collected. Through the input tax credit mechanism, tax applies only on the final value of sales to consumers, which ensures that almost all business inputs are relieved from tax, thus eliminating the cascading effect.

Registrants are subject to certain documentation requirements under the legislation. This documentation is necessary to enable purchasers to support input tax credit claims. Documents may include invoices, cash register receipts, formal written contracts, credit-card receipts, or any other document issued or signed by a registered vendor in respect of a purchase on which GST has been paid or is payable.

The GST is a destination-based tax. It is the destination of goods or services that determines tax liability. Goods or services consumed in Canada, including imports, are subject to GST; however, where the goods or services are consumed outside Canada or where supplies are made outside Canada, they are beyond the scope of the GST regime and are not taxable.

Although GST applies to most supplies of property and services, special rules often apply to supplies of different categories and particular kinds of property and services. For the purposes of the GST, there are three types of properties: real property, tangible personal property (often referred to as goods), and intangible personal property. The main components of real property are land, buildings, and fixtures. Any property that is not real property is either tangible or intangible personal property. Tangible personal property may be viewed as including all objects or things that may be touched, felt, or possessed and that are movable at the time the supply is made, other than money. Intangible personal property includes contractual rights, intellectual property, the right to recover a debt, rights in relation to goods that are not in possession, and other rights that may be enforced by the courts. Contractual rights include royalties and software licences. Intellectual property includes copyrights, patents, trade secrets, trade-marks, trade-names, industrial designs, and knowhow. Services include anything that is not property or money. Services provided by an employee to an employer are excluded from the definition of services for the purposes of the GST. Money is excluded from the definitions of both property and services.

The determination whether a particular supply is a supply of property or a service, and, when it is a supply of property, the classification of property according to the categories specified above, is particularly relevant for those involved with the software industry. The GST implications for various types of software may be affected by whether they are property or services. For example, it is likely that a custom software program developed for the specific needs of a particular customer would be classified as a service; a mass-marketed, prepackaged program sold at retail stores would be treated as tangible personal property (a good); and the right to use a software package would be intangible personal property.

VALUE FOR TAX

A sale of a licence for the use of software in Canada generally attracts GST on the full selling price. Where the use of software is governed by a licensing agreement that calls for periodic payments, each payment attracts GST. Importations of software will generally be subject to GST on the duty-paid value. However, there are certain circumstances in which only the value of the medium (disk or tape) is taxed on importation, such as under nonresident licensing arrangements. That situation is discussed later.

PLACE OF SUPPLY

GST applies only to supplies made in Canada. The legislation provides a series of rules to determine when a supply is deemed to be made in Canada and when it is deemed to be made outside of Canada. A number of supplies made in Canada are zero-rated if the goods or services are to be consumed or are considered to be consumed outside of Canada.

A supply of software in Canada by a nonresident person is treated as being made in Canada and therefore taxable only if the supply is made in the course of a business carried on by the nonresident in Canada or if the nonresident is registered for GST purposes.

A sale of tangible property (goods) is deemed to be made in Canada when the property is delivered or made available in Canada to the purchaser. Any other supply of goods, such as a lease, is deemed to be made when possession or use of the goods is given or made available to the recipient. A supply of intangible personal property, such as intellectual property or the right to use a software package, is deemed to be made in Canada if the property may be used in whole or in part in Canada and if the recipient of the supply is either a resident in Canada or registered for GST purposes even if not a resident of Canada.

Conversely, if the software may not be used in Canada, and the software relates to tangible property situated outside of Canada, or to a service to be performed wholly outside Canada, or when the recipient is a nonresident and is not registered in Canada, then it would be zero-rated. As an example, if a Canadian software company sells distribution rights to a Canadian company with a French subsidiary, for distribution in France and Quebec, the sale would be taxable because the purchaser is a Canadian resident and because part of the right relates to the fact that the software may be used in Canada (i.e., Quebec). Alternatively, if the rights were sold to the French subsidiary, no tax would be paid, as the French subsidiary is neither resident in Canada nor registered for GST purposes.

A service is generally deemed to be supplied in Canada if the service is performed in whole or in part in Canada. It is deemed to be supplied outside Canada if it is performed wholly outside Canada. As an example, suppose a

Canadian software company sells software to a client in France, and the software malfunctions. An employee of the United States-based parent company visits the client. The U.S. parent bills the Canadian company who in turn bills the client. There will be no GST charged to the client because the service was not performed in whole or in part in Canada — it was performed in France. In this case, the supply is not zero-rated, it is merely outside the scope of GST.

SALES BY CHARITIES (UNIVERSITIES)

Supplies by charities of property, real property, or services are exempt, unless specifically enumerated as being taxable. Since universities are often registered charities, the GST treatment of sales by charities is of particular relevance to the software industry. If a university that is a registered charity makes a supply of a copyright or other intellectual property, or any right, licence, or privilege to use any such property, the supply would be exempt. Similarly, if a university supplies a service related to a custom software package, the supply would be exempt. Sales of prepackaged software programs would be taxable because prepackaged programs are generally considered to be sales of tangible personal property (which is specified as being taxable when sold by a charity). Prepackaged software programs would include subsequent sales of custom software programs. In this case, the initial supply of the custom program is considered a service, whereas subsequent sales are considered to be sales of tangible personal property.

IMPORTS

In the case of the software imported into Canada, there has been considerable confusion as to whether it should be taxed as tangible personal property or as intangible personal property. The distinction is important since the way in which software is characterized will dictate how GST applies, including whether GST applies on the full value at the time of importation, whether a non-resident GST-registered supplier will be required to collect GST on the charges made to Canadian recipients and whether the Canadian recipients are required to self assess GST if they are not charged GST by the foreign supplier. In this regard, Revenue Canada issued a policy bulletin, that took effect December 1, 1994, outlining its official policy on the taxation of imported computer software. For the most part, this policy parallels the rules that were in effect prior to December 1, 1994; however, some important differences were announced.

The general rule is that all off-the-shelf, pre-packaged software imported into Canada on a physical medium is treated as tangible personal property and as such is taxable at the time of importation on its full value (the value of the carrier medium and the value of the program stored on the medium), with limited exceptions. The same rules apply to outright purchases of custom software. In both cases, the importer will be required to pay GST at the time of importation and the foreign vendor (providing the vendor is not the importer) will not be required to collect any GST given that the place of supply is outside Canada. The foregoing rules are the same as apply to any importation of goods into Canada.

Where custom software is acquired by way of licence from a nonresident, different rules apply. Specifically, GST will not be charged by Canada Customs on the full value at the time of importation. Instead, GST will only be payable on the value of the carrier medium. The software program contained thereon will be treated as intangible personal property, excluded in determining the value for GST purposes. However, if the nonresident supplier is registered for the GST and the software may be used in whole or in part in Canada, then the supplier will be required to collect GST on the value of the software program (including licence fees and lump sum payments) contained on the medium. If the nonresident supplier is not registered for the GST, the recipient of the software may be required to self-assess tax as described below.

When a service or intangible personal property is imported into Canada, it cannot be practically taxed at the border by Canada Customs. If a supply is transmitted electonically, there is no easy means of applying the tax. In such situations, taxable supplies are subject to tax on a self-assessment basis. Consequently, persons who import services — for example, an electronically transmitted customized software program — are required to assess and remit tax of 7% when the supply is for use in Canada other than exclusively in a commercial activity (for example, of the software package is to be used for providing an exempt service, such as provided by a university or a financial institution). Tax is not imposed when imported services or intangible personal property is for use in Canada "exclusively" in a commercial activity. The reason for not imposing tax on these importations is that tax will ultimately be collected by the importer on its subsequent taxable supplies. The cost of the importation will supposedly be included in the importer's selling price, and tax is therefore indirectly collected on the value of the imported software. The "exclusively" term is defined as all or substantially all of the consumption, use or supply of the property or service. Revenue Canada, Excise, has determined that "substantially all" means 90% or more.

SPECIAL CLASSES OF PURCHASERS

The following classes of purchasers have special provisions that relate to either their supplies or their purchases. Since these classes of purchasers often represent substantial customers, software suppliers of goods or services to them should be aware of the special provisions.

The federal government pays GST on its purchases like any other organization. Suppliers to the federal government who are registered for the GST are entitled to claim input tax credits for GST paid on purchases used in making taxable supplies sold to the federal government. The federal government receives a full rebate of the GST paid on purchases by means of a tax remission order, and therefore does not claim input tax credits. Therefore, the GST will not be a cost to federal government departments. Federal crown corporations are not included in the federal government entity for these purposes.

With respect to provincial governments, prior to January, 1991, reciprocal taxation agreements between the federal government and the provinces were in effect. Under these agreements, both levels of governments agreed to pay each other's taxes. However, these agreements were not renewed on January 1, 1991. As a result, provincial governments and certain of their agencies, boards, and commissions are not required to pay GST on their purchases. They will provide exemption certificates to suppliers that allow them to make purchases without having to pay GST. In effect, supplies that would otherwise be subject to GST are treated as if they were zero-rated. Thus, suppliers can obtain input tax credits in the normal manner.

As for financial institutions, in general, all financial services rendered to residents in Canada are exempt from GST. Financial institutions do not charge tax on the supply of exempt financial services to domestic consumers or businesses and do not claim input tax credits on their own purchases of taxable goods and services acquired for use in making the exempt supplies. Nonfinancial services, such as data processing, investment and financial management advice, and payroll administration, are generally subject to tax. Therefore, input tax credits are available on purchases with respect to these actions. As a general rule, an input tax credit is allowed to a registrant in respect of a property or service only to the extent it is for consumption, use, or supply in the course of a commercial activity. Since commercial activity excludes exempt supplies, registrants engaged in providing exempt financial services are restricted in their ability to claim input tax credits. For the software industry, this means the GST on the majority of sales to financial institutions will not be refunded and will increase the costs for the purchaser.

A final category of purchaser worth considering is the "public service body." The term public service body includes a nonprofit organization, a charity, a municipality, a public college or university, a school authority, and a hospital authority. A significant portion of the goods and services supplied by public service bodies is exempt from GST. These organizations are not entitled to claim credits for the GST paid on most of their purchases, and to that extent their costs increase. However, to mitigate this impact, rebates of a portion of the GST paid on purchases by specified public service bodies are provided. The rebate percentages for the public service bodies are as follows: universities 67%, schools 68%, hospitals 83%, municipalities 57.14%, and charities and qualifying nonprofit organizations 50%. These rebates reduce the GST cost of sales to this class of purchasers by the amount received as refund.

PROVINCIAL SALES TAXES

It is worth concluding this chapter by mentioning only very briefly the impact of provincial retail sales tax on software. With the exception of Quebec, who adopted a GST-like sales tax in 1992, generally speaking, the retail sales taxes imposed by the Canadian provinces apply only to chattels or tangible personal property and specified services. Sales of real property, fixtures, and most intangible personal property do not generally attract this tax.

Concerning computer software, with the exception of the province of Manitoba whose legislation specifically taxes most charges for computer software, and the province of Quebec, the legislation in the provinces is either silent on the subject or has been revised to include certain types of software in the definition of tangible personal property. Regardless, most provinces have developed administrative policies with respect to the taxation of software. As a general rule they differentiate between, on the one hand, custom software, and on the other hand, mass-produced prepackaged application software. The former is generally not considered tangible personal property and as such is not subject to provincial tax. The latter, however, is normally considered tangible personal property and any charges for such property, whether or not for a licence, are subject to provincial sales tax.

Because of the provincial variations in the provisions and the fact that taxation in this area continues to evolve, software companies should carefully review the applicable province's current administrative policy before charging (or deciding not to charge) sales tax in respect of customers located in that province.

3

Raising Money for Growing Software Companies*

By Linda Willis

Statistics say that three-quarters of Canadian software developers have under $2 million in revenue and are still coping with the demands that face young and growing enterprises. If your company is in this category, this chapter is designed for you. It takes a straightforward, practical business approach, and is meant to be read and used by people whose primary expertise is not finance or accounting. It covers the important concepts and the basic terminology you will hear used by the people you deal with in the financing community, but it avoids the worst of the complexity and jargon. The definition of "financing" used is a broad one — it includes any source that makes cash available to fund software development: it can be a cash inflow or a reduced cash outflow.

Software development is a business and must be run like a business if you are going to succeed. You or someone who works for you must understand the basics of the software business (R&D project management, marketing and distribution, finance, and people management) and take responsibility for them. This

---

*This chapter, an earlier version of which first appeared in *Business Basics for Software Developers* published by Software Ontario, is reprinted with the kind permission of Software Ontario.

chapter assumes you have a grasp of those basics. As your business grows, how-ever, the "basics" are no longer enough. "Management" is you and the rest of the team that runs your business and decides its direction. If your team needs to upgrade its management skills, you can learn them or hire them, but you can't expect to attract money from outsiders without them.

You may already have found that raising money for software development is no simple task. It devours management time and effort on a continuing basis. The sources of financing discussed here are to some extent alternatives to each other, and you should pursue the lowest-cost alternative available to you at any given time. You will usually have choices, but before focussing on one source or another read through this chapter once to understand the full range of options available and how to develop a financing strategy.

There are some common mistakes that young software companies make in their financing efforts. One of the aims of this chapter is to help you to avoid them. The first mistake is to underestimate how much time and effort it takes to finance a software business to maturity. Raising money is not a sideline. You may spend a third of your time developing your product, another third selling it, and the remaining time raising money to pay for the first two-thirds.

The second mistake is to underestimate how much money it will take to turn your dream into a profitable, self-sustaining business. To launch a packaged software product can take $1 million to $5 million or more, probably spread over two or three major financings. A third mistake is assuming that all businesses are alike when it comes to raising money and that what works for your neigh-bour the auto dealer will work for you. It isn't so. And the fourth mistake is clinging to unrealistic expectations about what motivates the investors and lenders whose money you want to attract. They lend or invest money to make money, according to decision rules that have worked for them in the past.

This chapter does not cover any of the financing topics exhaustively and will not turn you into a financial wizard overnight. It charts the maze of financing sources you have to choose from and describes how to reach the right source at the right time for your business. It will give you a more realistic understanding of what to expect, and make you more comfortable discussing your business and your financing options with potential funders. It will never be a substitute for good professional advice tailored to your needs.

WHY IT'S TOUGH TO FINANCE SOFTWARE DEVELOPMENT

Software industry participants consider that their industry has unique financing needs and in many ways they are correct. Let's look at the characteristics of the software industry in Canada that affect the availability of funds.

Success in software product development is driven primarily by the time it takes software writers to produce a new product. If development is slow because your firm is underfinanced, you may lose out to larger competitors in an industry characterized by short product life cycles. Software development costs can range from $100,000 to $10 million. Products typically take one to three years to develop and have a sales life of two to six years.

Research and product development together with marketing are by far the most significant costs in taking a concept to market in the software industry; production and administration costs are quite small in comparison. Financing a software enterprise through the research-and-development phase and the initial marketing phase is a daunting challenge. To be financeable any business must have the following:

- A product with the clear potential to be commercially successful

- A competent, well-balanced management team with demonstrated technical, marketing, financial and operating skills

- A clear and achievable strategic direction that is market driven

Assuming your emerging software business passes these fundamental tests, what is it about computer software development that makes software businesses, particularly in their early stages, a high financial risk to the investor?

- *Financing requirements are high.* Competitive advantages in packaged software are created by spending large amounts for marketing and R&D differentiating the product and gaining superior access to distribution channels. For a personal computer software package, costs for marketing are almost as high as development costs. Substantial amounts must be raised and spent for product and market development before there are significant commercial sales.

- *Assets are intangible.* The most valuable assets of a software business are the software product itself and its name recognition in the marketplace (the results of its investment in research and marketing), and talented people. These assets usually have less value as collateral security for a lender or investor than tangible property such as land, plant and equipment, or inventory.

- *Young businesses are more risky.* Many software businesses are relatively young, and often the key people are young as well. This lack of track record makes them more risky than established businesses.

- *Product life cycles are short.* Mistakes and delays can be fatal to the business. The business is also vulnerable if it cannot continue to develop successor products that are commercially viable.

- *The environment is complex.* The products and the markets are difficult for the outside investor to understand. The products are technically sophisticated and their success is tied to developments in the computer hardware sector, which is equally complex and subject to short product life cycles. Market behaviour in this environment is harder to forecast, and investors view the potential for missteps as a continuing risk.

These risks will decline over time as the industry and the individual players mature, but they will continue to be a factor in the decisions of existing and potential investors.

Canada has the potential to emerge as a major software developer and exporter. Among our strengths in an industry where people are the key ingredient is the high calibre of software professionals both in the industry and graduating from top schools, such as the University of Waterloo. The challenge will be for individual firms, many of which are small today, to grow to their full potential; to meet the challenge we must continue to build the financial infrastructure and teach the industry how to use it.

The Rules of the Financing Game

Raising money for a software business is an important responsibility that will consume more of your time and attention than you ever thought possible. To mount a successful financing effort, you must be realistic about the process of convincing outsiders to invest in your idea. Regardless of who you are approaching, the following rules of the game apply.

Management, management, management. More than anything else the investor needs a high level of confidence that your management team can be counted on to carry off its business plan. The investor is looking for a strong, well-balanced management group. If you scrimp on anything, don't let it be the key people. If you think you can't afford to invest in good marketing, research, project management, or financial talent (tick one or more as appropriate) who have scope to grow with the business, perhaps you need to raise more money.

The business plan is the selling document for the business. The fundamental tool for raising funds is a professional, crisp, current business plan that sells your business to the investor. Properly prepared, the plan and its supporting detail are also your operating blueprint for the business. The plan need not be long, but it must be persuasive. You market your product to customers with a keen eye to their needs, and you market your business to potential investors the same way. Articulate your strategic vision in a way that convinces the potential investor that the product will work, that customers will buy it at the price and in the quantities you project, and that customers will buy the product from you, rather than from your competitors. It isn't enough that you believe it; you have to convince the investor, like your customer, to write the cheque.

Know what the total financing commitment is. Your business plan and financing strategy must reflect a realistic understanding of the total amount that the business will need to raise, usually in a series of investments, before it becomes profitable and can finance itself from earnings.

Table 3:1 summarizes the typical capital requirements of a growing software start-up. Study it carefully. It shows, for each of the stages of development, the cash that must be raised from outside sources. Space is provided for you to pencil in your company's estimates. The names of the various stages, seed, startup, and development (collectively, the early stages), and expansion are commonly used and understood terms in financing circles to describe how a business grows, but with software the time frame for completing this growth cycle is compressed. Many Canadian software businesses would be classed as early-stage investments.

Table 3:1
FINANCING STAGES FOR A TYPICAL SOFTWARE START-UP

		EARLY STAGES		
		Seed	Start-up	Development	Expansion
Earnings and cash flow	+ 0 −				
Focus of company activity		• Initial R&D • Marketing feasibility studies	• Product development, prototyping and initial marketing • Begin commercialization	• Market development • Building distribution channels	• Full market development • Full-scale manufacturing
Use of capital		• To develop concept or technology	• To move product into market	• For expansion	• To prepare company for public offering or sale
Size of financing		$0 – $250,000	$250,000 – $500,000	$500,000 – $5 million	$5 million+
Your estimates here		$	$	$	$

The first point to note about Table 3:1 is that the total amount is large. It includes sizeable R&D and market development expenditures. Marketing costs are high because software markets for Canadian companies are, geographically at least, North American in scope to begin with and international shortly afterwards. The total amount for market development also depends on the dollar size of the markets you are trying to reach and the number of target buyers, since the key to success for many software developers is to dominate a particular market niche.

A second very important point about relating Table 3:1 to your software development project is that the total amount is not fixed. You can choose to scale your operations up or down to some extent based on your ultimate ambitions (how big do you want to be?) and the rate of growth with which you feel comfortable. Rapid expansion will eat up more capital than slow, steady growth and will attract a different breed of investor.

The choices you make about how big and how fast the business will grow have a ripple effect on every business decision you make. A $5-million project has very different needs for people and skills, premises, etc., than the same project scaled down to a $1-million total commitment. The larger project would also be financed differently from the smaller version, but the most important thing from a financing point of view is that your business plan tells the investor which of these businesses you are.

Use the financial forecast to plan your financing strategy. The value of the financial forecast is not that it is accurate; forecasts rarely are. Its value is in the thought process you go through to prepare it and to explain it to investors. A good financial forecast lets you estimate your total requirements for financing and other resources, and predict in advance when the business will next need to raise money. It also provides you and your investors with a basis for comparing actual results with those that were expected, and for responding promptly to adjust the company's plans.

It takes time to raise money (often four to six months) so allow for it. During an active financing effort your management team will be heavily committed to meeting and negotiating with potential sources and expediting their "due diligence" process, the exercise whereby investors, to the extent they consider appropriate, will independently investigate the claims made in your business plan about the business, its management, and its prospects.

It costs money to raise money. Raising risk capital is one of the more difficult tasks in financing; it requires time, experience, and careful negotiation. If you are fortunate enough to be able to arrange adequate, suitable financing without paying significant out-of-pocket costs for commissions and professional fees, you should, of course, do so. Financing costs are often a normal and necessary expenditure, however, which may range from 5% to 10% of the funds raised, particularly for equity capital. They can include the costs of preparing the business plan, preparing financial forecasts, negotiating with investors, and preparing legal documents. If an agent or underwriter is involved, there may also be a commission of up to 10% of the funds raised. You should allow for these costs in setting the amount to be raised, and carefully manage them like any other cost.

Use good professional advisors. Raising money is a sophisticated skill that many good operating managers lack, especially if they are just starting out. It is well worth the cost and effort to select professional advisors (investment advisors, accountants, and lawyers) who are experienced and recognized for their financing knowledge, preferably in the technology field. They can help you to avoid costly mistakes, and sometimes even to complete a financing that would otherwise fail. The role of your lawyer is particularly important, if you intend to issue shares, to ensure that the company complies with the securities laws (in some circumstances, for example, such laws will not allow you to distribute financial forecasts with your business plan). One thing you will not find in this chapter is an extensive list of the organizations that provide various kinds of financing. Any list is out of date almost as soon as it is committed to paper. New firms are created and the interests and appetites of existing firms change. One reason you rely on financing experts is that it's their business to know who is likely to be actively interested in financing your enterprise today.

There are good times to raise money, such as just before you need it and just after you reach a major milestone. In general, the value of the business increases and the cost of financing decreases as each research and commercialization milestone (e.g., Beta test, first commercial sale, signing a major distribution agreement) is reached. This is logical, since an element of business risk is eliminated each time a critical test is completed successfully. With each round of financing, your objective should be to raise enough to get to the next major milestone, plus enough to cover operating costs while the next round of financing is being raised. That way, financing efforts take place when the business is most attractive to investors.

And there are bad times to raise money, such as just after you run out of cash but before a major milestone is achieved. A company's desperation shows when it needs cash urgently, and investors can be merciless about terms when a company is in distress — if they consider investing at all.

You are known by the company you keep. This is particularly true in information technology, and in any financing arrangement. Build and maintain strong relationships. If you can refer in your business plan to credible individuals, and organizations who will act as references for you and your business, their credibility rubs off on you and makes the job of financing easier. Examples may be suppliers, customers, Beta test sites, members of your board, strategic partners, financing sources, and professional advisors. For obvious business reasons, as well as financing ones, choose these relationships carefully and nurture them. With respect to financing, the investor who is not prepared to invest today may well be receptive when it comes time to raise the "next round." It is important to feel comfortable working with the investors you do choose, because the relationship will likely be a long one, through good times and bad.

We're all grown-ups here. As an emerging software company you will frequently find yourself in business relationships where there is an elephant and a mouse, and you are not the elephant. Be realistic about your negotiating and financial clout and about the bureaucratic behaviour of large organizations. Since clout usually originates with money, one way or another, it is prudent to remember the golden rule — "He who has the gold, rules." It is naive to think that people who have clout won't use it.

What can you do? Choose partners carefully and protect yourself to the extent you can through contract terms. Be frank and honest with lenders and investors. They will find problems and weaknesses eventually, but unpleasant surprises make them wonder what else has been hidden. There is no substitute for competent performance and results to protect your position, but if things are not going well, you can still earn goodwill and respect by showing personal integrity and grace under fire.

We will next review which financing sources you might want to approach — and when, what they have to offer, and what they expect from you.

HOW SOFTWARE BUSINESSES ARE FINANCED

There was a time when understanding Canadian financial markets was much simpler than it is today. Deregulation of the financial services industry and global competition have changed all that. There is a bewildering array of sources, large and small, individuals and organizations, both Canadian and foreign-owned, that provide financing to business. The emerging software business is interested in those that serve small business. The legal mechanisms for investing in a growing company (such as debt, equity, leasing, and government assistance) are equally numerous and confusing — enough to thoroughly baffle an otherwise intelligent and competent entrepreneur. By concentrating on basic principles and avoiding jargon to the extent possible, we will discuss in this chapter how to search out the right source and what choices you have as a growing software company.

Table 3:2 illustrates, somewhat facetiously, the balance sheet of a typical software company.

Space is provided for you to slot in actual numbers from the financial statements of your own company. Table 3:2 highlights the financial facts of life for the emerging software business. The assets of the business are listed on the left in this typical balance sheet. You can expect to see the following:

- There may be a limited amount of accounts receivable, but only if the company has begun making commercial sales or does consulting; inventory is usually nominal.

- There will be only small amounts of fixed assets, usually limited to office furniture and research equipment; wherever leasing can be used instead of outright ownership, it is usually the wiser choice (see page 91).

- The real assets are largely intangible: the software product, the value of its market position, if any, and people. These are generally not recorded, and do not have collateral value for borrowing purposes.

Table 3:2

YER BASIC SOFTWARE COMPANY, INC.: BALANCE SHEET

ASSETS	TYPICAL COMPANY	YOUR COMPANY	LIABILITIES	TYPICAL COMPANY	YOUR COMPANY
Current • Accounts receivable • Inventory	$ If commercial sales Usually nil	$	Current • Accounts payable • Operating bank debt	50 – 75% of current assets	$
Fixed	Small		Long term • Term debt	50 – 75% of fixed assets	
Intangible • Software • Name recognition • People • Deferred R&D • Goodwill	Small		Equity • Subordinated debt • Share capital • Retained s earning	The rest	

The right side of the balance sheet shows how the business is financed, and illustrates the very real difficulty technology firms have raising money. The horizontal divisions and alignment with related assets are intentional. The available amount of each type of financing shown on the right is directly tied to the value of the corresponding asset category on the left. This same relationship holds for any business, but the lending ratios will be different. With respect to liabilities and shareholders' equity you can expect the following:

- Short-term credit from suppliers and a bank operating line of credit are typically available in amounts equal to 50% to 75% of the value of accounts receivable (and inventory, if there is any); the percentage depends on how easily the lender could liquidate these assets under distress conditions; the borrowing ratio can sometimes be increased for export receivables by government guarantees (see page 77).

- Term debt with a fixed term greater than one year, and preferably a fixed interest rate, can be raised against fixed assets (land, buildings, and equipment) to the extent of, say, 50% (up to 75% for real estate), again depending on the amount the lender could expect to receive if the assets had to be sold to recover the loan.

- The remainder of the financing for the business must typically come from "equity" or "near-equity": subordinated debt, share capital, and retained earnings; retained earnings is often negative because of start-up losses.

As the risk of loss to the lender/investor increases, so does the cost of financing to the business. Because even mature software businesses do not usually have "bankable assets" (assets with collateral value) in quantity, you can expect to work hard to raise the money you need, and it is usually expensive money.

The income statement for Yer Basic Software Company, shown in Table 3:3, reflects the high up-front investment in research, marketing, and administrative costs required to launch new software products.

This large and persistent cash outflow is a second reason why debt is an inappropriate financing vehicle for early-stage software development firms; all the business's cash is needed to fund development and is not available to make interest or principal payments on debt. Note that the profit margins on software products are high to recover the early investments in R&D and marketing. Government assistance, in the form of contributions and investment tax credits, reduces the costs it relates to, usually R&D.

Table 3:3

YER BASIC SOFTWARE COMPANY, INC.: INCOME STATEMENT

	TYPICAL COMPANY	YOUR COMPANY
Sales	$ Some	$
Less: Cost of sales	Low	_____
Gross profit	High	_____
Selling, general, and administration	More	
R&D	Potfuls	
Less: Government assistance	( )	
Less: Investment tax credits	( )	
Loss and deficit	$ ( )	_____

Table 3:4 summarizes the sources of financing commonly used by emerging software companies, their approximate cost, and the circumstances in which each is applicable. Table 3:4 and the rest of this chapter are your roadmap to the sources available to you now. Read it again a year from now and it will point you to different possibilities.

Financing Strategy

Financing strategy is your long-term plan for raising money. The following decisions are required:

- Estimate the total amount your business will need to raise to get it to the stage at which revenue exceeds expenses and the business can support itself. Use Table 3:1 and your financial forecast to build up the total of the amounts you need for each of the four stages of development (seed, start-up, development, and expansion).

- Identify the two or three major milestones you intend to use to launch a major financing effort. Examples might be completion of Beta testing or first commercial sales. These milestones determine the approximate amount and timing of major financing efforts. You need to raise enough in the first financing to get you through to the second, and so on.

- Using the balance sheet for your company and Table 3:4, select the lowest-cost financing sources that are likely to be available for your next financing, and prepare to approach them. Start thinking about future rounds, but there is no need to make decisions until the time comes.

Table 3:4

SOURCES OF FINANCING FOR EMERGING SOFTWARE COMPANIES

FINANCING TYPE/ MARKET SEGMENT	AMOUNT GENERALLY AVAILABLE	TYPICAL COST	WHEN AVAILABLE
Suppliers	Limited by credit terms	Free (until payment due)	Always, to the extent of nonsalary expenses
Founders' investment	As much as you can scrape together	Free (until company pays dividend)	Limited by personal finances of the owners and employees
Earnings	Sales and other revenue in excess of costs	Free (until company pays dividend)	The sooner the better
Strategic partnering	Varies, but can be substantial	Varies, but usually less than similar equity amount	Where a fit exists between a smaller and a larger organization
Government assistance	Varies, but can be substantial	Free or low	R&D, job creation, export, government procurement
Bank operating line	50–75% of receivables plus 50% of inventory	Prime plus 1 – 3%	Need customer quality and readily saleable inventories
Bank term debt	50% of equipment; 70–75% of appraised real estate values	Prime plus 3% Mortgage base rate	For funding readily saleable equipment and real estate
Leasing	Most fixed assets	Prime plus 3%	Almost always
Venture capital	$250,000 – $500,000 and up	30% – 60% per annum	Where the business has strong management and projects rapid growth
Subordinated debt	Usually accompanies venture capital	Prime plus 1 – 30% based on term and security	As for venture capital and for more mature businesses
Going public	$250,000 up to several million	25 – 35%	Depends on the state of the financial markets

- Be opportunistic about strategic alliances (see page 73) and government assistance (see page 76). These two possibilities can surface any time and can be used to extend the gap between major financings or to reduce the amount you would otherwise need.

Remember that financing is any source that makes cash available to fund software development: it can be a cash inflow or a reduced cash outflow. It only makes sense to exhaust the free and low-cost sources of funds, to the extent they are available, before the more expensive ones. One obvious way to maximize available cash is to hoard the cash you already have through careful project management and cost control. Missed deadlines and cost overruns in research and marketing programs cost money. Make use of supplier credit and collect accounts receivable. Explore government assistance and strategic alliances as lower-cost alternatives to venture capital. Lease, rather than buy, assets to conserve funds.

Young software companies often take on contract work for others as a way of covering fixed costs. While this makes sense, within limits, a word of warning is in order. There is a real danger of losing focus when you divert people's valuable time and attention, which are scarce resources, from the main software project. Some software companies maintain their focus and momentum by taking on only "strategic" consulting assignments: assignments where someone will pay them to do work they would have to do anyway to develop the product.

Basic Forms of Financing

The remaining sections of this chapter cover the commonly used options for outside financing that you can build into your financing strategy. Outside financing can come in one of three basic forms although, as you will see, hybrids are common and the boundaries between the categories can be somewhat fuzzy. Money may be provided in the form of debt, equity, or a contribution.

Debt, or borrowing, is financing with a fixed obligation to repay the amount borrowed plus interest. Debt may be "senior" or "secured" in that tangible assets are pledged as collateral and are expected to have a net realizable value (to the lender) on liquidation equal to or greater than the outstanding loan. The cost of debt is interest, and sometimes there are fees to put the loan agreement in place. "Subordinated" or "unsecured" debt has a claim to the remaining realizable value of assets, if there is any, once the senior debt has been repaid. Amounts owing to suppliers are a form of unsecured debt that has no interest cost. In a software company, it is not unusual for subordinated debt to have very little security protection for practical purposes and to be virtually equivalent to share capital or equity in terms of risk to the lender.

Equity is raised initially by selling shares. Common or preferred shares have no fixed repayment terms but entitle the investor to share in the ownership of the business according to the share terms (usually up to the amount contributed for preferred shares, or in proportion to their ownership in the case of common shares). Equity is increased by accumulated earnings and by any increase in the value of the business, and is decreased by accumulated losses or milestones missed. The cost of equity is its right to a proportionate share of the earnings and growth in value of the business. Subordinated debt is debt in legal form (there is an obligation to repay), but in substance it is often the equivalent of common share equity in a software business. Any repayment of principal and interest is dependent on the success of the venture, and preferential legal rights to income or security provide little practical protection. Debt with these characteristics is sometimes called quasi-equity or near-equity. It is frequently convertible into common shares.

A *contribution* includes, for example, most government assistance, investment tax credits, or up-front licence payments. It is more like equity than debt, because it does not have to be repaid, but it does not entitle the provider to participate in the earnings and growth in value of the business the same way a common shareholder would.

Government assistance and financing obtained from strategic partners can be debt or equity or a contribution. Venture capital and going public are sources of equity.

The Canadian Financing Environment Compared with the U.S.

Canadian software entrepreneurs operate in a North American market with United States competitors who have access to U.S. financing sources. Accordingly, you can quite properly ask how the availability of risk capital for Canadian software companies compares with that for their U.S. counterparts. It is fair to say that the private and public equity markets in Canada do not have the breadth and depth of the U.S. markets, but they do not lack for sophistication, either in using innovative financing techniques or in analyzing and evaluating investments. The market lacks breadth in that there are fewer sources in Canada, as you would expect, given the relative size of the two nations' populations and economies. There are fewer venture capital firms, individuals, and institutions whose investment criteria include early-stage technology investments. The market lacks depth in the sense that the amount these sources have to invest in such investments is relatively smaller, and they do not have the opportunity to spread risk that a larger fund might have. These constraints do not mean, however, that a strong, well-managed company with good potential cannot be financed.

The sections that follow are organized to discuss outside financing sources in the approximate chronological order in which they would be used by a "typical" software business. The lower-cost options are covered first, to the extent that they are available. Thus, debt follows venture capital, since, although it is cheaper, it is usually not available in sufficient amounts in the early stages of a company's growth.

STRATEGIC PARTNERSHIPS

Strategic partnering is commonly defined as a mutually beneficial alliance — between a large company and an innovative young company — which is built on the strengths of both parties. In financing your software company, it would involve obtaining funds from a large established company, combined with other benefits that would not normally accompany more traditional sources of funds. The financing aspect of corporate partnering may be any source of cash to fund the development process. It can be a cash inflow or a reduced cash outflow, such as loaned equipment or development equipment supplied at a deeply discounted price, or free technical or development support.

The most common form of strategic financing is "turf financing," and it illustrates very well the synergy that develops in these relationships. Turf financing, also called entitlement financing, generally involves the sale of a bundle of rights to the product being developed by the young software company, in addition to, or instead of, a direct equity investment. These rights may include, for example, rights to sell the product in a particular geographical area or in a particular limited market, or to use the product or further develop it in a way that is not the primary focus of your company.

For example, a Canadian company might fund North American market development by selling the rights to market its software product in Europe for an up-front payment and an on-going stream of royalties based on sales. The investor would be a European company in a related business that can critically evaluate the product and already has the infrastructure to market and support it in Europe. Now for the synergy: the European investor gets the rights to a software product that will round out its product offering, and earns the distribution profit on each sale. In effect the cost of this "investment" to the entrepreneur is lower because the European investor is getting part of his return from the marketplace, not just from the income generated by the Canadian software partner. The entrepreneur meanwhile has sold a bunch of rights that, realistically, the business couldn't have used for some time anyway.

Benefits sought by the investor include the following:

• Access to products it needs but does not now have — it can round out the product line, improve an existing product, or provide the next generation of products.

• Access to technology or people or creativity not otherwise available to it.

- Diversification, a priority for many mature industries, but in an area that is known and understood — many large Canadian companies, particularly in manufacturing and resource industries, are large users of advanced technology, including software, and have the engineering and scientific resources to understand and appreciate both the technological and the market potential of software innovations.

- A level of risk in new ventures that is manageable.

For you, the entrepreneurial technology company, there are also some big plusses:

- What is being given up has high value to others, but limited current value to you because you lack the resources to exploit it.

- The credibility that you achieve through your public association with a recognized and respected partner is worth its weight in gold.

- Your company gains faster entry to markets on a wider scale than would be possible otherwise. You stand a better chance of establishing yourself as a market leader than if you could only build volume at the pace your own resources permit. Typically, as a young company you have your hands full initially developing your primary markets in North America, without going further afield right away.

- Often the strategic investor can provide valuable business skills and resources with a depth that is not available to even the most capable small company management team. This may be as simple as having a senior executive of the strategic investor sit on your board, but can also include an ad hoc mentoring relationship that is useful in dealing with the stresses of rapid growth.

- The strategic investor is often there for the longer term. In contrast to the "pure" venture capital investor (see page 81), for whom a medium-term exit strategy is essential, a strategic investor may be quite content to maintain its position for as long as it makes business sense. While you may sincerely intend to see your venture investors taken out profitably, the need to provide them with liquidity can be awkward or expensive if the financial markets are not rosy or the timing is wrong for the company.

- The strategic investor may have deeper pockets or a faster response time in reacting to subsequent financing needs (because you are a known quantity) and does not have the same need as a venture capital investor to spread risk or syndicate investments.

The last two factors can be very important to an early-stage company with a steep growth curve. Strategic partnering, if available, can be particularly valuable in the earlier stages of a software company's development — Beta test, preproduction prototype, or initial commercialization — because the investor is taking a calculated strategic risk rather than a venture capitalist's portfolio risk, and may also be comfortable with a longer-term view.

Besides turf financing there are many other strategic relationships that have a direct or indirect financing component. These are limited only by the ingenuity of the parties involved in finding ways to benefit from synergy. Financing can mean finding new and better ways either to make cash flow in, or to reduce cash flowing out — while still accomplishing the same objective. Using the existing sales force or distribution channels of an established company to mutual advantage keeps costs down.

The way in which contract R&D is carried out can have a big impact on total costs. Say you want some development work done on a hardware component for your product, such as a robot, which will eventually have to be manufactured in quantity. You could buy the special equipment, hire people, and do the work yourself. That might cost $300,000. Or you could contact a potential supplier of the component, convince it to provide the equipment, and engage them to do contract research for, say, $100,000. Or you could get them so excited about the potential for the product that they do the research at their own expense and license it to you in exchange for future royalties.

In the computer industry the major hardware manufacturers, through seed capital programs and other means, support companies that provide software, networks, and peripherals that enhance the manufacturer's total package. These programs may involve direct investment, providing development hardware at little or no cost, consulting and development assistance, prime/sub-contractor agreements, designation as a qualified software supplier, or joint marketing and value-added reseller agreements.

Successful long-term relationships are the key to success for a software business, and a significant strategic financing partner can be among the most important of those relationships. The following considerations should be borne in mind in selecting and negotiating with a potential partner, and in living with that partner afterwards.

Management is the key. Your business plan should provide your potential partner with a strong comfort level in terms of your technical and management ability to carry off the business plan, your management's ability to work together, and your ability to report to the partner monthly in a prompt, reliable way what is going on in the business and how the partner's investment is doing. Corporate investors often require control or outright acquisition. If you can convince your partner that you have strong financial and operating control of the business, it may forego this requirement. Some excellent partnerships have been rejected outright because the entrepreneurial principals would never agree to become employees.

The business plan. Strategic partnering is just another form of financing — no one plunks down a few million dollars without a thorough analysis and understanding of the investment. The time frame for making an investment decision is no shorter, and may well be longer, than with other financing sources.

Lead times are long. Good strategic relationships take time to build. Allow for that in your financing timetable, and nurse them along. Someone who is unwilling to commit today may be in your corner a year from now when you've passed a couple more milestones or they have come to know you.

Be sure you are dealing with a decision maker. You can waste a lot of time selling your business to the wrong person in the organization. Find out who you have to convince, be sure to meet them, however briefly, and ascertain what their key criteria are and what you have to do to satisfy them.

Establish a beach-head. If your potential strategic partner is a customer or a supplier, sometimes an effective way to establish credibility is to convince their internal operating people of the capabilities of your product, so they'll be your allies. Instead of making a cold call, you may be upgrading an existing business relationship into an investment relationship.

The use of strategic alliances is not yet as prevalent in Canada as in the United States, which seems to indicate untapped business opportunities for Canadian technology companies, large and small.

GOVERNMENT ASSISTANCE

Notwithstanding the current climate of fiscal austerity in government, there are still some government agencies providing financial assistance to encourage businesses to undertake activities that will further their governments' economic and social objectives. While the total amount of assistance is not what it once was, such assistance is still available from federal, provincial, and municipal agencies and through the income tax system, and may take the form of grants, loans, loan guarantees, tax concessions, or equity investment.

The federal and provincial governments currently assign a high priority to the renewal and expansion of Canada's scientific, technological, managerial, and production base. Government's objective is to promote the international competitiveness of Canadian industry, and small business is viewed as having an important role to play. Financial assistance is available to encourage industrial research and development, technology transfer, and the use of advanced technology.

These benefits can only be realized if the project is commercially viable, however, so the case you build in the business plan is important here also. Government assistance can significantly lower your cost of financing in circumstances where government policy and your business objectives mesh. A government's objectives should be viewed as its lending criteria. Your business plan and application should clearly demonstrate the benefits to government of supporting your project. A successful application promises economic growth, which leads to increased tax revenue, advancement of technology, job creation and training, improved balance of payments through exports or import replacement, and technology transfer. Certain levels of private-sector funding are usually also required. Governments view investment by the private sector as further evidence that the project has commercial merit. Agencies also require that you establish the need for the funds; you should not have made any firm financial commitments to the project prior to submitting the application.

Any published reference source for government assistance programs and their criteria, including this one, quickly becomes dated as programs are added or deleted, or as a particular program runs out of funds from time to time. The following is a list of the federal and provincial assistance programs that are most frequently used by software companies operating in Ontario. Much of this discussion of financing applies regardless of where in Canada a software business is located. In this section, however, the provincial programs available in Ontario have been used for illustration purposes. The array of programs offered by other provinces is similar, and you should explore what is available locally if you operate elsewhere in Canada. Tax-related incentives, such as the R&D tax credit, are not discussed here as they have been explained in Chapter 2.

NRC Industrial Research Assistance Program

The National Research Council's (NRC) Industrial Research Assistance Program (IRAP) provides assistance to Canadian small and medium-sized businesses to tap the scientific and engineering expertise in government laboratories, specialized research centres, universities, and consulting engineering firms, or to acquire foreign technology which will help you to build a strong, competitive business. Grant assistance is available to pay a percentage of the salaries of students for short work terms or a percentage of the direct and contract costs of approved research projects. Both large and small projects are eligible.

Business Development Bank of Canada (BDBC) (formerly Federal Business Development Bank)

Along with management-help programs to assist businesses with exporting and achieving ISO 9000 certification, the BDBC has several programs that are available to provide financing to businesses in Canada.

- *Term Loans.* The BDBC provides term loans to businesses in Canada that are unable to obtain financing from other sources on reasonable terms and conditions. The loans are generally granted to fund capital expenditures, but the BDBC also provides money to replenish working capital (particularly when a business has used its working capital to undertake capital expenditures).

- *Venture Loans.* Venture loans are available to entrepreneurs who offer established earnings and a strong growth potential.

- *Venture Capital.* The BDBC has become a major force in the venture capital field, assisting both new and established businesses to achieve a high growth potential. Often such assistance is provided in conjunction with conventional private sector sources of venture capital.

- *Patient Capital.* The patient capital program was established to provide loans from $50,000 to $250,000 to new high technology firms lacking the collateral for conventional financing. Payments on account of principal and interest can be postponed for up to three years. Interest is calculated using a base interest rate plus royalties on sales.

- *Micro-Business.* The micro-business program was established to provide loans of up to $25,000 to very small businesses and entrepreneurs who have completed a BDBC-run training program and developed a realistic business plan.

- *Working Capital.* This program offers term loans for supplementary working capital for businesses that have discovered opportunities for expansion or growth. The program provides any additional funding, in the form of working capital loans, that is needed over financing from conventional lending sources. Small and medium-sized Canadian-owned businesses may be eligible for funding if they have identified new or expanded markets for their products, but need working capital to take advantage of these growth opportunities. The maximum loan available is $100,000.

Investment Canada Investment Development Program (IDP)

IDP works to attract investment that makes Canada more innovative and increases its international competitiveness. The program is especially interested in attracting investment that introduces new technology. Diplomatic staff in about 50 of Canada's missions abroad actively promote investment in Canada and respond to inquiries of both foreign investors and Canadian companies. The program attempts to meet the specific needs of Canadian companies searching for foreign sources of investment and technology.

Small Business Development Corporations

The Ontario Small Business Development Corporation (SBDC) program is designed to encourage investment in certain types of Ontario small businesses by combining the concepts of venture capital and government assistance. The SBDC investor resident in Ontario receives a 25% grant (to an individual) or tax credit (to a corporation paying tax in Ontario), thus reducing the amount at risk to $0.75 for each dollar invested ($0.70 in northern and eastern Ontario where the grant or tax credit is equal to 30% of the amount invested). One or more SBDCs may invest up to $2.5 million in any one small business that is primarily engaged in an eligible activity. Software development and "computer services" are eligible activities for SBDC purposes.

There are detailed, often complex, requirements governing how a SBDC and the companies it invests in conduct their affairs, but if these are acceptable to you and the SBDC investors, a SBDC can be a useful mechanism for raising up to $2.5 million.

Industry Canada Microelectronics and Systems Development Program (MSDP)

MSDP is part of InnovAction, a comprehensive Canadian government strategy to promote the research and development of innovative technologies in Canada. MSDP is a cost-sharing program that provides financial support to encourage Canadian companies to undertake technologically innovative ventures in microelectronics and systems development. Eligible projects include software development for communication, processing and display of information in real-time, and applications in production and process control. MSDP covers 50% of eligible costs to a maximum of $5 million, with repayment required for amounts over $500,000.

Program for Export Market Development (PEMD)

Administered by Foreign Affairs and International Trade Canada, PEMD's objective is to increase Canadian exports. To this end, PEMD will share the cost of various types of export promotion activities, such as visits, trade fairs, missions and project bidding that businesses could not or would not undertake alone, thereby reducing the risks to the business. Support is limited to small or medium-sized businesses with annual sales of less than $10 million and/or less than 100 employees for a manufacturing firm and less than 50 employees for a service firm. Participation in government-sponsored trade fairs is cost-shared for smaller firms, based on a sliding-scale formula.

A related project is WIN Exports. WIN Exports is a computer database of Canadian exporters and their capabilities, implemented to help exporters find opportunities by registering with it. The database is used by government trade staff at over 100 offices around the world. A foreign buyer calling WIN Export's trade staff in any country can quickly receive a Canadian company's information. The database is also used to invite Canadian exporters to trade shows and missions, and to receive foreign market information and intelligence.

Business Improvement Loans/Small Business Bond

The *Small Business Loans Act* (*SBLA*) is a federal government initiative designed to help new and existing small business enterprises obtain term loans from chartered banks and other lending institutions to help finance the purchase and improvement of fixed assets. Loans are made directly by lenders to small businesses. The *SBLA* provides for any loan losses to be shared between the federal government and its lenders. The maximum loan amount available is $250,000, and must be used for the purchase of land, construction or extension of premises or the purchase of equipment (which includes software).

Export Development Corporation (EDC)

The EDC is a financial services corporation dedicated to helping Canadian business succeed in the global marketplace. The EDC's programs fall into four major categories: a) export credit insurance, covering short- and medium-term credits; b) performance-related guarantees and insurance, providing cover for exporters and financial institutions against calls on various performance bonds and obligations normally issued either by banks or surety companies; c) foreign investment insurance, providing political risk protection for new Canadian investments abroad; and d) export financing, providing medium- and long-term export financing to foreign buyers of Canadian goods and services.

The advancement of technology, the development of related skills and the nurturing of strong, technology-based Canadian enterprises are likely to remain government priorities through the latter half of the 1990s. Government financial assistance may be an important source of funding that you should explore fully at all stages in your company's development.

It should also be noted that the Government of Canada Web sites on the INTERNET are chock full of useful information for the exporting or otherwise entrepreneurial software company owner or manager. The Government of Canada site (http://canada.gc.ca) offers links to many federal organizations that have their own Web sites, and additional links are planned as more federal organizations come on-line. The Canada site is very well organized, with good graphics and informative and helpful links. Industry Canada's Strategis Web site (http://strategis.ic.gc.ca) is also relevant to software companies. It provides access to Industry Canada's extensive enterprise and information resources, including 60,000 reports, 500,000 pages of searchable text, 2 gigabytes of statistical data and links to Canadian and international business information databases. Information is divided into six categories: markets trade & investment, industrial perspectives, technology & innovation, microeconomic research and analysis, managing your business, and marketplace services.

VENTURE CAPITAL IN ALL ITS FORMS

Venture capital is the term used in this chapter to describe private equity investment in a closely held corporation. You will recall that equity is raised initially by selling shares. Common or preferred shares have no fixed repayment terms but entitle the investor to share in the ownership of the business. Equity is increased by accumulated earnings and by any increase in the value of the business, and is decreased by accumulated losses. The cost of equity is its right to a proportionate share of the earnings and growth in value of the business.

To understand venture capital, start with the word "venture": it means risk. A software developer with good potential for strong, rapid growth is the type of investment that attracts the venture capitalist. The venture capitalist shares the founders' high risk and wants to see a clear prospect for growth and, ultimately, a high return on the investment (typically 30% to 60% a year, or more).

There are three sources of venture capital equity investment: the founding management group, wealthy individuals, and the firms in the venture capital industry. Most of this chapter is devoted to the formal venture capital industry, which operates by decision rules that are reasonably consistent across firms. The first two sources, the founding shareholders and wealthy individuals, may have less rigid criteria. They may also be the main or only sources of equity investment available to you if you are in the seed or start-up stages of development, or if your growth aspirations are not ambitious enough to appeal to the venture capital investor.

The Founders

The initial investors in almost any business are the owner or management group and their relatives, friends, and associates. Their initial capital, supplemented by government assistance, is required to establish the business, to develop the idea for the software product into an early prototype in order to demonstrate that the concept works, and to accumulate information to prove that a market for the product exists. As owners, you should contribute as much of your own capital as possible to the business, and strain your personal resources to the limit to do so. Ownership should extend to all the key people in the business. Outside investors judge the amount of this contribution in relation to your personal resources, rather than as a dollar amount: for a young management group, $30,000 each might represent a significant contribution, while a group of senior executives would be expected to provide, say, $200,000 each.

For you, the owners, this contribution supports your entitlement to retain a larger interest in the business. Money counts more in the eyes of the outside investor than the founders' contribution of time, energy, sweat, and talent. With a bigger investment, you can also bring the business further along and increase its value before asking outside investors to buy in. Outside investors view your cash investment as important evidence of your commitment to the project. If the people who are key to the success of the business have most of their personal financial resources tied up in it, it is also harder for them to walk away when times get tough, leaving the venture capital investor holding the company and not much else.

Wealthy Individuals

The most elusive outside investors who provide venture capital in small but useful amounts to emerging businesses are wealthy individuals (sometimes called "angels") willing to invest in promising young companies. There is little in the way of an organized market for identifying these sources, however, which makes it difficult to find one, let alone the one or ones whose investment criteria happen to include emerging software companies. A number of government and private-sector organizations operate "matching services" that list, usually for a nominal fee, businesses seeking investment capital or for sale, and correspondingly, potential investors or purchasers. Your business is briefly described, as are the investment criteria of the investors/purchasers. Making contact and negotiating a successful transaction are usually up to the two parties.

While there will no doubt be many false starts and blind alleys in trying to strike this type of match, the following organizations operate in Ontario and may be of assistance. Similar local forums exist in other parts of the country. You should also talk to business associates, particularly those in your industry, and professional advisors such as accountants and lawyers to obtain referrals.

- The Ontario Ministry of Economic Development, Trade & Tourism operates a confidential matchmaking service for Ontario companies. The purpose of this database is to link investors and businesses seeking investment. A brief, confidential description is provided of the opportunity offered or the investment sought, with advisors arranging for interested parties to meet.

- The Computerized Ontario Investment Network (COIN) is a computer database that matches entrepreneurs looking for capital with investors offering funds. Venture capital in amounts from $5,000 to $500,000 can be offered or sought. A computer search lists the matches, and the investor is contacted. An executive summary of the business plan is provided if the investor is interested. Names are then exchanged if the parties wish to proceed. A six-month listing for an entrepreneur costs $300, and for an investor $200. Contact Venture Link Canada for information.

- The Ontario Ministry of Revenue Small Business Development Corporation (SBDC) program is described on page 79. Officials of the program will also advise existing SBDCs of eligible investment opportunities. The service is free of charge. The maximum investment by SBDCs in any one business is $2.5 million

The Venture Capital Industry

At December 31, 1994, the capital under management by the Canadian venture capital industry amounted to $4.96 billion, up $934 million from 1993. The firms in the industry include independent private corporations or partnerships, venture capital subsidiaries of corporations, and federal and provincial crown corporations. The independent, private firms are funded by pension funds, insurance companies, and other financial institutions, corporations, individuals, and foreign sources. The corporate subsidiaries and crown corporations are funded by their sponsors.

Venture capital pools are managed by professional investment managers who are experienced in venture capital investing. It is the track record of these individuals that attracts investors to the private firms. Funds are committed to the private firms for periods of from seven to ten years or longer, after which the returns are distributed to the investors.

Investments are spread across industries and between stages of growth of portfolio companies (early-stage, expansion, buyout/acquisition, turn-around, etc.). Sometimes the investment criteria of the fund limit its participation in certain types of investments; for example, some funds' investment criteria specify second-round or later financings, but not early-stage or turnaround financing.

Venture capital investors look for certain critical characteristics in an investment candidate, including a highly skilled and committed management team with entrepreneurial spirit, a competitive market advantage, and a clearly defined and achievable strategic plan. We've already identified these as necessary ingredients for any successful growth business. There are other features of venture capital investing that you should understand.

The venture investor needs rapid, explosive growth to generate target rates of return. You will recall that in discussing the rules of the financing game (page 62) we advised you to make clear decisions about how big you want your business to be and how fast you are prepared to grow, and to reflect those decisions in your business plan. Entrepreneurs are often puzzled or offended when they get a lukewarm reception from the venture capital community. While there is nothing wrong with adopting a sure and steady, slower-growth strategy, you should be aware that your company may not have the growth potential to qualify as a venture capital investment.

The venture capitalist does not participate in day-to-day management, but is not a passive investor. One of the characteristics of venture investing, and one of the benefits to the investee of the right venture partner, is the value added to the business through active participation by the venture capitalist. By receiving and responding to regular reports on the business, and often through being represented on the board of directors, the venture capitalist provides valuable guidance as well as business and entrepreneurial expertise. If problems or delays develop, the venture investor may become more actively involved for a period of time until they are resolved. The role and rights of the venture capital investors are usually formalized in a shareholders' agreement.

There is considerable interaction and co-operation among venture capital firms, which is most evident in their practice of syndicating investments. One way in which venture capitalists spread risk in their portfolios is to invite other firms to participate in larger investments. A $3.5 million investment might be split among three firms, with one firm taking the lead role. The lead investor will typically take a strong enough liking to the investment opportunity (perhaps the manager knows the product and is attracted by its potential or is impressed with the management group) to do the bulk of the due diligence effort and to negotiate the terms of the investment. The other two firms would piggyback on the work done by the lead investor, but would reciprocate by taking the lead role in some other investment. This process benefits you, because the lead firm ensures that the full amount is raised, although it is not prepared to provide it all itself. You also have three investors to approach in subsequent financings, rather than just one.

The venture investor will want to see one or preferably more than one route to exit (sell his holdings) in the medium term, say five to seven years. Venture capital is not permanent capital, but it is long-term capital. Among the exit methods commonly used by venture capitalists are (a) an initial public offering (IPO) (see page 87); (b) shares purchased by the company itself or by the other shareholders; (c) private sale of their interest to other outside investors; or (d) acquisition or merger of the company with a larger firm.

The venture capitalist's strategy to exit a particular investment depends on the conditions prevailing at the time. An investment in a successful business may be a suitable candidate for a public offering, if market conditions are favourable. Moderate winners may become acquisition targets for larger companies. The exit of choice from the venture capitalist's point of view is the one that provides the highest value for the investment, although sometimes considerations of liquidity enter into the equation. An all-cash offer may be preferable to an IPO, where the venture capitalist's shares will be subject to escrow requirements (trading restrictions) for a number of years, or to an acquisition for cash and debt. The ideal timing of the exit, again from the venture capitalist's point of view, is illustrated in Figure 3:1.

The right time to exit is when the company has reached the peak of its fast-growth phase. At this point the company has gotten the maximum use from the venture funds, and the investor has maximized his return.

If you have a venture capital investor, you will have to accommodate the investor's need to exit, which results in part because the venture capital fund has a limited life. You should be prepared to finance the purchase of the holding using either the company's own funds or those of the other shareholders, or outside money raised for the purpose. An established, mature software company with good cash flow may be a candidate for a leveraged buyout (buying the shares with borrowed money, then using the company's future cash flow to pay the interest and principal) or a private placement of equity, awaiting the appropriate time for an IPO.

Figure 3: 1

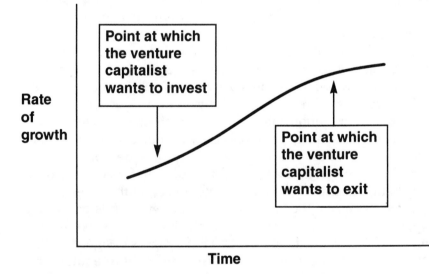

The issue of control is often contentious in negotiations with venture investors. Most entrepreneurs are aghast to hear the percentage ownership of the company that venture investors require for providing funding, especially early-stage funding. This disagreement may arise from a genuine difference of opinion as to the value of the founders' contribution or from your psychological aversion to giving up legal control of your business and your destiny. The value of your contribution legitimately includes (a) the cash you have invested in the project; (b) the collective experience and talent of the management team and its ability to achieve the business plan, so-called "sweat equity"; (c) an ill-defined ownership right arising from having the guts and entrepreneurial drive to put the project and the team together and to hold it together this far; and (d) the value of the product at its current stage of development.

You are, however, asking the venture capital investors ultimately to provide several million dollars, over two or three rounds of financing, which is also critical to the project's success. It is reasonable for them to expect to share in the rewards and to build controls into the business relationship to protect their investment. The right venture partner also offers broad business experience, which can mean the difference between surviving and failing in troubled times. The percentage of the company the investors need to acquire is driven by their rate-of-return targets, and takes into account that not all investments are spectacularly successful. Those targets, in the range of 35% to 60% per year or higher, are a fair return to compensate for the financial risk.

It is also important that your management group retain enough of a stake to motivate them to build the company into a superior performer, but in a mature company, after two or three rounds of financing, this stake might be reduced to 15% to 25% at the stage of going public. If you are successful, that stake should be quite valuable, and if you do not perform, you should expect to be held accountable by the other investors.

The legal form of venture capital investment may be common or preferred shares, or subordinated debt, but in substance it is the equivalent of common-share equity in an emerging software business. Any return on disposition or earlier depends on your success. Preferential legal rights to income or security provide little practical protection. Subordinated debt with these characteristics is sometimes referred to as quasi-equity or near-equity. If your company is more mature and has commercial sales, you may be able to provide your venture investors with part of their return in the form of a regular preferred-share dividend or interest payment, but usually it is in the interests of all the investors for the company to reinvest its cash in the business to fuel growth. While part of the investment may appear to involve a lower return to the investor (a subordinated loan bearing interest at 10%, say), the total investment package is designed so that overall return is consistent with the venture capitalist's target "hurdle rate." This may be accomplished by using debt that is convertible into common shares or that is accompanied by options or warrants entitling the investor to additional shares.

How much venture capital investment is available to the software industry in Canada? Of the amount invested by the Canadian venture capital industry at December 31, 1994, 18% is in the category of Computers and Software, up from 16% in 1994. Amounts disbursed in 1994 to early-stage and expansion-stage businesses were 25% and 56% respectively, compared to 29% and 39%, respectively, in 1993. Generally speaking, venture capital investing is somewhat cyclical, not in the strict sense of following the business cycle, but in shifting its emphasis to find the best opportunities. Nevertheless, there are Canadian firms with an interest in the software industry. The level of interest in software investment is quite respectable, and new funds are formed from time to time. There is no reason that a well-managed company with strong growth potential cannot be financed. At any time, though, you need persistence, effort, and a professional approach.

GOING PUBLIC

The public stock markets are highly regulated, and therefore represent a financing and operating environment for a business that is very different from private venture capital sources. Most business people follow the cyclical ups and downs of the public stock markets. When the stock market is hot and share prices are high, it is very attractive for business to go to the stock market to raise money. When times are good, risk capital is easier to find, and the market's tolerance for risk is sufficient to accommodate initial public offerings (IPOs) by relatively young, untested companies, like those in the technology sector. When the public's appetite for buying shares begins to cool, however, it is the higher-risk stocks, such as the young technology companies and the recent or imminent IPOs, that lose favour first. Nevertheless, there is now a long list of Canadian companies in the software field that have gone public both in Canada and the U.S., including Corel, Cognos, Hummingbird, PC DOCS, Architel and InContext.

In the right circumstances, however, a public issue of shares can be an attractive financing option for a software company. Going public is one of the preferred routes for venture capital investors to liquidate profitable investments; if investors need to be bought out but neither the company nor the other shareholders have the resources, going public provides an alternative. Shares or stock options held by key management and employees become more attractive as an incentive to motivate and retain good people, since their value is readily determined in the public market and shares are more easily traded than they could be when the company was private. The liquidity provided by having publicly traded shares may also increase the value of management's block of shares, although they will be subject to escrow requirements (trading restrictions) for a period of time.

One of the benefits of going public is that the company becomes more visible and acquires the prestige customarily accorded to public companies. Through press releases and other public announcements, and through listing in the stock market tables each day, your company and its software products become known to the business and financial community, investors, and the general public.

There are also disadvantages to going public. A public company is required by law to publish timely and reliable financial information, and your management information system may need to be strengthened to permit reporting of reliable quarterly financial information, typically within 60 days of the end of each quarter. There is an immense time commitment from senior management in preparing the initial public offering, which will divert attention from managing your day-to-day operations. A public company is required to disclose extensive information about its operations at the time of the initial offering and on a continuing basis thereafter. Some owners and managers are more perturbed than others at losing their privacy and disclosing sensitive competitive information.

The cash cost of a public offering can be substantial, although presumably this cost will be included in determining the amount to be raised. The largest single cost will be the underwriters' commission, which would normally be in the 5% to 7% range for larger issues, ranging upward beyond 10% for smaller or more speculative issues. The expenses of the issue, in addition to the underwriters' commission, vary considerably, but can range from as little as $60,000 for a small, simple issue on a junior stock exchange to $150,000 to $250,000 or more for such items as professional fees, printing and stock exchange listing fees. Opinion varies as to the minimum size of offering, but to justify the expenses and the effort involved, most advisors suggest that at least several hundred thousand dollars be raised, and often considerably more.

Perhaps the most serious risk to a developing software company is going public too early, before your business is strong enough and stable enough to withstand public scrutiny of its quarterly earnings. If product development plans slip behind schedule, or a market launch falters, it is a very public event. As a private company, your relationship with your investors, who are mainly sophisticated venture capital or institutional investors, may be better able to withstand this sort of stumble (and they aren't uncommon), but the loss of credibility in the public market may take a long time to fade. If you go public too soon, you may find that you have inadvertently foreclosed some future financing options or made later rounds of financing very expensive. If you can tap other financing sources at reasonable cost, you may be wiser to delay going public until your company is more established.

In an IPO, choose your team of advisors carefully. Complex rules apply and the process can be intimidating; you will rely heavily on the experience of your advisors. These include the company's lawyer and accountant, an investment dealer who acts as underwriter or agent, and the dealer's lawyer. Your lawyer and accountant should have experience in offerings of this kind and be able to work effectively with the securities regulators.

In selecting an underwriter or agent, you can turn to a number of trusted sources for guidance — professional advisors, outside directors on your board, or other companies that have gone public recently, particularly those in your own industry. Look for a firm that has a good general reputation, that understands the important characteristics of the information technology industry, and that has experience with offerings of the size and type you are planning.

Over-the-Counter Trading

Publicly traded securities may be listed on a stock exchange or may trade in the over-the-counter (OTC) market (in Canada, known as the Canadian Dealer Network). Preparing and filing a prospectus with the securities commission qualifies the shares offered for sale in the unlisted or OTC market. If the primary objective in going public is to raise capital, but there will not be broad public interest in the shares, you may choose not to obtain an exchange listing. The OTC market consists of a network of securities dealers that trades unlisted securities based on negotiated prices. While these negotiated prices are published in the daily newspaper, trading is usually very light, and there is no assurance that these prices can be realized.

Stock Exchange Listings

The major stock exchanges in Canada are Alberta, Montreal, Toronto, and Vancouver. Each of these exchanges has established minimum listing requirements to maintain the integrity of the securities traded on its facilities.

The listing requirements of the Vancouver and Alberta exchanges are less onerous than those of the so-called senior exchanges in Toronto and Montreal and have been designed to attract junior companies. Vancouver and Alberta have thus developed a relatively high-risk, venture capital type of market, where it is possible to raise smaller amounts at lower cost than on the senior exchanges. The main risk in listing on the junior exchanges is that the float of shares that trade freely is usually a small proportion of the shares outstanding, making prices quite volatile.

Private Placement

If you are contemplating an IPO, you may want to discuss the possibility with an investment dealer, even if the timing seems premature. They may suggest a private placement as an intermediate step if the markets are not right or if the company has good future prospects but doesn't yet have a history of earnings or dramatic growth in revenues and profits. Private placement investors tend to be sophisticated financial institutions or individuals who are able to form their own assessments of the company's short- and long-term prospects and are prepared to be patient. Investment dealers are eager to be involved in private placements for promising companies, as they are then well positioned for any subsequent public offering.

BORROWING

This section focusses on conventional debt financing for software companies, that is, borrowing that is supported by collateral security and that bears interest.

Borrowing is the last financing option presented because as a software development business you have limited capacity to borrow in significant amounts until the more mature stages of your growth, commencing when you begin to sell your product.

Debt is financing with a fixed obligation to repay the amount borrowed plus interest. Debt may be "senior" or "secured" in that tangible assets are pledged as collateral and are usually expected to have a net realizable value, on liquidation, which is equal to or greater than the loan outstanding. The cost of debt is interest. "Subordinated" or "unsecured" debt has a claim to the remaining realizable value of assets, if there is any, once the senior debt has been repaid.

The following types of debt financing may be used:

- An operating bank line of credit secured primarily by accounts receivable and perhaps by government guarantees if applicable

- Term debt collateralized by fixed assets

- Leasing where the leased assets are owned by the leasing company

- Bridge or leveraged buyout financing, which may be available to mature businesses with stable earnings and cash flow from established products.

Operating Bank Line of Credit

You can typically borrow from 50% to 75% of accounts receivable, depending on the creditworthiness of your customers, with an operating line of credit from a bank or similar lender on normal commercial terms. If you also have inventory, for example because you sell some hardware components as well as software, 40% to 60% of the inventory value may be similarly financed with bank borrowings. This would apply, for example, to businesses with manufacturing productivity or telecommunications or defence-related products that have a hardware or equipment component together with a substantial software component. Many software developers export their products. The administrative and legal costs to a lender of realizing the value of its security are greater in a foreign country than they are in Canada; consequently, foreign receivables, even receivables from blue-chip customers, are less attractive as security.

Term Debt and Leasing

Software development businesses have minimal investment in fixed assets. The fixed assets that you do use are not special purpose, so there is little need to custom-design and own your premises or equipment. Software businesses therefore rarely use term debt to buy fixed assets. If your company also manufactures sophisticated hardware components that are operated by your proprietary software, and the two are sold as a package, however, the land, building, and equipment for the manufacturing facility could be financed with term debt, just as they are in other industries.

Most software businesses opt to lease their office space and to lease the equipment they require, such as computers (if they are not provided by hardware vendors), telephones, and fax machines. Leasing makes it easier for you to expand your premises or to upgrade your equipment as the need arises. It also conserves scarce cash, as lease payments are made monthly over time as the space and equipment are used.

Bridge or Leveraged Buyout Financing

A mature software business that has one or more established products and that is profitable and generates reasonably stable and predictable cash flow may be a candidate for bridge financing, either as an intermediate stage prior to going public, or to buy out a venture capital or other investor. Bridge financing may involve borrowing, or private placement equity financing (see page 89).

The term "leveraged buyout" refers to buying a business with borrowed money and then using its future cash flow to pay the interest and principal. This type of transaction is certainly not common in the software industry, but can happen where management of a mature software business buys the business from its parent company. To be a candidate for a leveraged buyout, the business has to be successful and viable as a stand-alone business. Occasionally these businesses are sold because, even though they are successful, they no longer contribute to the parent company's main business strategy.

Since the debt in bridge or leveraged buyout financing is usually not well secured, the lender will rely primarily on the business's cash flow to repay the principal and interest. The risk would be relatively high from a lending perspective, and the lender's interest rate and other terms would reflect the risk.

Sources for conventional borrowing are the same as those for business generally and include government-sponsored and private-sector financial institutions such as Canadian and foreign banks, trust companies, credit unions, leasing companies, and term lenders. It is wise to obtain referrals from your associates in the industry or from your professional advisors, however, to identify sources with which they have good working relationships. Ask to be introduced to an organization and the people in it who have experience and comfort with lending to software companies. They are more likely to be receptive and to support a well-conceived borrowing application.

4

Some Legal Aspects of Strategic Partnering

Strategic partnering is an increasingly common phenomenon in the computer industry. Hardware manufacturers, software developers, developers and distributors of multimedia products, computer products distributors, and others are getting together in a multitude of forms — in a number of different kinds of strategic partnerships — for a whole host of reasons and to pursue a number of different objectives. This chapter gives an overview of several forms of strategic partnerships used today in the computer industry, as well as some legal/business issues that software developers and other participants in such partnerships ought to consider when entering into these forms of arrangements.

REASONS FOR STRATEGIC PARTNERING

As noted by Willis in Chapter 3, high-technology companies enter into strategic partnerships for a number of different reasons. Some companies do it to obtain access to the research and/or technology of others. In some sectors of the computer industry this is becoming a compelling reason indeed as R&D costs increase and customers become more demanding about the functionality and performance of computer products. A similar rationale is to gain access to management expertise in the product development or marketing areas. In some strategic partnerships there is also a strong element of financial assistance; for instance, an established, larger player in the computer industry may make a debt or equity investment in a start-up software developer.

Perhaps the most common reason for a strategic partnership is to permit a hardware manufacturer or software developer to gain timely access to product distribution channels. The computer industry is one of the truly global businesses. A Canadian software developer who creates a reliable, cost-effective computer program will have potential markets in the four corners of the world. Getting the product to these markets, however, can be very difficult, and expensive, if the only structure contemplated is direct selling by the developer. Going it alone may also take a long time, perhaps longer than it takes for the particular product to be superseded by new technology from competitors. Accordingly, strategic partners in far-away places may be a relatively inexpensive and quick way of putting the product before customers worldwide.

FORMS OF STRATEGIC PARTNERSHIPS

Strategic partnerships come in all shapes and sizes. If the objective is to obtain access to research and development, a software developer could entertain several options. It might participate in some form of technology transfer with another software company, perhaps one whose products are complementary in function but are based on common technology. Another option might be some form of participation in a private or public research consortium. These entities are becoming increasingly popular, and the federal and some provincial governments, particularly Ontario's, have placed great emphasis (financial and otherwise) on them recently. Consider the workings of the Information Technology Research Centre (IRTC).

This centre is one of seven "Centres of Excellence" funded by the Ontario government to link universities with private-sector interests through government funding. Ontario has created such centres in the following areas: space and terrestrial science, advanced laser and lightwave research, integrated manufacturing, groundwater research, materials research, telecommunications, and information technology. All of these centres operate on roughly the same principles, namely, the Ontario government gives each centre a research budget, which is allocated by the centre's participating universities and private sector members. The government's objective with the centres is to ensure that the laboratory and other R&D work being performed in Ontario's universities finds its way into the Canadian and international marketplace, to the long-term benefit of the high-technology sector of Ontario's economy.

The IRTRC has five principal areas of endeavour: information systems and knowledge management, hardware design and architecture, networks for information services, modelling and software design. All these areas, as well as many of the research programs at the other centres, have significant software components. Accordingly, a software supplier whose products fall into any of these areas would do well to explore a linkage with the centre, either to join in the general research program, or perhaps to apply the centre's special expertise to a particular project or product being created by the supplier.

There are several other public and private research consortia as well. The federal government has created its own "centres of excellence" program which operates largely along the lines of Ontario's. Private research consortia have also come into being, such as PRECARN Associates Inc., based in Ottawa. PRECARN focusses on intelligent systems and advanced robotics work, again an area where software is critical.

A variation on the research consortium is the software developer that participates in some way in the research efforts of a university, perhaps by sponsoring some specific research project. Particularly those educational institutions with strong computer science departments can serve as important research partners of software companies. And particularly as public funding for universities decreases in the current climate of deficit cutting and general fiscal restraint, universities are looking to undertake more commercial interaction with the private sector, including by incubating entrepreneurs on campus who can then make a go of it outside of the halls of academe.

Where the objective is to obtain access to international distribution channels, a software company can look to several potential strategic partners. The most common tend to be foreign software companies, ideally those with a product complimentary to the one being supplied by the Canadian software developer. On many occasions, however, the distributor in fact produces a competitive product or at least intends to in the near future. The production of such competitive products, particularly when the distributor is given access to the source code of the supplier's computer program, can cause serious friction. The matter is discussed below.

One less common form of access to international markets involves the software developer's partnering with one or more of its customers. For example, a smaller software company may have several large customers with significant operations in the United States, Europe, or elsewhere. In such a case the software developer might retain the customer, through its international affiliates, to serve as a demonstration site and to perform other marketing and support services for the software developer's product. Such a relationship may also be accompanied by some form of equity infusion by the customer in the software developer. Over time, the customer may also come to consider the software developer as the "in-house" R&D facility of the customer in respect of the customer's software requirements. In short, great scope exists for mutually beneficial partnering arrangements between software developers and their clients.

One variation involves a software developer's recruiting current users of the developer's products to assist in the creation of new products. In such an arrangement the user partners would agree to provide the software company with assistance in developing the functional specifications for the new software, as well as to serve as Beta-test sites for the resulting product (Beta testing is explained in Chapter 11 under "Beta-Test Licences"). In this way the software company receives extremely relevant input and feedback regarding its product, from the high-level planning and analysis phase right through to the testing and debugging of the final software product, and hence can create a product that truly responds to the needs of the marketplace. The arrangement also benefits the user partners, inasmuch as they are given the ability to shape the structure and organization of the software, something that might save them significant modifications costs later on. As well, in some of these deals the user partners are given a significant discount on the ultimate licence fee — provided they pay the lower fee before the software is even developed.

AVOIDING THE PITFALLS OF PARTNERING

While the strategic partnership option can be extremely attractive for many smaller software companies — this is why so many strategic partnerships are entered into each year in the computer industry —these agreements are not without their disadvantages or dangers.

A major risk in a strategic partnership is the possible loss of intellectual property rights, such as trade secrets or assets that are subject to copyright or patent rights. Virtually all forms of strategic partnerships involve the exchange of confidential technical, scientific, or commercial information. Accordingly, each participant in such a venture should ensure that its ownership rights in the material contributed to the strategic partnership are clearly delineated; for instance, does the discloser of such information continue to own it, or does ownership pass to some other party?

Equally important, if not more so, is the need to set out in writing among the partners who will own any intellectual property rights developed in the course of the strategic partnership, and what other rights short of ownership, such as exclusive or nonexclusive licence rights, will accrue to the other participants. The importance of dealing with this question in writing cannot be overstated, particularly where computer software is the asset resulting from the joint activity. This is so because the *Copyright Act*, which applies to computer programs, provides that the author of a copyrighted literary work (such as software) is the first owner of the copyright in such work (except where the author is an employee who creates the work in the course of his employment, in which case the employee's employer is the first owner of the work). Accordingly, if a software developer participates in a research consortium and wishes to own the copyright in a work produced by the consortium, it must obtain a written assignment of the copyright; otherwise the consortium will end up owning the resulting work if, for example, the consortium's employees authored the particular software. Failure to deal with such ownership and related questions in writing, and in advance, has resulted in the derailment of many strategic partnerships.

A similar issue arises when a software developer enters into a distribution arrangement whereby a competitor or potential competitor agrees to market the developer's software. It is a common occurrence in such circumstances that the distributor, after a period of time, develops a software product that is competitive with the one for which it has distribution rights. The two parties then have a falling out over whether, or to what extent, the distributor illegally copied the supplier's product in developing the competing product. Given the current, somewhat uncertain scope of copyright protection for computer software (as discussed in Chapter 5), such a dispute between the supplier and the distributor can become a severely protracted one. One way to avoid such problems is to have the distributor agree, in writing, that it will not develop, market, or otherwise be associated with a product competitive with the supplier's as long as it is distributing the supplier's product and for a certain period, say, one year, thereafter. A related option is for the distributor to adopt a "clean room" approach to developing its competitive software (see Chapter 5 under "Creation of Competitive Software").

In certain R&D-oriented strategic partnerships some particularly creative solutions are called for to deal with proprietary rights protection and ownership issues. For example, if a university is involved with the R&D consortium, there will generally be a desire on the part of the professorial participants to publish as soon as possible the results of their research, given the "publish or perish" dynamic at work in the university environment. By contrast, the private-sector partners will be extremely reluctant to publish research results that may jeopardize the acquisition of patent protection, or the maintenance of trade secret protection, for the particular product of the research. This is a very common tension when the private sector enters into partnerships with universities and other public-sector research bodies. One means of resolving this conflict is to allow professors to publish their research results, but only after the research has been rigorously reviewed by the representatives of the private-sector party for the purpose of deciding whether to make patent applications based on the research. And if the research indeed has commercial potential, then perhaps the form of the publication might be modified so as not to disclose the most sensitive parts of the research.

Another danger that strategic partners should try to guard against is the loss of personnel to the joint venture or any other partner involved in it. To this end, a software developer might consider having the partners agree to nonsolicitation and nonemployment provisions, though great care must be taken in the drafting of these clauses, as they may be held to be unenforceable as being an unreasonable restraint on competition. An alternative approach taken by some companies is to establish a more positive and remunerative provision that provides that if a partner hires one of the developer's employees during the term of the arrangement and for a period of, say, six months thereafter, the hiring company will pay to the developer, as a form of employment-agency and training fee, an amount of money equal to some percentage of the employee's first-year salary with the new employer. The benefit of this mechanism is that it allows employees to choose freely where they want to work (subject to their duties not to use or disclose confidential information and, in the case of certain employees, their fiduciary obligations as well), but it also recognizes to a degree the cost incurred by the developer in losing a valued member of its staff.

Another danger area worth noting briefly about strategic partnerships relates to the *Competition Act* (this statute is discussed in greater detail in the context of the computer industry generally in Chapter 9). With respect to strategic partnerships, it is sufficient here to point out that a participant in a strategic partnership, particularly one that includes numerous private-sector entities, should be extremely careful that the activities of the partnership do not violate one or more of the provisions of the *Competition Act*. For example, a research consortium should limit its activities to research; if the members participate in discussions regarding prices, production, customers, markets, or other nonresearch matters, they may be committing the criminal offence of conspiring to limit competition unduly. Or if the strategic partnership involves accessing another entity's distribution mechanism, great care must be taken by the software developer not to influence the resale prices of the distributor in light of the criminal offence of resale price maintenance provided under the *Competition Act*. In short, a company contemplating entering into a strategic partnership should review with legal counsel the various provisions of the *Competition Act* that may be relevant to the particular activity.

It was noted above that universities are becoming increasingly entrepreneurial through strategic partnering and other means. One risk related to this trend is illustrated in a recent case involving an Ontario university. This university had as the head of one of its computer facilities a Mr. Hanis, an entrepreneurial person who, in addition to his university duties, began a software business using a number of university resources. For example, Hanis had persons who were on the university payroll, write and support the software product that he was success-fully selling to users in North America. Over a few years Hanis's computer soft-ware venture turned into a thriving business, all the while utilizing university resources.

Initially, Hanis notified the university of this venture, but only vaguely. Years later, when the extent of Hanis's personal operations became apparent to it, the university immediately fired him. Hanis brought a lawsuit against the universi-ty; after a lengthy trial, the judge found that the university had cause to termi-nate him because of inadequate notification of his activities to the university. The court also held that the university owned the software that Hanis argued was his: the people were employed by the university and, as discussed in Chapter 5, their copyright was owned by their employer. The court refused to accept Hanis's argument that he had overridden this general rule in the *Copyright Act* because he had an agreement with each person purporting to give him the copy-right in the software. It was held that the only agreement that could displace the general copyright employee-employer ownership rule would be an agreement between the employee and the employer, and Hanis' agreements were therefore of no effect.

The *Hanis* case illustrates only some of the risks that can confront universities, other public sector entities (such as governments), and others who get involved in strategic partnerships. All of these players can reduce the risks associated with their participation in strategic partnerships if the terms and conditions rele-vant to the relationship are clearly set out in writing in a balanced and well-thought-out contract. The agreement should address the proprietary rights issues mentioned above, as well as the ongoing operational aspects of the strate-gic partnership. A prudent agreement will also contemplate the eventual termi-nation of the relationship, and will set out what happens when the relationship comes to an end, particularly if it is terminated prematurely as a result of the default of one of the partners.

PART

II

Protecting Software

5

Protecting Intellectual Property Rights in Computer Products and Related Technology

By Barry B. Sookman
(bsookman@mccarthy.ca)

In a market economy, competition is the norm rather than the exception. The vitality of companies doing business in information-technology-related products necessitates an understanding of the products, of evolving technology, and of the standards being developed and applied by competitors. Technology-based industries abound. At the heart of these industries are products that are based upon and embody intangible information, and their intangible nature makes them vulnerable to concerted efforts by competitors and others to copy them. The creation of designs, data, drawings, and computer programs can be time consuming and costly. It is of the utmost importance, therefore, for companies in the computer and related high-technology industries to understand and utilize the laws available to protect their investments in technology. Businesses also need to know the type and scope of protection that applies to the technology of their competitors.

This chapter describes Canada's intellectual property laws as they relate to the protection of computer products and related technologies. In particular, the applicable laws governing trade secrets, copyrights, industrial designs, trademarks, patents, and integrated circuit products will be reviewed.

TRADE SECRETS

What is a Trade Secret?

There is no Canadian legislation defining what is or is not a trade secret in this country. The class of matters capable of forming part of the information protected by the common law is therefore not restricted by any limiting definition. In general, it has been recognized that a trade secret may consist of any information including but not limited to a formula, pattern, compilation, program, method, technique, or process that is or may be used in a trade or business, that is not generally known in that trade or business, that has economic value from not being generally known, and that is the subject of efforts that are reasonable under the circumstances to maintain the secrecy of the information.

To be recognized as a trade secret, neither novelty, in the patent sense, nor complexity is required. Trade secrets lie somewhere on a continuum from what is generally known in a field to what has some degree of uniqueness. They can exist in a method, idea, or process, and may exist even though other forms of protection, such as copyright and patent protection, may not be available. The term of protection can continue for as long as the trade secret is kept secret.

Information Technologies Protected as Trade Secrets

Most information technologies that are created through the expenditure of time and money and that are inaccessible to competitors can be protected as trade secrets. Computer hardware components, including peripherals, transistors, memory devices, disc controllers, display devices, semi-conductor chip products, and circuitry, have been protected in cases decided in the United States and would be protected in Canada as well. Computer software for financial cost accounting, reservation handling, security monitoring, construction industry management, medical and dental management, retail merchandising, time-sharing, performing structural analysis, hospital management, speech synthesis, and other diverse purposes have also been protected under trade-secret laws. Communication interfaces, designs and design methodologies, mathematical models, procedures, statistical assumptions, specifications, program architectures including program organization, structure, logical flow, data structures, and protocols, and systems consisting of both hardware and software have also been protected in cases decided in Canada and the U.S.

In several cases decided in the United States, unique features relating to the engineering, logic, coherence, design, and efficiency of computer programs have been the bases for protecting them. In other cases, courts have protected a combination of elements, each of which, by itself, was in the public domain, but the combination of which afforded the owner thereof a competitive advantage in the marketplace. In still other situations courts have protected computer products by pointing to the effort and expense made by the trade-secret owner and the general inaccessibility of the product in the marketplace.

Jurisdictional Basis for Protecting Trade Secrets

The law in Canada relating to protecting trade secrets is judge-made law and reflects the willingness of judges to provide a remedy to protect people from being taken advantage of by those they have trusted with confidential information. Although the jurisdiction of the courts to protect trade secrets is not disputed, the basis of the court's jurisdiction remains unsettled. In some cases the jurisdiction has referred to property, in others to contract, and in still others it has been treated as founded on an obligation of conscience arising from the circumstances in or through which the information is communicated or obtained. Recently, one of the judges of the Supreme Court of Canada suggested that the foundation of the court's jurisdiction does not rest solely on one of the traditional jurisdictional bases of contract, equity, or property, but rather has its own composite jurisdictional basis.

Persons Who are Subject to a Duty to Respect the Trade Secrets of Others

The cases show that the duty of confidence does not depend on any contract, express or implied, between parties, or some wider fiduciary duty or other special relationship. In general, a duty of confidence arises when confidential information comes to the knowledge of a person in circumstances where the person has notice, or is held to have agreed, that the information is confidential, with the effect that it would be just in all of the circumstances that the person should be precluded from disclosing the information to others. A duty of confidence may therefore arise between manufacturers and distributors, licensors and licensees of technology, intending partners and joint venturers, partners and joint venturers, employers and employees, and persons standing towards each other in a fiduciary relationship. It is also clear that duties of confidence may apply to parties who are involved in arms-length commercial transactions if information of a commercial or industrial value is given on a businesslike basis and with some avowed common object in mind.

Importance of Secrecy

The duty to maintain information in confidence applies only to the extent that the information is confidential. Once information has entered the public domain (which means no more than that the information in question is so generally accessible that, in all the circumstances, it cannot be regarded as confidential), then, as a general rule, the principle of confidentiality can have no application to it. Something that is public knowledge cannot be a trade secret. On the other hand, absolute secrecy is not a precondition to obtaining trade-secret protection for information. In general, the question of whether public accessibility of the information sought to be protected is fatal to an attempt to restrain the use or disclosure of that information will depend on the circumstances of the particular case, including the nature of the information, the nature of the interest sought to be protected, the relationship between the discloser and the recipient, the manner in which the recipient has come into possession of the information, and the circumstances in which and the extent to which the information has been made public.

A product made generally available in the marketplace and lawfully acquired may generally be studied and reverse engineered by a competitor. Marketing of a product that is capable of being taken apart and reverse engineered does not by itself prevent the owner of the trade secret from claiming it has not been lost. However, the time needed to reverse engineer a product is a factor in determining whether information is readily ascertainable and is therefore related to whether, at a given point in time, a trade secret embodied in a product still has the necessary quality of confidence about it to remain a trade secret.

Many companies involved in marketing and distributing computer products attempt to restrain competitors and customers from reverse engineering them in order to preserve the general inaccessibility of their trade secrets. This is frequently accomplished by requiring buyers or licensees of products to sign agreements requiring them to maintain the confidentiality of information disclosed and not to use documentation supplied with the products for any purpose other than for using or maintaining the product. Software licences frequently also contain terms prohibiting licensees from reverse compiling and reverse engineering software supplied under such licences.

Secrecy in the Employment Context

A company is most vulnerable to loss of its trade secrets through its own employees. It is not uncommon for those engaged in developing computer products to move from one employer to another or to form, either alone or in conjunction with other former employees, another company to compete in the employee's area of expertise. Because of the intangible and ephemeral nature of the knowledge of employees, use of such information by them after their employment comes to an end or disclosure to third persons is usually foreseeable. The law governing use of information by former employees balances the interest of employers in maintaining the confidentiality of their trade secrets and the public policy of the law, which favours the right of scientific and technical personnel to use their training, experience, and knowhow to benefit themselves and society as a whole after the termination of their employments.

While employed, an employee has a duty of good faith or, as it has sometimes been called, a duty of "fidelity" to his employer. This duty is reflected in three main obligations that subsist during the employment:

- The employee is bound not to disclose, or to use for purposes that are inimical to his employer's interests, confidential information received by him in his capacity as an employee.

- The employee must not compete with his employer during the term of the employment relationship.

- The employee is bound to disclose to his employer valuable information that he receives by virtue of his being an employee and that is unknown to his employer.

The employee's obligation with respect to confidential information is more restricted in scope after the termination of his employment. It is clear that the obligation exists not to use or disclose information that is a trade secret, or is of a sufficiently high degree of confidentiality as to amount to a trade secret. The obligation does not extend, however, to cover all information that is given to or acquired by an employee while employed and in particular may not cover information that is only confidential in the sense that an unauthorized disclosure of such information to a third person during the course of employment would be a breach of the duty of good faith.

In order to determine whether a particular item of information falls within the employee's continuing duty to his former employer, so as to prevent its use or disclosure after his employment has ceased, it is necessary to consider all the prevailing circumstances. The nature of the employee's employment is one factor. Employment in a capacity where "confidential" material is regularly handled may impose a high obligation of confidentiality because the employee can be expected to be aware of its sensitive nature to a greater extent than if he were employed in a capacity where such material reached him only occasionally or incidentally. The nature of the information itself must also be considered. In order for the continuing obligation of nondisclosure and nonuse to exist, the information must be a trade secret or material that, while not a trade secret, is in all the circumstances of such a highly confidential nature as to require the same protection as a trade secret.

Although the law may be easy to state, it is extremely difficult to determine what information known by a former employee may be used by him after his employment ends. The issue is particularly difficult in the context of skilled employees involved in the design and implementation of information-technology products. The former employee's knowledge of the employer's technology will frequently be intimate, with the consequence that the employer will claim that such knowledge is highly confidential and require it to be protected as a trade secret. Employees, on the other hand, will often assert that their intimate knowledge of their employer's technology has become part of the general skill and expertise of the employee and may therefore be freely used by the employee after the employee's employment has come to an end. Given the wide range of matters that have been held to be trade secrets in the context of information technology, such as source codes, designs, specifications, methodologies, mathematical models, procedures, program architectures, structure, sequence, organization, logical flow, data structures, protocols, and interfaces, employees who disclose to third persons or who use such information, and new employers receiving such information from former employees, take the risk of being liable for trade-secret misappropriation.

Employment Contracts

Companies engaged in developing computer products often develop internal policies and procedures to protect their intellectual property rights. Such a program for protection of proprietary rights is discussed at some length in Chapter 7. One component of such a plan includes written contracts with employees who have access to, or knowledge about, confidential matters and who may have intellectual property rights in inventions and other works subject to intellectual property laws. Such agreements, as well as similar ones with independent contractors, such as consultants and computer programmers, are discussed in some detail in Chapter 8, but it is worth mentioning a few key aspects about them here as well.

One purpose of employment contracts is to settle, as between the employee and the employer, who will be the owner of intellectual property rights that come into existence during the term of employment. Ordinarily, if a patentable invention or a work in which copyright subsists is developed by an employee in the course of employment, on the employer's time and with the employer's materials, the agreement will reflect the law and provide that these rights will be owned by the employer. Because the relationship of an employer to an employee is constituted by contract, the parties may, if they choose, alter or vary the normal incidence of the relationship. In consulting arrangements, on the other hand, an agreement concerning ownership of intellectual property rights in inventions, copyrights, and trade secrets is even more important. In such situations, except in limited circumstances, absent an agreement in writing to the contrary, the copyright in works created by an independent consultant is owned by the consultant and not the person commissioning the work. However, patent and trade secret rights may be owned either by the commissioning party or the independent consultant, depending on the circumstances. Employment contracts frequently also contain waivers of moral rights by all persons who are likely to create any works that may be published or altered by others.

Employment agreements frequently also contain terms that require the employee both during and after his employment to maintain the employer's trade secrets in confidence. Nondisclosure of such information can be particularly important in matters relating to inventions and patent applications, because if the details of an invention are made publicly known the invention may be considered to have fallen into the public domain and be therefore unpatentable and not protectable as a trade secret.

Experience has shown that often it is not satisfactory simply to have a promise from an employee not to disclose confidential information, because it is very difficult to draw the line between information that is confidential and that which is not, and that it is very difficult to prove a breach of confidence when the information is of such a character that an employee can carry it away in his or her head. In a case where an employer has legitimate interests to protect, such as proprietary rights and trade connections, a covenant not to compete will provide the employer with greater protection than merely a promise not to disclose or use confidential information. A promise not to compete, however, is void and unenforceable unless it is reasonable in going no further than necessary to protect the legitimate interests of the employer and is not injurious to the public. To be enforceable, a promise not to compete must be reasonable in terms of time, geographic restriction, and scope.

Competition in the computer industry often transcends national boundaries. In some situations, therefore, geographically unlimited covenants not to compete might be necessary to protect an employer's legitimate interest. Although such a restriction may sometimes be enforceable against a former employee, the reasonableness of such a clause will always depend on the places in which the employer's business is carried on and how the employee's potential activities pose a risk to the employer's legitimate interests. If worldwide protection is not required to protect the employer's interest, a territorially unlimited noncompetition clause will not be enforceable.

Other Methods of Preserving the Confidentiality of Trade Secrets

It is impossible to list all of the ways in which a company can protect the confidentiality of its trade secrets. Some of the following procedures should be considered, however, in developing corporate policies in this area:

- Restricting access to areas in which computer products are being developed

- Limiting access to confidential information on a need-to-know-only basis

- Limiting access to confidential documents such as designs, specifications, flow charts, computer codes, and manuals to essential personnel only, and applying proprietary legends to such materials

- Maintaining a register of technology that is considered to be a trade secret and routinely advising employees of the confidential status of such technology

- Requiring employees and independent consultants to sign proprietary rights protection agreements

- Conducting exit interviews with departing employees to remind them of their duties to respect the trade secrets of the company

- Maintaining a strict policy of not disclosing business or technical information outside the corporation without first obtaining a nondisclosure agreement

- Requiring customers who license or acquire technology from the company to sign agreements containing nondisclosure provisions and prohibiting them from reverse engineering products

- Distributing computer software pursuant to license agreements and where feasible, in object-code form only

- Using passwords and other access-restricting techniques to limit access to computer programs and data centrally available

COPYRIGHT

Copyright law is governed by the *Copyright Act*, federal legislation that is concerned with the protection of qualifying works. Its most important aspects are the right to make copies, and the associated right to prevent others from making copies. Traditionally, copyright has protected literary, dramatic, musical, and artistic works in print or in written form. Examples of works protected by copyright are tables, compilations, books, pamphlets, sheets of music, records, choreographic works, motion pictures, paintings, drawings, maps, charts, plans, photographs, engravings (including etchings, lithographs, and prints), sculptures, works of artistic craftsmanship, and architectural works of art.

Today copyright law is relied upon by almost all computer-based industries to protect works, including computer programs and computer databases. The development of electronic networks and other communications technologies has raised significant issues as to the ability and appropriateness of traditional principles for protecting works in digital form. Any work, however originally created, and whether in the form of film, writing, print or a musical CD, can easily be digitized and then stored and used in that digital format. The work can be easily copied, manipulated, and transmitted over networks such as the INTERNET to many members of the public. Various studies have been commissioned in Canada and elsewhere to assess whether changes to copyright protection for works created or manipulated in a digital environment are needed.

Formalities Required to Protect Computer Programs and Other Machine Readable Works

Copyright in a work does not depend on registration. It arises automatically from authorship and continues, for most literary works, for a period equal to the life of the author plus 50 years. Although registration is not required in Canada, it is nevertheless recommended, because a certificate of registration of copyright in a work is evidence that copyright subsists in the work and that the person registered is the owner of the copyright. Registration also prevents an infringer from alleging at trial innocent infringement, which is a defence to a claim for damages.

Canada and many of its trading partners have adhered to the Berne Convention. A work published in Canada or in any other country that has adhered to the Berne Convention will generally be protected in that country in accordance with domestic copyright laws. Although the formality of marking a work is not required in Canada, placing notices on copyrighted works, consisting of the symbol "©," or the word "Copyright," or the abbreviation "copr.," the year of first publication of the work, and the name of the owner of the copyright in the work is still often done, to obtain protection in countries that adhere to the Universal Copyright Convention (U.C.C.). The United States is now a member of the Berne Convention. Consequently, it is no longer required (although it is still advisable) to comply with the U.C.C. marking requirements in order to obtain copyright protection for computer programs in that country.

Protection for Computer Programs Before June, 1988, in Canada

Until the June 8, 1988, amendments, no explicit reference to computer programs was contained in the *Copyright Act*. Considerable doubt existed as to whether computer programs could be protected under Canadian copyright laws. In fact, until a decision of the Federal Court of Canada in the *Apple* case, in which the copyrightability of computer programs was confirmed, the Copyright Office circulated pamphlets to the general public that expressed uncertainty as to whether computer programs on discs were covered by the Act. Because of the unsettled state of the law, the Copyright Office accepted for registration only the "written directions" for a computer program. Before the amendments to the Act, it was widely believed also that computer programs in their object-code form might not be protected under the Act, in view of jurisprudence that required "literary works" to afford either information and instruction or pleasure in the form of literary enjoyment and to be in print or in writing. However, the Federal Court of Canada in two cases concluded that copies of computer programs in object-code form stored in Read Only Memory (ROM) silicon chips were protected under Canadian copyright law.

Protection for Computer Programs Under the *Copyright Act*

Under the present *Copyright Act* computer programs are protected as literary works. A "computer program" is defined as "a set of instructions or statements, expressed, fixed, embodied, or stored in any manner, that is to be used directly or indirectly in a computer in order to bring about a specific result." This definition follows closely the definition in the United States Copyright Act which defines "computer program" as a "set of statements or instructions to be used directly or indirectly in a computer in order to bring about a certain result."

The definition of "computer program" clearly applies to source codes which cannot be used directly in a computer to bring about a specific result. Computer programs written in human-readable source code such as FORTRAN and BASIC are protected under the *Copyright Act*. Programs in machine-readable form that can be used directly in a computer in order to bring about a specific result, such as object codes, are also clearly eligible for protection.

The protection of instructions or statements, however "expressed, fixed, embodied or stored," suggests that computer programs will be protected in a wide range of media. Given the wording of the definition, it is expected that computer programs will be protected when copied onto computer printouts, floppy discs, ROMS, CD-ROMS, and EPROMS, punch cards, magnetic tapes, bubble memories, and other tangible forms. Documentation in traditional printed or written forms, such as flow charts, specifications, and designs, are also protected under the *Copyright Act* as literary or artistic works. It has not yet been judicially determined in Canada whether computer programs or data stored only in Random Access Memory (RAM) will be protected. It is quite arguable, however, that the presence of a computer program or other work in machine readable form in such memory will be considered to be sufficiently permanent or stable to be protected under the Act.

Protection for Databases

The widespread use of computers has led to the creation of a multitude of information that is stored in digital form. This information will, if it has the necessary quality of confidence about it, be protectable under the laws relating to trade secrets. Compilations of information are also capable of being protected under the *Copyright Act* if the creator of the compilation has expended a sufficient amount of labour, time, expense, skill, or judgement in assembling facts or in selecting or arranging them.

In January, 1994 the *Copyright Act* was amended to explicitly protect certain types of compilations. Under the *Copyright Act* a work resulting from the selection or arrangement of literary, dramatic, musical or artistic works, or work resulting from the selection or arrangement of data, if original, is capable of being protected. Many multimedia works, which are in essence compilations of works in digital form, and computer databases will now be explicitly protected as compilations under the Act.

The marvel of computer technology has made it relatively easy to copy compilations of information in both printed or machine-readable form and to rearrange the information. Canadian case law suggests that, notwithstanding that an owner's copyright in such information exists in the selection and arrangement of the information, the rearrangement of a database by an unauthorized person will be an infringement of copyright. However, in the United States the extraction of facts from a database is not considered to be an act of infringement. This was the holding in a controversial decision of the United States Supreme Court, *Feist Publications Inc.* v. *Rural Telephone Services Co.*, where it was held that the copying of information from a white pages telephone directory did not infringe the copyright of the owner of the directory. The European Union has recognized the importance of protecting the raw data in a database and has passed a directive addressed to all member states to create a special right by which the creator of a database will be able to prevent the unauthorized extraction or reutilization of the contents of the database for commercial purposes.

Protection for Structure, Sequence, and Organization of a Computer Program

The definition of the term "computer program" in the *Copyright Act* makes it clear that what is protected under the Act is the "set of instructions or statements". The definition makes no reference to other valuable aspects of a computer program, including its overall design, architecture, structure, sequence and organization, file layouts, and data structures. These elements may be more valuable than the program codes, and a plagiarist can save a substantial amount of time, effort, risk, and expense by taking a completed and proven design instead of developing an original one. The protection of the structure, sequence, and organization (SSO) in a computer program raises two fundamental copyright issues. Firstly, can the structure, sequence, and organization in a computer program be protected as a work in its own right under the Act in the way that preliminary sketches of artistic works are protected? Secondly, is the copying of only one or more parts of a program (other than source or object codes) in the creation of a second program an infringement of copyright?

Many American cases have addressed the issue of the scope of protection for computer programs and have held that copyright protection for computer programs is capable of protecting the program's structure, sequence and organization. A leading case in this area in the United States is a decision of an appellate court in *Computer Associates International Inc.* v. *Altai Inc.* There it was explicitly recognized that nonliteral structures of a computer program could be protected by copyright. The *Altai* case has been considered and quoted from extensively in several Canadian cases which have addressed whether nonliteral aspects of computer programs can be protected by copyright. In two of the Canadian cases, the courts accepted that copying of parts of the computer program other than the source and object code could lead to infringement, but did not find infringement of copyright on the facts. In a third case, a British Columbia court held that the rewriting of a computer program from one computer language to another where there had been extensive copying of the overall design, field, record and data structures, menu screens and the structure and sequence of execution did infringe the copyright of the plaintiff.

Although nonliteral aspects of computer programs have been protected, the exact contours of that protection in any case is often difficult to determine. This is because there may be ideas, methods, processes, or algorithms embodied in the program and these components — as contrasted with the statements and instructions of computer programs which implement them — are not protected by copyright. Many decisions in the United States have struggled to articulate tests to separate the protectable from the nonprotectable parts of a computer program. The recent trend in the United States on this issue is to apply a three-step analysis to determine if an allegedly infringing program has reproduced nonliteral aspects of another program. This test is sometimes referred to as the "Abstraction – Filtration – Comparison Test." First articulated in the *Altai* case, it has, with some changes, been embraced by several other American appellate courts. This test was recently summarized by an American appellate court as follows.

> First, in order to provide a framework for analysis, we conclude that a court should dissect the program according to its varying levels of generality as provided in the abstractions test. Second, poised with this framework, the court should examine each level of abstraction in order to filter out those elements of the program which are unprotectable.

Filtration should eliminate from comparison the unprotectable elements of ideas, processes, facts, public domain information, merger material, scenes a faire material, and other unprotectable elements suggested by the particular facts of the program under examination. Third, the court should then compare the remaining protectable elements with the allegedly infringing program to determine whether the defendants have misappropriated substantial elements of the plaintiff's program.

Protection for User Interfaces

The user interface of a computer program, sometimes referred to as the "look and feel" of the program, is generally the design of the video screen and the manner in which information is presented to the user. User interfaces employed in computer programs include all the means by which the human user can interact with the computer in order to accomplish the task the computer is programmed to perform. Screen displays of images and text are the most important components of the user interface.

A significant amount of the creative work in designing a computer program lies in the conceptualization of the program and its user interface, rather than in its encoding. In fact, creating a suitable user interface is often a more difficult intellectual task, requiring greater creativity, originality, and insight, than converting the user interface design into instructions to the machine. Software publishers, particularly in the United States, have litigated to protect the "look and feel" of their programs on the basis that their creation is dictated primarily by artistic and aesthetic considerations. For instance, Lotus Development Corporation sued Mosaic Software, Paperback Software International, and Borland International over the "look and feel" of Lotus's 1-2-3 spreadsheet program, and Apple Computer Inc. sued Microsoft Corp. and Hewlett-Packard Co. over the look and feel of the Macintosh Interface. Xerox Corporation also sued Apple Computer Inc., alleging that Xerox's Star Interface was infringed by Apple Macintosh Interface.

Plaintiffs in these "look and feel" actions have focused on "expressive" material in their interfaces that makes them appeal to users, an aesthetic appeal that results in sales. These interfaces have been characterized as "fanciful," "artistic," and "aesthetically pleasing." Defendants on the other hand have argued that these interfaces are essentially functional devices designed to enable people to interact with computers. The courts in the United States have provided some degree of protection for these interfaces by characterizing them as literary works in the form of compilations or as part of the structure, sequence, and organization of the underlying program, as manifested in the menus presented on the screen displays.

Several American decisions have emphasized that the scope of protection for user interfaces will not extend to components not protected by copyright. For example, in the American litigation between Apple and Microsoft, Apple alleged that its copyright in the Macintosh user interface was infringed by several versions of Microsoft's Windows and Hewlett-Packard's NewWave programs. In the action, Apple sought to protect five principal features of its desktop metaphor. These consisted of:

> (1) use of windows to display multiple images on a computer screen and facilitate interaction with the information contained in the windows; (2) use of icons to represent familiar objects from the office environment and facilitate organization of information stored in the computer's memory; (3) manipulation of icons to convey instructions and to control operation of the computer; (4) use of menus to store information or functions of the computer in a place that is convenient to reach, but saves screen space for other images; and (5) opening and closing of objects as a means of retrieving, transferring or storing information.

The American appellate court which decided the case characterized "Apple's desktop metaphor" as unprotectable ideas — something not protected by copyright in that country.

Another American case which has caused considerable controversy in the United States involves a decision of an appellate court in *Lotus* v. *Borland*. There, the court ruled that Lotus's menu command hierarchy in its 1-2-3 spreadsheet program was not protectable by copyright and that Borland's literal copying of it in Quattro and Quattro Pro's "Lotus Emulation Interface" and "Key Reader" programs was not infringing. According to the court, Lotus's menu command hierarchy was not protected by copyright because it served as the basis for running 1-2-3 macro files. Under United States law, "methods of operation" are not protected by copyright. Therefore, according to the court, Lotus' command hierarchy was not protected. The court likened Lotus's menu command hierarchy to buttons used to control machines. The court's reasoning on this issue is, in part, contained in the following portion of the opinion:

> In many ways, the Lotus menu command hierarchy is like the buttons used to control, say, a video cassette recorder ("VCR"). A VCR is a machine that enables one to watch and record video tapes. Users operate VCRs by pressing a series of buttons that are typically labelled 'Record, Play, Reverse, Fast Forward, Pause, Stop/Eject." That the buttons are arranged and labelled does not make tham a "literary work," nor does it make them an "expression" of the abstract "method of operating" the VCR.

Infringing Acts in Relation to Works Protected by Copyright

Copyright in a work is deemed to be infringed by any person who, without the consent of the owner of the copyright, does anything that, according to the *Copyright Act*, only the owner of the copyright has the right to do. In relation to computer programs the most important right conferred by the Act is the sole right to reproduce a computer program or any substantial part of it in any material form. The concept of reproduction involves two elements: resemblance to, and actual use of, the copyright work. In order to establish infringement of copyright by reproduction two elements must therefore be established. Firstly, the infringing work and the copyrighted work must be shown to be substantially similar, and secondly, the similarity must be shown to be due to substantial copying of the copyrighted work in the creation of the allegedly infringing work.

The right to reproduce a work is one of the most important rights given to the owner of a copyright. For computer programs and other works in machine readable form, this right is particularly important, given the ease with which copies can be made and transmitted electronically over computer networks. A variety of acts may infringe the reproduction right unless done with the consent of the owner of the copyright. Copying of all or any substantial part of a computer program can infringe the reproduction right. The modification or adaptation of a work in machine readable form also usually involves the making of reproductions. The creation of multimedia works by scanning other works such as photographs, motion pictures, or sound recordings into a digital file may be infringing. So may digital sampling of musical works. Whenever a digitized file is uploaded from a user's computer to a bulletin board system or downloaded from a computer bulletin board system to a computer, a copy is made. When a file is transferred from one computer network user to another, multiple copies are made. All of these activities in theory can infringe the reproduction right.

Rental of Computer Programs

The owner of the copyright in a computer program has the sole right "in the case of a computer program that can be reproduced in the ordinary course of its use, other than by a reproduction during its execution in conjunction with a machine, device or computer, to rent out the computer program." Thus, under the *Copyright Act*, the rental of a computer program without the consent of the owner of the copyright may be an infringing act. Because the prohibition applies to a computer program that "can be reproduced in the ordinary course of its use," the rental right will not be infringed where computer programs are distributed in forms that cannot ordinarily be copied in the course of their use, such as video games stored in ROM chips. Also, the rental right applies only to commercial lending, and not to transactions entered into without a profit motive.

Under the *Copyright Act*, "an arrangement, whatever its form, constitutes a rental of a computer program if, and only if, (a) it is in substance a rental, having regard to all the circumstances; and (b) it is entered into with motive of gain in relation to the overall operations of the person who rents out the computer program." A person who rents out a computer program with the intention of recovering no more than the costs, including overhead, associated with the rental operation, does not by that act alone have a motive of gain in relation to the rental operations.

Right to Reverse Engineer Software

Reverse engineering is a process that starts with the known product and works backwards to define the process of its development or manufacture. Different processes can be used to reverse engineer computer programs. One method involves the conversion of object code into a form that more closely resembles the source code to the program. Another involves a process of working backwards from the source code to determine the design on which the computer program was based. In many instances, the process of reverse engineering a computer program will result in a reproduction of all or a substantial part of the program being examined.

Although no Canadian court has dealt expressly with the issue, several Commonwealth and American courts have, and they suggest that, because making one or more reproductions of a computer program during reverse engineering is involved, the reverse engineering process may be infringing. Several American courts have, however, ruled that copying in the process of a legitimate reverse engineering activity may constitute a "fair use" under United States copyright law. It is possible that a Canadian court would consider that copying in the course of a legitimate reverse engineering project for the purpose of extracting only the ideas contained therein for the purpose of creating an original competitive or interoperable program would constitute a "fair dealing" with the program for the purpose of private study or research. In Canada, such acts of fair dealing do not constitute an infringement of copyright.

Another unresolved issue is whether a computer program derived in part from the study of a disassembled program would infringe the copyright of the owner of the disassembled program. Although each case will depend on its own facts, the resolution of the issue will depend upon whether the allegedly infringing program is substantially similar to the disassembled program and whether the substantial similarity is due to copying from parts of the disassembled program.

Creation of Competitive Software

A problem faced by developers of software is the extent to which they may study and analyze the programs of a competitor and use features of the competitor's program in designing and developing a second competitive or compatible program. The issue in each case is difficult to resolve and depends upon the answer to three related questions. Firstly, which parts of the original program may not be copied because they are protected by copyright? Secondly, which parts of the original program may be freely copied because they are ideas, processes, or methods that are not protected by copyright? Thirdly, how much of the original program which is protected by copyright may be copied before the original program and the competitive program will be considered as substantially similar?

It is clear under Canadian law that two computer programs may be substantially similar without one infringing the copyright of the owner of the other unless there has been copying. For instance, in the *Solartronix* case, the resemblance between two computer programs used for automating a concrete factory was not sufficient to render the defendant liable for copyright infringement, because the resemblance was not due to copying of protectable elements of the plaintiff's program, but to features that any such program would contain. Similarly, in the recent *Delrina* case, the similarity between two computer programs for monitoring the performance of a machine was not sufficient to make the defendant liable for copyright infringement where the resemblances between the two programs were the result of constraints imposed upon the defendant.

Some companies that develop competitive or compatible software attempt to do so through a procedure known as a "clean room." The purpose of the procedure is to separate the process of extracting the "ideas, methods, and processes" of the original program from the detailed design and coding of the new competitive program. Often two groups are established within the same company and kept completely separate from one another so that if the competitive program is challenged as being substantially similar to the original program due to copying, evidence will be available to establish precisely what parts of the original program were copied in the development process. In the United States *NEC* case, the use of a clean-room procedure helped NEC to establish that the similarities in its microcodes were not due to copying of Intel's microcodes. Because of the difficulty in separating the parts of a program that are protected by copyright from the parts that are not, there is always the possibility that the specifications developed by the team analyzing the original software will be so detailed that the new software will closely resemble the original program. In that event, the new software may infringe the copyright of the owner of the original program.

Making Adaptations to Computer Programs

The June, 1988, amendments to the *Copyright Act* specifically exempted the following from infringement of copyright:

The making by a person who owns a copy of a computer program, which copy is authorized by the owner of the copyright, of a single reproduction of the copy by adapting, modifying or converting the computer program or translating it into another computer language if the person proves that

- *the reproduction is essential for the compatibility of the computer program with a particular computer,*

- *the reproduction is solely for the person's own use, and*

- *the reproduction is destroyed forthwith when the person ceases to be the owner of the copy of the computer program.*

This amendment to the Act was made in recognition of the need for computer programs to be adapted or modified to meet the needs of end users. As can be seen, this exemption from infringement of copyright is subject to two important qualifications. Firstly, the exemption applies only to a person who "owns" a copy of a computer program. Since most software is licenced and not sold (see Chapter 11), there is a question as to whether a licensee "owns" the copy of the program licensed. Secondly, if the reproduction of the computer program is not essential for the compatibility of the program with a particular computer, the exemption does not apply. It would seem, therefore, that an owner of a copy of a computer program who wants to make modifications to it for maintenance purposes may not do so unless authorized, expressly or by implication, by the owner of the copyright in the program to do so.

Right to Make Backup Copies of a Computer Program

The magnetic media upon which computer programs are stored are susceptible to damage due to mechanical and electrical failure and physical abuse. For this reason the 1988 amendments to the *Copyright Act* created the following exemption from infringement:

The making by a person who owns a copy of a computer program, which copy is authorized by the owner of the copyright, of a single reproduction for backup purposes of the copy ... if the person proves that the reproduction is destroyed forthwith when the person ceases to be the owner of the copy of the computer program.

It should be noted that this amendment to the Act does not create the general right to make a backup copy of a computer program. It is limited to exempting from infringement the making of a backup copy of a computer program in certain instances. Therefore, if a computer program is licensed under terms that expressly prohibit any reproduction of the program except for specified purposes, this amendment may not apply. As with the amendment to the Act that permits the making of adaptations, this amendment will also not apply unless the person in possession of the computer program is considered to be a person who "owns" a copy of the computer program

Other Infringing Actions

Under the amendments made to the *Copyright Act* in June, 1988 it is now an infringement of copyright to communicate any literary work, including a computer program, to the public by telecommunication. The term "telecommunication" is broadly defined in the Act to mean "any transmission of signs, signals, writing, images or sounds or intelligence of any nature by wire, radio, visual, optical or other electromagnetic system." It is not, however, an infringement of copyright in some instances to retransmit a local or distant signal that is lawful under the *Broadcasting Act*.

It is generally an infringement of copyright for any unauthorized person to exercise any of the exclusive rights of the owner of the copyright, whether the infringement is done intentionally or unintentionally. Subsection 27(4) of the *Copyright Act* also stipulates that copyright in a work is

> deemed to be infringed by any person who (a) sells or lets for hire, or by way of trade exposes or offers for sale or hire, (b) distributes either for the purposes of trade or to such an extent as to affect prejudicially the owner of the copyright, (c) by way of trade exhibits in public, or (d) imports for sale or hire into Canada, any work that to the knowledge of that person infringes copyright or would infringe copyright if it had been made within Canada.

Infringement of Moral Rights in Computer Programs

The 1988 amendments to the *Copyright Act* conferred upon authors of a work the right to "the integrity of the work" and the right, where reasonable in the circumstances, "to be associated with the work as its author or under a pseudonym and the right to remain anonymous." An author's right to the integrity of a work is infringed only if the work is, to the prejudice of the honour or reputation of the author, (a) distorted, mutilated, or otherwise modified, or (b) used in association with a product, service, cause, or institution. Given the industry need to maintain computer programs, it is not clear why Parliament extended moral rights to creators of computer programs. In the United Kingdom, which recently revised its copyright legislation, the moral right to be identified as the author of a work and the right not to have the work subject to derogatory treatment under the *Copyright, Design and Patent Act*, 1988, does not apply to computer programs.

Moral rights in a computer program may not be assigned by an author, but may be waived in whole or in part by the author. Where a waiver of any moral right is made it may be invoked by any person authorized by the owner or licensee to use the work, unless there is an indication to the contrary in the waiver. In view of the moral rights of authors of computer programs, companies should make a practice of obtaining waivers from all persons involved in creating computer programs for the company.

Fair Dealing

The *Copyright Act* provides an exception for infringement where the otherwise infringing act constitutes a fair dealing with a work for the purposes of private study, research, criticism, review, or a newspaper summary. For the exemption pertaining to private study or research to apply, the conduct must be capable of being characterized as "private study" or "research" and there must be a fair dealing for either of those purposes. It should be noted that while a number of copyright cases in Canada have addressed the fair dealing exemption, none have done so in the context of software and therefore it is not yet clear how this exemption would be applied to particular situations involving computer programs.

PROTECTION FOR INDUSTRIAL DESIGNS

The design of computer hardware and packaging for computer products may in some instances be protected under Canada's *Industrial Design Act*. The Act gives protection for a period of up to ten years to designs in a finished article that are registered under the Act. Designs that are capable of being registered under the Act are "features of shape, configuration, pattern or ornament and any combination of those features, that, in a finished article, appeal to or are judged solely by the eye." The Act does not extend protection to features applied to a useful article that are dictated solely by a utilitarian function of the article or to any method or principle of manufacture or construction.

In some cases the shaping of computer hardware may distinguish the computer hardware from other hardware manufactured, sold, or leased by others. In this event, the owner of the hardware may be entitled to register its shape as a distinguishing guise under Canada's *Trade-Marks Act*. The registration of a distinguishing guise may not, however, interfere with the use of any utilitarian feature embodied in the distinguishing guise. Similarly, if the shape, size, colour, wrapping, and appearance of a computer product has acquired a reputation in the marketplace, the owner of it may have a right to prevent a second person from adopting and using its particular "get-up," if to do so might cause confusion in the marketplace as to the source of the goods.

TRADE-MARK PROTECTION FOR COMPUTER PRODUCTS

Companies in the computer business often use words, names, slogans, symbols, designs, and distinctive product guises or get-ups for the purpose of distinguishing their products from those of their competitors. If the words, names, slogans, symbols, designs, and distinctive product guises or get-ups distinguish or are capable of distinguishing the products or services of a company, they may be registrable under Canada's *Trade-Marks Act*.

Selecting a trade-mark to be used in conjunction with a product or business is often a difficult task. One important objective is to make the trade-mark as distinctive as possible so that the ambit of protection for the trade-mark will be wide, i.e., APPLE for computers and computer software. Picking a word mark that contains commonly used words in the industry such as "DATA" or "COMPUTER" or that contains letters only (such as ABC for a software product) will give only limited protection against encroachment by other marks with comparatively small differences.

A common objection to the registration of a trade-mark is that it may be easily confused with an existing registered trade-mark or with a trade-mark that has been previously used in Canada or made known in Canada by another person. Whether two trademarks may be confused is a matter of first impression and imperfect recollection, considering each of the trade-marks in its totality. In assessing the likelihood of confusion between two trade-marks, all of the surrounding circumstances are considered, including the following factors:

- The inherent distinctiveness of the trade-marks or trade names and the extent to which they have become known

- The length of time the trade-marks or trade names have been in use

- The nature of the wares, services, or business

- The nature of the trade

- The degree of resemblance between the trade-marks or trade names in appearance or sound or in the ideas suggested by them

The registration of a trade-mark in Canada gives to the owner of the trade-mark, with certain exceptions, the exclusive right to use it throughout Canada in respect of the products or services for which it is registered. This includes the right to prevent other persons from using the same trade-mark, or one that is confusingly similar. The right of the owner of a registered trade-mark to its exclusive use is deemed to be infringed by a person not entitled to its use under the *Trade-Marks Act* who sells, distributes, or advertises products or services in association with a confusingly similar trade-mark or trade name.

The growth of communication networks and the increasing commercial activity over such networks has raised a series of novel issues related to the registrability of and use of trade-marks over communication networks. The phenomenal growth of commercial activity over the INTERNET, for example, has raised considerable interest among owners and users of trade-marks as to the registrability of domain names, whether the display of a trade-mark over the INTERNET constitutes domestic or foreign use of the trade-mark, whether the display of a trade-mark at a company's INTERNET site constitutes use of a trade-mark, whether the display of a trade-mark in a foreign country constitutes use of the trade-mark in the country or can render the user of the trade-mark liable of trade-mark infringement. These issues are likely to become even more important in the future.

An important right conferred by the *Trade-Marks Act* is the right to prevent a person from using a trade-mark registered by another person in a manner likely to have the effect of depreciating the value of the goodwill attaching to it. To depreciate the value of goodwill means, simply, to reduce in some way the advantage of the reputation and connection attaching to the trade-mark, and to take away the whole or some portion of the custom to be expected. Certain forms of derogative and nonderogative advertising (for example, comparative advertising), may have the effect of depreciating the value of the goodwill attaching to a trade-mark and care must be taken in referring to the trade-mark of a competitor so as not to depreciate the value of the goodwill that attaches to it.

PATENT PROTECTION FOR COMPUTER PRODUCTS

Difference Between Patent, Copyright, and Trade-Secret Protection

The *Patent Act* governs the right to obtain patents for inventions in Canada. Under the Act, an inventor may, on compliance with all of the requirements of the Act, obtain a patent granting to him an exclusive property in an invention for a term of 20 years from the date of the filing of the application in Canada. The *Patent Act* defines the term "invention" to mean "any new and useful art, process, machine, manufacture or composition of matter, or any new and useful improvement in any art, process, machine, manufacture or composition of matter."

Patent protection is the strongest form of intellectual property protection available for computer-related products. Copyright protects only the expression in a work; it does not extend to the ideas, methods, or processes embodied in it. Copyright cannot be used, therefore, to prevent the unauthorized copying of "ideas" in a work. A patent, on the other hand, can protect an idea as embodied in a process or device whether or not there has been copying. Patent protection is also much stronger than trade-secret protection, which lasts only as long as the secret remains relatively inaccessible to others.

Although patent protection has distinct advantages over copyright and the protection accorded to trade secrets, many computer-related inventions will not meet the rigorous statutory requirements of novelty, nonobviousness, and the degree of utility required for patentability. Patent protection also requires that an application be made for protection. This can be a time-consuming and expensive process, in contrast to the lack of any statutory registration requirement for copyright and trade secret protection. The right to patent an invention may also be lost if certain statutory formalities are not complied with. For instance, the application for the invention must be filed less than one year after any disclosure of it by the applicant or by a person who obtains knowledge of the invention, directly or indirectly, from the applicant, in such a manner that the invention becomes available to the public in Canada or elsewhere. If the invention is, before the date of filing of the application, disclosed by a person other than the applicant or a person who obtains knowledge from the applicant, in such a manner that it becomes available to the public or elsewhere, the right to obtain a patent for such invention is also lost. It is also important to bear in mind that the formalities for applying for patents for computer-related inventions differ from country to country. In some countries any disclosure of the invention to the public before the filing of the application for the patent will render the invention unpatentable. It is very important, therefore, for commercial enterprises to identify patentable inventions as soon as possible and to make applications for patents before any public disclosure of the invention is made.

Patentability of Software-Related Inventions

There has been an accelerated trend, particularly in the United States, towards obtaining patent protection for computer program-related inventions. Patents have been issued claiming inventions for operating systems programs such as operations control and monitoring, programs for data/file management, compiler programs, and application programs. Many of these patents are "pure" software patents that specifically disclose and claim software technology without directly referring to hardware other than a conventional computer and peripheral devices. Patents have also been issued relating to the user/computer interface and to business methods employing computers. These patents, which have been issued to some of the largest American computer companies as well as financial institutions, demonstrate the importance of this type of protection for computer-program-related inventions.

Some controversy exists concerning which computer program-related inventions can be protected by patents. As stated above, under the *Patent Act* an invention may be patentable if it constitutes a new and useful machine, article of manufacture, or a statutory process. Generally, a computer or other programmable apparatus whose actions are directed by a computer program or other form of software is a "statutory machine." A computer-readable memory that can be used to direct a computer to function in a particular manner when used by the computer is a "statutory article of manufacture." A series of specific operational steps to be performed on or with the aid of a computer is a "statutory process."

In the United States, a significant amount of debate has arisen as to the patentability of a computer-related invention that recites one or more mathematical algorithms. In that country, mathematical algorithms *per se* are nonstatutory. However, a claim drawn to subject matter otherwise statutory does not become nonstatutory simply because it uses a mathematical formula, computer program, or digital computer.

In 1981 the Canadian Federal Court of Appeal considered the patentability of claims involving computer programs for the first time, in the *Schlumberger* case. Although the court declined to lay down specific guidelines to assist the Patent Office in determining which computer-program-related inventions are statutory subject matter, it ruled that there is nothing in the *Patent Act* that excludes inventions involving computers. It also ruled that the fact that a computer is used to implement a discovery does not change the nature of that discovery for patent purposes. Each application must therefore be considered to determine exactly what, according to the application, has been discovered.

Decisions following the *Schlumberger* case have recognized that certain types of applications containing computer programs, such as data manipulation and information enhancement systems control systems and operating software, may be patentable if the other criteria for patentability, such as novelty and utility, are met. In June of 1993, the Patent Examination Branch of the Canadian Patent Office developed a set of guidelines designed to reflect the view of the Patent Office as to the patentability of computer-related inventions in Canada. The guidelines state:

1. Unapplied mathematical formulae are considered equivalent to mere scientific principles or abstract theorems which are not patentable under section 27(3) of the *Patent Act*.

2. The presence of a programmed general purpose computer or a program for such computer does not lend patentability to, nor subract patentability from, an apparatus or process.

3. It follows from 2, that new and useful processes incorporating a computer program, and apparatus incorporating a programmed computer, are directed to patentable subject matter if the computer-related matter has been integrat-

ed with another practical system that falls within an area which is traditionally patentable. This principle is illustrative of what types of computer-related applications may be patentable, and is not intended to exclude other computer-related applications from patentability.

PROTECTION FOR INTEGRATED CIRCUITS

Integrated circuits, often called "chips" or "microchips," are manufactured devices in which highly miniaturized and very complex electronic circuits are integrated. They are incorporated into a wide variety of commercial and industrial products and are at the heart of modern computer, telecommunications, and other advanced technologies.

Statutory initiatives in other developed countries have been taken to protect integrated circuit technologies. The United States passed legislation in 1984, called the *Semi-Conductor Chip Protection Act*, which provides legal protection to owners of "mask works" which are fixed in semi-conductor products. Legislation was also passed in Japan to provide specific protection for semi-conductor integrated circuits. In 1987, the European Economic Community passed a directive requiring its member states to provide protection for topographies of semi-conductor products. More recently, on May 26, 1989, the World Intellectual Property Organization (WIPO) adopted a treaty for the protection of integrated circuits.

In Canada, on June 28, 1990, royal assent was given to the *Integrated Circuit Topography Act* to give intellectual property protection to the topography of integrated circuits. This legislation protects the original design of a topography, whether or not it has been embodied in an integrated circuit product, and whether the integrated circuit product is in a final or an intermediate form. Under the legislation an "integrated circuit product" is a product, in a final or intermediate form, that is intended to perform an electronic function and in which the elements, at least one of which is an active element, and some or all of the interconnections, are integrally formed in or on, or both in and on, a piece of material. The term "topography" is defined to mean the design, however expressed, of the disposition of (a) the interconnections, if any, and the elements for the making of an integrated circuit product or (b) the elements, if any, and the interconnections for the making of a customization layer or layers to be added to an integrated circuit product in an intermediate form.

To be registrable under the Act a topography must be original. A topography is original if (a) it has not been produced by the mere reproduction of another topography or of any substantial part thereof, and (b) it is the result of an intellectual effort and is not, at the time of its creation, commonplace among creators of topographies or manufacturers of integrated circuit products. Where a topography consists of a combination of elements or interconnections that are commonplace among creators of topographies or manufacturers of integrated circuit products, the topography will be considered to be original only if the combination, considered as a whole, is original.

The *Integrated Circuit Topography Act* provides protection by giving the owner of a topography exclusive statutory rights for a specific period of time to reproduce the topography, manufacture an integrated circuit product incorporating the topography, and import or commercially exploit the topography or an integrated circuit product that incorporates the topography. These exclusive rights do not confer on the owner of the topography any rights in relation to any idea, concept, process, system, technique, or information that may be embodied in a topography or an integrated circuit product.

The exclusive rights are subject to several important exceptions. The first permits the reproduction of a topography or the manufacture of an integrated circuit product incorporating the topography for the sole purpose of analysis or evaluation or of research or teaching with respect to topographies. Any person may also exercise any of the exclusive rights of the owner of the topography where they are done for a private and noncommercial purpose. Another exception relates to the doctrine of first sale and exhaustion of rights applying to integrated circuit products legitimately manufactured anywhere in the world, and put on the market with the authorization of the owner of the topography. After the first legitimate sale of such a product the topography owner will have no statutory right to control its resale.

The Act will protect a registered topography for a term of up to ten years. The term will commence on the filing date of the application for registration of the topography and end at the end of the tenth calendar year after either the calendar year in which the topography is first commercially exploited in any place in the world or the calendar year of the filing date of the application in Canada, whichever is earlier.

REMEDIES FOR INFRINGEMENT OF AN INTELLECTUAL PROPERTY RIGHT

Canada's intellectual property laws governing copyrights, patents, industrial designs, trade secrets, trade-marks, and integrated circuit topographies allow a broad range of remedies to a plaintiff in an infringement action. Depending upon the circumstances of the case, a plaintiff may be entitled to one or more of the following remedies: damages, an accounting of profits, the imposition of a constructive trust, and an interim, interlocutory and/or final injunction. The plaintiff may also be entitled to obtain an "Anton Piller" order.

Anton Piller Orders

In piracy actions involving intellectual property, where it is established that the defendants have in their possession incriminating documents or things and that there is a real possibility that they may destroy such material, the courts have granted what have come to be known as "Anton Piller" orders. These orders are the civil equivalent of criminal search and seizure orders. This form of relief, which originated in England and was first recognized in the *Anton Piller* case, has been obtained or applied for in numerous cases throughout the Commonwealth involving alleged infringements of intellectual property rights in video games and computer programs.

Interlocutory Injunctions

An interlocutory injunction is an extraordinary remedy designed to protect a very real threat to an enforceable right of a party. Generally, to obtain such an injunction the applicant must satisfy the court that the case against the defendant is not frivolous or vexatious, that the applicant will suffer harm for which it will not be adequately compensated by damages if it is successful after a trial and an injunction is not granted, and that the balance of convenience is in its favour. In matters involving clear violations of copyrights the Federal Court of Canada has granted interlocutory injunctions, without concerning itself with irreparable injury or the balance of convenience, to protect property rights against encroachment.

The Federal Court of Canada has set out the following guiding principles to be used in assessing the balance of convenience on an interlocutory injunction motion where there is a substantive dispute over whether copying or other infringement of proprietary rights has occurred:

- Where a plaintiff's recoverable damages resulting from the continuance of the defendant's activities pending trial would be an adequate remedy that the defendant would be financially able to pay, an interlocutory injunction should not normally be granted.

- Where such damages would not provide the plaintiff an adequate remedy but damages (recoverable under the plaintiff's undertaking) would provide the defendant with such a remedy for the restriction on his activities, there would be no ground for refusing an interlocutory injunction.

- Where doubt exists as to the adequacy of these remedies in damages available to either party, regard should be had to where the balance of convenience lies.

- Where other factors appear to be evenly balanced, it is prudent to take such measures as will preserve the status quo.

• Where the evidence on the application is such as to show one party's case to be disproportionately stronger than the other's, this factor may be permitted to tip the balance of convenience in that party's favour provided the uncompensable disadvantage to each party would not differ widely.

• Other unspecified special factors may possibly be considered in the particular circumstances of individual cases.

This chapter has only summarized the most salient aspects of Canada's intellectual property laws as they relate to computer products and related technologies. The subjects discussed in this chapter have been comprehensively treated in other works, listed in the Notes to this chapter, to which the reader may wish to refer.

6

The Software Business and the Criminal Code

Software developers can be the victims of computer crime in many different ways. Their computers can be accessed by unauthorized parties such as "hackers" involved in a prank or, more ominously, by competitors intent on industrial espionage, who then proceed to destroy or otherwise abuse (or misuse in the case of competitors) important research results or financial data. Or a disgruntled employee may implant a "virus" in the software developer's computer program, which causes the software to malfunction some time after the individual has left the employment of the developer. Or there are the more traditional computer crimes, such as the production and sale by a "software pirate" of unauthorized copies of the software company's products.

Another traditional crime is theft of a computer company's hardware. This type of crime is becoming almost endemic with smaller machines, especially the portable laptop computers, which can be easily swiped from cars and even off desks if they are not securely fastened by some means. And the thieves are becoming more sophisticated, "fencing" the laptop machine only after they have resold to the original owner the various data files in the laptop's memory, under the threat of disclosing this material to the owner's competitor.

Canada's general criminal law, contained in the federal *Criminal Code*, includes several provisions that may be utilized by software companies to combat these and other computer-related crimes. This chapter discusses briefly the key provisions of the *Criminal Code* that may be used to fight computer crime. These provisions are in addition to civil remedies that may be available, as well as some other criminal sanctions that may be relevant to the particular objectionable activity, such as the offences relating to certain types of unauthorized copying provided in the *Copyright Act*.

UNAUTHORIZED USE
OF A COMPUTER

The *Criminal Code* makes it an offence for anyone to obtain fraudulently any computer service. The term "computer service" is defined broadly in the *Criminal Code* and includes data processing and the storage or retrieval of data. The same section of the *Criminal Code* also prohibits the interception of any function of a computer system. A person found guilty of an unauthorized use of a computer may be fined and/or imprisoned for up to 10 years.

This *Criminal Code* offence was enacted in 1985 to combat what was perceived to be a growing phenomenon in the computer age, the predilection of hackers and others to gain unauthorized access to computer facilities. This is precisely what had happened in the *McLaughlin* case, which went all the way to the Supreme Court of Canada. Given the negative outcome of this case from the government's point of view, it was likely an impetus for amending the *Criminal Code* to include the unauthorized use of a computer as an offence. In the *McLaughlin* case a student at the University of Alberta gained access, in an unauthorized fashion, to the university's computer. At the time (late 1970s) there was no offence called "unauthorized use of a computer" and thus the student was charged with fraudulent use of a telecommunications facility.

The Supreme Court of Canada acquitted the student because it concluded that a computer is a data-processing apparatus and not a telecommunications facility. The court determined that while data may be transmitted within the computer system, from one device to another, the *Criminal Code*'s offence of theft of a telecommunications service was aimed at the theft of external transmission signals between a sender and a receiver. The court reiterated a long-standing rule of interpretation in criminal law, that criminal statutes should be construed narrowly and that where there is any uncertainty or ambiguity as to whether a certain type of activity is criminal or not, the person accused of an offence must be acquitted. In short, the Supreme Court of Canada found that, at the time, there was no section of the *Criminal Code* that could be used to stop merely the unauthorized operation of a computer.

Partly in response to the *McLaughlin* case, Parliament enacted the section of the *Criminal Code* relating to the unauthorized use of a computer in 1985. As a result, facts similar to those found in the *McLaughlin* case would, today, likely secure a conviction under this new section of the *Criminal Code*. Thus, software companies, as well as other users of computers, now have a criminal law provision with which to deter potential hackers and other unauthorized users of their computer systems.

MISCHIEF IN RELATION TO DATA

The 1985 *Criminal Code* amendments added another offence: "mischief in relation to data." This section makes it a criminal offence for anyone to wilfully destroy or alter data, or to render data meaningless, useless, or ineffective or to obstruct, interrupt, or interfere with the lawful use of data, or to deny access to any person entitled access to data. The term "data" is defined quite broadly to mean representations of information or concepts that are being prepared or have been prepared in a form suitable for use in a computer. This definition would include computer programs, given that the *Criminal Code* defines "computer program" as being "data" representing instructions or statements that, when executed in a computer system, cause the computer system to perform a function. A person found guilty of committing mischief in relation to data may be fined and/or imprisoned for up to ten years.

One of the kinds of activity at which this new offence is aimed is illustrated by the facts which gave rise to the *Turner* decision. In this case an individual in Toronto dialled up a service bureau computer located in Milwaukee and implemented an encryption device on the bureau's computer. This encryption device caused the computer to refuse a certain customer of the service bureau access to its data, which was resident on the computer. The implementer of the encryption device was charged with, and convicted of, the general offence of mischief, which includes obstructing, interrupting, or interfering with any person in the lawful use, enjoyment, or operation of property.

At the time of this prosecution, the offence of mischief in relation to data was not yet enacted but was before Parliament as proposed legislation. The judge noted that the defendant likely could also have been convicted under the offence of mischief in relation to data if it were in force. The net effect of the new section, therefore, is to expand the scope of the mischief offence to include, in addition to property, "data" as an item that can be the subject of a mischief charge. This is a useful development, given that certain types of information-based assets of a software company may not be considered "property" for the purposes of the *Criminal Code*, as will be seen below in the discussion of the *Stewart* case.

THE *CRIMINAL CODE* AND COMPUTER VIRUSES

One very useful result of the addition to the *Criminal Code* of the offences of unauthorized use of a computer and mischief in relation to data is that these two sections, and especially the latter one, will assist Canadian law-enforcement agencies in combatting computer viruses. The computer virus is a disturbing phenomenon in the computer industry. The term "virus" was coined to describe the malicious actions of certain employees of computer software companies who, when creating software, purposely implant within it errors that will be triggered at some time in the future, usually long after the particular employee has left the software company. The word "virus" was adopted because many of these consciously programmed booby traps can spread themselves from computer to computer by means of telecommunications links. Some significant recent computer failures caused by computer viruses have focussed attention on this dangerous activity, essentially an act of industrial sabotage performed by disgruntled employees. The virus problem has become so serious that several years ago *Time* magazine devoted a cover story to the issue.

Employees are not the only ones who can perpetrate damage with computer viruses. Several years ago in a highly publicized case in the United States, Robert T. Morris, a former Cornell University graduate student, was convicted under the U.S. *Computer Fraud and Abuse Act* for letting loose a "worm" (a variation of a virus) into the INTERNET computer network. This worm caused the INTERNET system to grind to a halt; estimates of the damage caused by this virus attack range from $500,000 to $90 million. Morris was sentenced to three years probation, fined $10,000 plus the costs of probation, and ordered to perform 400 hours of community service.

The implantation into software of a computer virus in Canada would likely fall within the activity prohibited by the sections of the *Criminal Code* relating to unauthorized use of a computer and/or the mischief in relation to data. Where the virus destroys data it would clearly be covered by the latter section. It is perhaps somewhat more problematic whether "benign" viruses would also be captured under the two *Criminal Code* provisions. For example, some viruses do not destroy data or software, but merely convey a message, such as "Merry Christmas," as was the case with a virus that displayed this greeting on countless microcomputer programs on December 25 several years ago.

While such a virus seems to be harmless, in fact it still causes users serious anxiety and trouble. While it may not destroy data, it does take up some memory capacity and denies a user, for however short a period of time, access to the user's preferred screen (substituting for it the one with the unexpected message). Moreover, the existence of even a seemingly benign virus means that the program has been infected with unwanted elements, and hence generally leads users to expend money and time to eradicate it, inasmuch as they cannot know the nature or extent of the infection. For example, a recent *Globe & Mail* story documented the time and effort — and anxiety — expended by the Toronto Stock Exchange in preparing for the infamous "Michaelangelo virus", even though the TSE was never actually hit by it. In effect, what a hacker might have meant to be an innocuous joke turns out to cause significant damage. Even a benign virus, therefore, should be caught by the *Criminal Code*'s computer-abuse provisions because it obstructs, interrupts, or interferes with the lawful use of data.

Viruslike elements can sometimes be programmed into software by developers for ostensibly legitimate purposes. Generally known as "time bombs," these are devices that software companies might include in a program to combat unauthorized copying of the software. The time bomb would be set to go off on a particular date, perhaps causing the software to seize up and cease functioning — in some cases it may even destroy data — unless the user of the program renews its software licence with the supplier. This then would be a technical mechanism to thwart software piracy because, of course, unauthorized users would not have their bootleg software program reactivated by the supplier, unless they paid the required fee and entered into an appropriate software licence agreement.

This type of "legitimate" software virus could pose a problem under the section of the *Criminal Code* dealing with mischief in relation to data, particularly if it caused the destruction of data in addition to disabling the supplier's software (i.e., if it actually deleted the user's data). There may also be legal risks outside the criminal law in using such a software repossession device, as discussed in Chapter 11 under "Restrictions on Copying." As a result, it is generally not advisable for software companies to use such a technical mechanism to counteract illegal copying of software. If it is used, however, the time bomb should be designed not to destroy a user's data. As well, clear, written notice should be given to users that the software contains such a time bomb, in order to deter unauthorized copying of the program. Such a notice should be displayed prominently on the packaging of the software, in the related documentation, and on at least the first screen of the program itself. In short, a software company utilizing a time bomb should take great pains to notify the users — whether authorized users or not — about the time bomb, its consequences if the user causes it to be activated, and how it can be avoided, namely, by paying the required licence fee and entering into an appropriate licence agreement in a timely manner.

It is worth noting, in respect of such "legitimate" viruses, a recent press report that described how a freelance computer programmer in the U.S. made novel use of a time-bomb device. The programmer was hired to write a computer program. He inserted into it a time bomb, which he then activated when the client refused to pay the programmer for his services. Ostensibly the programmer was merely using self-help to "repossess" his property because of nonpayment. The local law-enforcement agency disagreed with this characterization of his actions, and he was charged with destroying computer data and causing damage under the particular state's computer crime law. While the programmer's actions may have been understandable, he should have restricted his legal claim to a breach of contract recovery of his fees for services rendered rather than, in a sense, taking the law into his own hands in a very crude and inflammatory way. Again, this case illustrates the dangers involved in using viruslike devices to achieve seemingly legitimate goals.

THEFT OF CONFIDENTIAL INFORMATION

The sections of the *Criminal Code* dealing with unauthorized use of a computer and mischief in relation to data have given software companies two new important tools for fighting computer crime. By contrast, the 1988 decision of the Supreme Court of Canada in the *Stewart* case has taken away what might have been another significant form of *Criminal Code* protection.

It is clear that if a software company's physical assets, such as an item of computer hardware, is stolen, the thief could be convicted of theft under the *Criminal Code*. By contrast, in the *Stewart* case the narrow issue to be decided was whether confidential information — an intangible item — could be stolen for the purpose's of the *Criminal Code*'s theft provision. In this case an agent of a union paid a hotel employee to divulge the names, addresses, and telephone numbers of the hotel's employees in order to assist the union in an organizing drive. The employee did not comply with the request, and indeed turned in the requester of the information to the police, who charged him with, among other things, counselling theft.

The Supreme Court of Canada acquitted the union's agent on the theft charge, holding that confidential information (the employee information was considered confidential by the hotel) cannot be stolen for the purposes of the *Criminal Code*'s theft section. The court noted that copying confidential information may be illegal under the *Copyright Act*, and in certain circumstances, where information was disclosed without authorization, the civil law may allow parties to bring claims. For an activity to be considered theft under the *Criminal Code*, however, it must involve a physical taking of a tangible object, the court decided, and this would not happen where confidential information, albeit through unauthorized disclosure, merely lost its confidential quality. The court, in a manner reminiscent of the *McLaughlin* case, construed the *Criminal Code* narrowly; the court said it was up to Parliament to amend the *Criminal Code* if Parliament wished the unauthorized disclosure of confidential information to constitute theft or some other offence under the *Criminal Code*.

Commentators within the legal and high-technology communities have criticized the *Stewart* decision for not showing sufficient flexibility in that it refused to extend an old *Criminal Code* offence, theft, to a new set of circumstances. On the other hand, since the date of the *Stewart* decision the computer industry has not lobbied vigorously enough for a change to be made in the law. Officials in the federal and provincial departments of justice have proposed new criminal trade-secrets legislation that would cover not only a physical taking, but also economic deprivation caused by the unauthorized disclosure of confidential information. Unfortunately, this reform initiative has not received adequate backing from the private sector and hence has not been seen by government to be a priority item.

FRAUD

While the Supreme Court of Canada made it clear in the *Stewart* case that confidential information cannot be stolen for purposes of the theft section of the *Criminal Code*, the offence of fraud may be committed by someone who makes unauthorized copies of a copyrighted work, such as a computer program. This was the important conclusion in the *Leahy* case, which was decided after the *Stewart* case and which was a preliminary inquiry to decide whether the unauthorized copying of computer software, in addition to constituting a violation of the *Copyright Act*, could also constitute fraud under the *Criminal Code*.

In the *Leahy* case an owner of a so-called software evaluation club would rent to members of the club copies of software and documentation at a fraction of their regular retail price. Members were supposed only to evaluate the software, and then to destroy it. The evidence of several customers of the club showed, however, that in fact the software was never deliberately erased after being evaluated. In effect, the court found the club to be merely a facade, by which, through dishonesty, software and documentation was being copied and sold for a profit without the authorization of the developers of the software. As this deliberate dishonesty caused economic deprivation to the software developers, the court found there was sufficient evidence to put the accused software evaluation club owner on trial for fraud. It should be noted that since January 1994 the activities described in the *Leahy* case, a software rental business, would have contravened the *Copyright Act* given that since that date the renting of certain computer software for commercial gain may only be done with the consent of the owner of the copyright in the software.

USING THE CRIMINAL LAW TO FIGHT COMPUTER CRIME

The foregoing discussion of the *Criminal Code* in the computer age may be summarized as follows: the unauthorized disclosure of confidential information does not constitute the offence of theft, but numerous other activities detrimental to the software company may be caught by the *Criminal Code*'s provisions for unauthorized use of a computer, mischief in relation to data, and fraud. It should be noted, however, that a software company wishing to interest the Crown in bringing charges under these latter provisions faces numerous procedural obstacles.

There is the difficulty of detecting many kinds of computer crime, or in finding the individual who perpetrated a particular incident of computer abuse. While this problem also arises in civil lawsuits brought in respect of the same objectionable activity, the problem may be manageable in a civil case where a claimant merely has to prove his case "on a balance of probabilities"; in a criminal matter, where the much higher onus of the Crown is to prove the case "beyond a reasonable doubt," the problem of detection and the lack of paper trails and other traditional forms of evidence can often be fatal to a computer-abuse prosecution. In a similar vein, a further obstacle is posed by the rule, which was mentioned above in the context of the *McLaughlin* and *Stewart* cases, that courts construe criminal statutes narrowly, and if the objectionable activity cannot be placed squarely within a section of the *Criminal Code*, the accused will be acquitted.

These difficulties are further compounded when the criminal activity is perpetrated over computer networks such as the INTERNET. Virtually all of these networks, and in particular the INTERNET, are international in their scope, and therefore the criminal is often outside of Canada, making it difficult for Canadian authorities to track him or her down and bring the accused to justice. As well, criminals (even those in Canada) who use the INTERNET to commit offences often do not leave evidence of their wrongdoing. Finding electronic fingerprints can be a fiendishly difficult task.

This problem was illustrated in a recent Canadian criminal case involving a young person who was accused of transmitting obscene child pornography over the INTERNET. The primary defence of the alleged offender was that it was not proven beyond a reasonable doubt that in fact he had been the individual responsible for downloading and uploading the offensive material. In particular, the defence argued that it was possible for another network user to "impersonate" the accused and to have been responsible for originating the offensive material. The court did not accept this argument because of the existence of circumstantial evidence at the accused's home. In other cases, however, the relative anonymity of the INTERNET will invariably make it more difficult for authorities to track down and bring to justice cybercriminals.

There is the additional problem that many software companies, and their clients, unfortunately, are extremely reluctant to report computer crime, or are unwilling to become involved in a computer-crime investigation, the results of which may become public. For example, a software company may be unwilling to blow the whistle on a former employee for implanting a virus in the company's software because of the negative impact of such a proceeding on the reputation of the relevant software product. Similarly, a user of the software who suffered damage resulting from the virus, say a financial institution, will be extremely reluctant to let the public know that its computer system was the subject of a virus attack, as this could bring into question the organization's reputation for reliability.

Notwithstanding these difficulties, the *Criminal Code* can be a useful ally of the software company in combatting computer crime. Where activity that threatens the reasonable business interests of the software company is covered by the *Criminal Code*, a criminal proceeding can be a relatively inexpensive and effective way of obtaining relief, given that the government pays for the investigation and prosecution, and that the government's extensive search and seizure and investigatory powers can be brought to bear on a particular problem. The publicity surrounding a criminal proceeding can also be extremely effective in deterring others from engaging in similar acts, particularly given that most people attach a certain social stigma to a criminal conviction.

The other benefit of the *Criminal Code* provisions is that they permit a software company to impress upon its employees that activities such as implanting viruses are illegal. This message ought to be conveyed forcefully to all employees. The limitations of the criminal law pointed out above, however, make it important that such an employee-communication program not focus exclusively on the *Criminal Code*. Rather, as discussed in greater detail in the next two chapters, it should present a comprehensive proprietary rights protection policy that covers all forms of relevant intellectual property, such as patents, trade secrets, copyrights, and trade-marks. The policy should discuss how these assets are to be identified, obtained (where formalities are required), and protected. Such a proprietary rights protection policy could prove valuable, assuming it was followed by employees and enforced by the software company, if the software company had to take civil action to protect a particular intellectual property asset — whether or not such action was accompanied by a criminal proceeding.

GIVING AN ILLEGAL BENEFIT

Another *Criminal Code* offence that software companies should be aware of is the one that makes it illegal for a software (or any other company), when it is marketing or selling its products or services, to give an employee of the prospective customer a benefit, such as a gift — in kind or in cash — that is not disclosed to the employee's superiors. Such a giving of a secret benefit is commonly known as a bribe. The rationale for the offence is to prevent the situation where the employee is in a conflict of interest; namely, where he or she might suggest selecting a particular vendor of computing resources based not on the objective merits of the products or their respective prices, etc., but because he or she has received a secret benefit and now feels beholden to the person who gave it.

This offence, which has application across a wide range of businesses, came into focus for the computer sector a few years ago when a computer supplier was charged with allegedly providing several municipal politicians with personal computers for their own home use. An embarrassing trial — both for the supplier and the politicians — followed. At the end of the trial the supplier was acquitted on the basis of a finding that the computers belonged to the municipality and were merely being loaned to the politicians. Notwithstanding the final result in this case, it serves as a useful reminder to software companies to behave in a manner that can in no way be construed as providing secret benefits to employees of their customers, whether the customer is in the private or public sector.

7

A Proprietary Rights Protection Policy for the Software Business

The software and related documentation of a software company are, almost by definition, the company's most critical assets. It is essential to protect these and related items, and the legal mechanisms available for doing so are discussed in Chapters 5 and 6. It is not enough, however, merely to understand the fundamentals of copyright and other intellectual property protection laws afforded by the legal system. Owners and managers of software businesses must also design and administer a proprietary rights protection policy that implements these legal rules in the work place.

Such a policy will have two major written components. One is a document that is distributed to employees and that sets out clearly, concisely, and in easy-to-understand terms the various policies and procedures of the software company regarding the protection of proprietary and other confidential information. The main areas to be addressed by such a document are discussed in this chapter. The second written component is a proprietary rights protection agreement that should be signed by all the employees of the software company, as well as the consultants, independent contract programmers, and other similar people or entities that the company may utilize for particular projects from time to time. This type of agreement is discussed in Chapter 8.

THE IMPORTANCE OF PROPRIETARY INFORMATION

The proprietary rights protection policy should begin by listing the various types of intellectual and other proprietary property that will come into the hands of employees. It would include the company's software and documentation, of course, but would also encompass a number of other items, such as trade secrets, research and development work-in-progress, technical knowhow, confidential business or financial information, marketing plans, customer lists, and the confidential information of others entrusted to the company (such as client data, or software licensed to the company by other software companies).

After describing the relevant proprietary information, the policy should state how important these assets are to the company and that, accordingly, all staff are to protect them by, among other means, the procedures described in the policy. It is important to stress to employees that inadvertent, let alone conscious, disclosure of confidential information to persons outside the company can cause great harm to the company — as well as to the livelihood of the people employed by it; in short, the protection of proprietary rights is every employee's business, and every employee should take the task seriously.

The policy should note that some of the proprietary information handled by the company is in fact owned by others and is typically provided to the company for a particular purpose only. The policy should emphasize that it is imperative to treat this material also with the utmost care, particularly because the company is invariably obligated by contract to keep such third party material confidential and because an improper disclosure of it by an employee could expose the company to a breach-of-contract or breach-of-confidence claim.

MEASURES TO PROTECT SECURITY

After noting why the protection of proprietary rights is so important, the policy should describe the actual procedures and practices utilized to ensure such protection, especially the physical security measures instituted to safeguard trade secrets and confidential information. As noted by Sookman in Chapter 5, trade-secret protection can be easily lost if adequate measures are not taken to keep the particular item secret.

Some basic examples of physical security measures are cleaning desks at the end of each day and keeping the hard-copy versions of the proprietary material in locked filing cabinets; locking the doors and otherwise limiting access to areas where proprietary material is kept, perhaps by an "access card," key, or similar system; and implementing visitor control procedures, such as keeping a visitors' log, issuing visitor badges, and excluding visitors from areas where trade secrets or other confidential material are kept. This is not an exhaustive list by any means. Each software company will have to carefully review its own operations and "corporate culture" to institute the right mix of physical security measures, which should then be clearly described in the policy so that all staff will know exactly what is required of them in this important area.

The importance of these kinds of physical security measures cannot be overstated. In a recent case, a small software company won a judgment against a much larger software company when the former was able to demonstrate to a judge that the latter had misappropriated the former's trade secrets. In order to find in favour of the small company, the court had to conclude that that company had trade secrets in the first place, and it did this largely on the strength of evidence which showed that the company took protective measures in respect of its software similar to those noted above and elsewhere in this chapter.

Of course, these kinds of physical security measures are no longer sufficient to protect the trade secrets and other important assets — and reputation — of the software company, given that so much of the company's critical information and knowledge resides on computers and is communicated over a broad range of public and private networks. To address challenges posed by these new technologies and circumstances, the proprietary rights policy should enumerate a number of computer and network protection rules, including requiring employees and other staff to use various passwords and personal identification number systems for all computers; to utilize software encryption technologies when appropriate; to implement "firewalls" between the company's computers and internal networks, on the one hand, and external networks such as the INTERNET on the other; and to exercise extreme caution when downloading material from public networks or INTERNET Web sites, first to ensure that it can in fact be freely downloaded and used, and second by subjecting the material to virus scanning software to detect any electronic infection with it.

SECURING INTELLECTUAL PROPERTY PROTECTION

The proprietary rights protection policy should briefly explain the terms "trade secret," "copyright," "patent," and "trade-mark," and how each is obtained and maintained. It should also point out that to obtain trade-secret, patent, copyright, and trade-mark protection for proprietary information certain formal requirements must be met. For example, documents of the company containing trade secrets or confidential information should be clearly marked with the following or a similar notice:

TRADE SECRETS/CONFIDENTIAL INFORMATION

THIS MATERIAL CONTAINS TRADE SECRETS AND/OR CONFIDEN-
TIAL INFORMATION OF [name of company] AND MAY NOT BE
USED, DISCLOSED, OR COPIED WITHOUT THE PERMISSION OF
[name of company].

The policy should also note that, in addition to being properly marked, materials containing trade secrets or confidential information should be treated in accordance with the physical security measures outlined elsewhere in the proprietary rights protection policy.

The policy should explain that the process of obtaining a patent or a trademark registration usually commences with a search of the applicable public register to determine the availability of such protection for the relevant invention or proposed trademark. It is common to provide that such procedures, as well as the filing of patent and trade-mark registration applications, will be coordinated and supervised by a particular officer of the software company and that all requests or enquiries relating to patent or trade-mark matters should be directed to this individual.

It is important that the individual at the software company given responsibility for patents and trade-marks understand at least in a general way how these two systems work. This individual should be allowed to interact closely with the lawyers, patent agents, and trade-mark agents who will be assisting the company in registering these important intellectual property rights. This individual must also think internationally when considering applying for patent or trademark protection. At the very least, consideration should be given to applying for protection in the United States at the time that registrations are filed in Canada.

Indeed, for patent rights it is often sensible to search and file an application in the U.S. first. An international patent-law treaty provides that if the applicant files in certain other countries that are parties to the treaty within twelve months of its filing in any country that is a party to the treaty, including the U.S., the filing date in the subsequent countries will be the filing date in the first treaty country (it should be noted, however, that certain countries are not parties to this treaty and would therefore have to be filed in immediately). It is wise to file in the U.S. first; because the American patent register contains the largest number of patents of any country, the review given an application by the U.S. Patent Office tends to be quite thorough and can usually give a good indication of how easy or difficult the processing of the application will be around the world, or indeed whether it stands a chance of succeeding at all. If the U.S. response to the application is negative, and the applicant withdraws the application, at least it saves the filing costs in the other treaty jurisdictions (in which filing would take place likely only if and when a positive response from the U.S. Patent Office was received, assuming a response was received from the U.S. Patent Office prior to the filing deadlines in other countries.).

A similar international, or at least North American, pitfall in the area of trade-mark registrations is described in the following scenario. A Canadian software company dreams up a trade-mark for its new flagship product. The product is initially intended to be marketed in Canada only, so the company orders a trade-mark search at the Canadian Trade-Mark Office. The search reveals no conflict-ing mark, so the company commences what proves to be two years of significant advertising and marketing effort for the product under the new trade-mark, which becomes registered in Canada. The product does very well in Canada and after two years the software company decides to distribute it in the U.S. as well. A search is done of the U.S. trade-mark register and, to the horror of the compa-ny, the trade-mark is not available in the U.S. (although it was in Canada).

This presents the company with an agonizing dilemma. Should it change the name of the product altogether so that it can be marketed in both Canada and the U.S. under the same name (thereby losing the goodwill built up in Canada in the first name)? Or should a different name be used for the copies of the product marketed in the U.S. (thereby probably causing confusion among a number of users, given that under such a scenario the product would be marketed under two different names in what is in many respects a single North American mar-ket)? Neither option is attractive; indeed, either one could lead to significant con-fusion in the marketplace — just what the Canadian software company doesn't need. What should have happened, of course, is that the Canadian and U.S. trade-mark registers should have been searched simultaneously to ensure that the product name was clear for use throughout North America before any marketing or advertising dollars were spent on either side of the border. The point of this example is that a software company's proprietary rights protection policy, in the section on trade-marks, should require simultaneous trade-mark searches con-ducted in both Canada and the U.S. if there is even the remotest possibility that the product will find its way into the U.S. market (which is likely the case for the lion's share of software developed in Canada!). Of course the same steps should be taken at the same time in respect of any other countries, such as those of the European Union, that are likely to become target markets for the software com-pany's product; indeed, acquiring trade-mark protection in Europe is now sim-pler with the recent introduction of a European Union trade-mark which, with a single trade-mark application, covers all 15 countries of the European Union.

The proprietary rights protection policy should also note the most important rules related to proper use of a trade-mark, from a legal perspective, in order to protect as fully as possible the company's exclusive interest in it. For example, a registered trademark should be printed with the registration symbol, "R" in a circle, ®, beside it, so that the public (and competitors) can see that it is a regis-tered trade-mark (some companies also put the symbol "TM" on unregistered trade-marks, which is probably a sensible idea, though not as important legally as putting the registration symbol on registered trade-marks). As well, the policy should note that trade-marks should be used only as adjectives, never as nouns. For instance, if the particular trade-mark is "XYXIS" then the relevant product label or advertisement might read "XYXIS Financial Software," but should never say "A XYXIS." The latter usage, as a noun, may make the trade-mark descriptive of a generic item or technology rather than of the company that produces the particular product or service, with the result that the trade-mark could lose its exclusive legal effect and others may be able to start to use it. The trade-mark landscape is littered with well-known trade-marks that, through improper usage and inadequate enforcement, have become too closely associated with generic products to allow their owners effective protection, much to the owners' dismay.

The proprietary rights protection policy would also contain the form of copyright notice that is useful to place on the software company's copyrightable works, including software and related documentation, before it is delivered to a customer or anyone else outside of the company. The notice should contain three elements: the copyright symbol, "c" in a circle (not merely in brackets), ©; the year of first publication; and the name of the owner of the copyright in the material. The symbol should appear prominently on the first page of written material, such as the user's manual, and should be embedded in software so that it appears on the first screen visible to a user of the program. As noted in Chapter 5, while this copyright notice is no longer required in the U.S. for new works, it is useful nonetheless because, among other things, it makes it difficult for a copier of the software to argue that it did not know the material was copyrighted, and hence greater damages can likely be recovered from the infringer.

LIMITING COPYING

The proprietary rights protection policy should encourage employees to strictly limit the number of copies made of documents containing trade secrets or confidential information. The indiscriminate copying of such materials greatly increases the risk that the sensitive information contained in them will be disclosed to unauthorized parties. To this end, such documents should be made available only to selected employees on a strictly "need-to-know" basis. In some circumstances it may also be useful to keep a log of authorized copies and to prohibit the further reproduction of such copies. When such copies are no longer required, they should be shredded or otherwise destroyed rather than merely thrown out with the regular waste. While some of these measures may seem extreme, the policy should explain that these and other measures, such as the physical and computer security measures discussed above, are required in order to help the software company protect its valuable information-based assets.

The software company should also take great pains to ensure that computer software licensed by it from others is strictly controlled so as to prevent its unauthorized copying. As explained in Chapter 11, software is almost always licensed rather than sold. This means that the software used by the company for administration, research, and other purposes will be licensed to the company, often on the basis that only one production copy of it can be made for use at the company. In such a case, if the company makes additional, unauthorized copies of the software, it is breaching its licence agreement as well as committing a violation of the *Copyright Act*.

Accordingly, the proprietary rights protection policy should state in no uncertain terms that the company does not condone the illegal copying of software and that employees engaging in such activity will be disciplined by appropriate measures, up to and including dismissal. The policy should point out that if multiple copies of a software program are required, options such as "site licences" or "institution licences" should be explored with the supplier of the software so that the company can operate with greater flexibility, all the while complying with the law.

Failure to implement, and enforce, such rules against illegal copying of software could cost the software company dearly. A number of American suppliers of personal computer software have formed the Software Protection Association in order to combat illegal copying of software by corporate entities and other organizations. Originally active mainly in the United States, this association is now bringing legal action against illegal copiers of software in many other countries — a similar type of group, the Canadian Alliance Against Software Theft (CAAST), has also been established in Canada. The cases brought by these software rights protection groups are aimed to achieve a high profile in the media, and they are often successful in doing so. It would be extremely embarrassing if a software company were ever the target of these groups' copyright enforcement activities, not least because of the coverage the press would likely give to such a story, given that one software company (which should know better) would be seen to be ripping off another one. For these reasons it is important that the software company teach its employees about the ethical use of software. In this regard it should be noted that the RCMP, at the behest of CAAST, has raided the premises of and charged several commercial resellers of computers for illegally copying software onto the systems they were selling. Apropos the discussion of computer/network protection rules elsewhere in this chapter, it should also be noted that the RCMP have brought prosecutions against persons who illegally copy and transmit software over the INTERNET.

For an anti-copying policy to be effective, the software company must be prepared at all times to enforce it and to take appropriate steps immediately upon learning of any unauthorized software-copying activities. Having the policy on paper without enforcing it could be worse than having no written policy at all, because it might lead to the conclusion that the written policy is just a smokescreen. The following case illustrates well the need to take suitable measures quickly against employees who participate in illegal software copying.

In this case, a software developer was unable to get full compensation from a person who had been making illegal copies of the software developer's product while an employee of a certain company to which the developer's product was licensed. As a result, the software developer tried to impose liability on the employer company, mainly on the basis that an employer is generally responsible for the acts of its employees. The judge dismissed the software developer's claim against the company, concluding that the company using the software, under its licence agreement with the software developer, was required to take only reasonably diligent measures to protect the software; that the company did take reasonable steps to supervise the employee's work; that the company uncovered the employee's irregular conduct in a reasonable and timely way; and that the company had acted to minimize the damage caused by the employee with reasonable speed and thoroughness. The point of this case is that for an organization to be in the clear in the event of an employee's unauthorized copying, it is not enough that the organization simply not encourage or participate in the illegal act; nor can an employer merely turn a blind eye to the problem. Rather, employers must take active and effective measures to deal with the problem and to try to ensure that it does not recur.

In a similar vein, the proprietary rights protection policy should make it clear that staff must respect the intellectual property rights of other software companies when staff are creating software. The policy must encourage "independent creation," which is always a defence to a competitor's claim of copyright infringement, and to this end the policy should indicate what kinds of records each staff member should keep of his or her creative efforts. These records are important not only for intellectual property rights protection purposes, but also for claiming R&D tax incentives, as discussed in Chapter 2. The policy might also require that searches of newly issued software patents be conducted periodically to help ensure that the software company's product development plans do not inadvertently come to infringe a third party's patent.

CLEARING MULTIMEDIA RIGHTS

If your company produces multimedia and related products, the proprietary rights policy should highlight the following issues related to acquiring the necessary rights to use other people's intellectual property. There are typically two ways in which your company would obtain the rights to use an intellectual property in one of your multimedia products: ownership, which means you would own the actual intellectual property rights (i.e. the copyright, etc.); or licence, which is a right granted by the owner of the intellectual property permiting you to use the particular property for a specific purpose. The proprietary rights policy should indicate that if you intend to own certain intellectual properties, you should have the author transfer to you in writing the copyrights and other rights. This document should also have the author waive, or give up, his or her moral rights in the property. This is important because in all likelihood you will alter or modify the property. Everyone involved in the creation of the multimedia product should sign an appropriate assignment where it is intended that you own the intellectual property in the product.

Where it is not intended that you own the property, you must obtain a licence for the property. The proprietary rights policy should stipulate that the licence must be broad enough to cover all of the possible uses that you will make of the property, including video, film, and book formats, for exploiting merchandising rights, etc. Of course, you will also want to be granted very broad "electronic rights" in the property, encompassing not only CD-ROM but also on-line distribution. With respect to the type of rights granted to you, you will want to ensure that you have a licence to the following copyright rights: copy, perform publicly, communicate by telecommunication, publish, translate, adapt, control public exhibition and rent. The licence should also give you the rights to exploit the property in technology and under intellectual property rights "not now known", so as to allow the product to be used in future electronic and other applications. Of course the owner of the property will likely resist such a broad licence, and hence securing licence rights can involve lively negotiations!

Particular issues relevant to the licensing of specific types of properties that would be addressed in the proprietary rights policy are set out below :

- *Text.* The publisher of a book may not have the "electronic rights" to the book, in which case you would have to deal directly with the author or his or her estate. Where a publisher says it has the electronic rights, ask to see the its underlying contract with the author (i.e.- do not just take the publisher's word for it).

- *Film.* Again, whoever holds the copyright in the film (i.e. the film studio, film director or film producer, etc.) may not have "electronic" or "interactive" rights to the underlying book. As well, the copyright in the soundtrack may be held by another entity. Or the actors may not have signed releases covering "multimedia" rights. Getting the rights to use a clip from a film in a multimedia work can be very difficult.

- *Photos.* The publisher of a magazine that contains a photo does not usually have the copyright, or even the electronic rights, in the photo. Again, you would have to approach the original creator of the photograph. And if the photo includes people, you will need releases from them.

- *Music.* There are several, separate rights that may have to be licensed for a particular piece of music. A "synchronization licence" is required if the music is to be used in conjunction with video or other images. In Canada, these rights can sometimes be cleared through CMRRA (Canadian Musical Reproduction Rights Agency). If the music is to be put on a separate, stand-alone soundtrack release, either on CD or cassette, etc., then a "mechanical licence" would also be required. Both the synchronization and mechanical licences only apply to the musical composition itself. If use of a particular recording is required, then a further "recording licence" is needed. For music on tape or CD, this would typically be obtained from the relevant record company. A fourth music right applies if the multimedia product is to be used or shown in public, such as in a kiosk located in a public place. In this case a "performance licence" would be required. In Canada, these rights can be cleared through SOCAN (Society of Composers, Authors and Music Publishers).

- *Software.* When you license the software you use to author your multimedia product, you should ensure that you obtain whatever rights you need to distribute run-time versions of the software with the copies of the CDs on which your product is resident. Again, you should ensure that this software licence is broad enough to cover all the different ways you might get your product to end-users.

- *Union talent.* When union actors, script writers or musicians are used, additional rights need to be secured and payments made to unions or guilds In Canada, the union for performers and writers would be ACTRA (Association of Canadian Television and Radio Artists), and for musicians the AF of M (American Federation of Musicians).

UNSOLICITED PRODUCT PROPOSALS

The software company from time to time may receive unsolicited ideas for new products or suggestions for improvements to existing products. The proprietary rights protection policy should provide that in most cases such proposals be returned immediately without even a cursory review. The danger in reviewing such a proposal lies in what is known as "proprietary rights contamination." The software company may already be working on the same product idea, and by reviewing and then declining to accept the unsolicited idea, the company may in some fashion become obligated to pay for the proposal, when in fact the company's eventual product is not derived from the unsolicited proposal at all.

If, however, some review of an unsolicited product idea is warranted, then the software company should have the person who is proposing the idea sign a carefully drafted waiver. This document would have the person proposing the idea acknowledge that the software company is engaged in R&D in an area similar to the product proposal. It would also provide that the software company need not hold in confidence the disclosed idea, that the company shall have no obligation to the discloser of the idea unless the company desires to acquire from the discloser the idea or some right in it, and that only in this latter situation would the company be required to pay any compensation for the product idea.

ACCESS-TO-INFORMATION LAWS

If the software company does or intends to do business with any government department or public agency, whether at the federal, provincial, or municipal level, including certain Crown corporations or utilities and the like, the proprietary rights protection policy should explain that there is federal legislation and similar laws in Ontario, Quebec, and the other provinces (which often cover municipalities and related local public entities as well), that give third parties access to information submitted to these public entities. These "access-to-information" or "freedom-of-information" laws, as they are usually called, can be extremely important because there are all sorts of ways that a software company can come to provide the government or related agencies with sensitive information. It may be given in support of an application for funding or some other financial assistance, or as part of a response to a call for tenders for a procurement by the public entity. The access-to-information laws raise the very real possibility that a journalist or, perhaps more importantly, a competitor of the company or someone else may gain access to information that the company has deposited with a government or some public agency.

Access-to-information laws, however, do generally limit or prohibit altogether the disclosure of certain trade secrets or confidential technical, scientific, and business information of a company to a third party requesting access under the relevant law. To take the fullest advantage of these exemptions, and to help prevent the software company's sensitive information from falling into the hands of strangers by means of access-to-information laws, the company's proprietary rights protection policy should encourage employees to keep in mind the following when contemplating providing information to a government department or public-sector agency:

1. Does the material really have to be sent to the government? Many businesses routinely provide the government with more information than is required by

the government. In many cases it is sensible to be initially modest about the amount of information given to the government, and perhaps to wait until asked for additional information before submitting extremely sensitive material, inasmuch as the government may not make such a request.

2. If the material has to be provided to government, can it be sent in a manner that discloses less about the company? For example, data might be compiled selectively so as to provide less sensitive details about operations while still satisfying the government's request. Or, if the government asks to see gross sales figures only, do not give a full profit and loss statement; rather, disaggregate the data to provide only the gross sales figures.

3. Rather than sending the information to the government, is it feasible to have the government officials review it at the company's premises? If the material must be sent, can it be retrieved after the government no longer needs it? For example, in certain circumstances it may be possible to have the government return certain documents relating to a government contract bid where the company is not awarded the contract.

4. When submitting trade secrets or confidential material to the government, the cover of such material should be clearly marked with the following or a similar notice (tailored to the relevant access-to-information legislation):

THIS DOCUMENT CONSTITUTES CONFIDENTIAL INFORMATION AND MAY ALSO CONTAIN TRADE SECRETS OR OTHER MATERIAL THE RELEASE OF WHICH MAY CAUSE PREJUDICE OR LOSS TO [name of company]. IF ANY GOVERNMENT DEPARTMENT OR AGENCY INTENDS TO DISCLOSE THIS INFORMATION, OR ANY PART THEREOF, WRITTEN NOTICE SHALL BE PROVIDED TO [name of company] TO THE ATTENTION OF [name of head of the group submitting the material or officer responsible for access-to-information or proprietary rights matters] AT THE FOLLOWING ADDRESS: [give full address, including fax number].

5. Respond promptly to any request from the government; for example, if a federal government request for disclosure of company information is received by the company, it must generally be responded to within 20 days of receipt of the request and, accordingly, the person who receives such a request should immediately contact the legal counsel of the company or the individual responsible for access-to-information matters.

6. It is important to note that merely marking a document as a trade secret or as confidential as noted in item 4 is not sufficient — such materials must be consistently treated by the company as secret or confidential in accordance with

relevant physical security and other procedures. Such security measures might include the measures enumerated above under "Measures to Protect Security" as well as making such material available to employees, customers, and others only after the recipients have signed nondisclosure agreements. Of course, these security and other measures should be taken in respect of all proprietary information of the company, whether or not it is to be submitted to the government.

PROPRIETARY RIGHTS PROTECTION AGREEMENTS

A key plank in any proprietary rights protection policy will be the proprietary rights protection agreements that will be signed by the software company's employees, consultants, contract programmers, customers, distributors, and anyone else that comes into contact with the company's software and other critical information-based assets. Such agreements are so important that Chapter 8 is devoted to a discussion of these types of agreements in relation to employees and independent contractors, and in Chapters 11 and 13 there is a discussion of the kinds of proprietary rights protection clauses that should be included in agreements between a software company and its customers and distributors.

The policy, however, should do more than simply remind employees when such proprietary rights protection agreements or provisions should be utilized. The policy should also stress the practical information-handling aspects of these agreements. For example, just as procedures should be instituted to ensure that employees return the software company's proprietary information in their possession or control upon their departure from the company, so too employees should ensure that other persons or entities — such as independent contractors or distributors — who have been given sensitive company information return it when they have finished with it. As well, employees should make sure that third-party proprietary information is returned to its rightful owner after the software company is done with it.

An important part of the proprietary rights protection agreement will be the "computer and network protection rules" established by the company, to which each employee or contractor is required to adhere. If, for whatever reason, the computer and network protection rules are not attached to the proprietary rights agreement, they can be distributed to staff as a stand-alone document. In either case, the key objective is to bring these rules to the attention of personnel so they understand that a failure to comply with them can cause damage to the company, and may result in the employee being disciplined.

ADMINISTRATION OF THE PROPRIETARY RIGHTS PROTECTION POLICY

It is not enough that a software company merely have a proprietary rights protection policy and a set of computer/network protection rules; it must also implement and enforce them. A policy that is written down but then left to languish on some dusty shelf is of no use to the company. Rather, the policy should be widely distributed, and life should be breathed into it by a senior officer, or a committee of managers in a larger company, so that the protection policies and procedures become second nature to all staff.

In many respects employee education is the key to a successful proprietary rights protection policy. Periodic seminars on the subjects covered by the policy are invaluable, particularly when such a seminar addresses new issues not adequately covered by the existing policy. And of course the policy must be enforced. The individual or group responsible for the policy should review its implementation to ensure that all relevant employees, independent contractors, and consultants are aware of the policy; that appropriate pre-hiring interviews (to help ensure that new staff do not bring third-party proprietary rights to the software company) and exit interviews (to help ensure that departing staff do not take with them any of the software company's proprietary rights) are held with all staff; that suitable physical and computer/network security, document marking, and other measures, including proper patent and trade-mark searches, are being taken in respect of the company's proprietary information; and that an inventory is being kept of, and appropriate measures are being taken to preserve and protect, the company's trade-secret, patent, copyright, and trademark assets.

8

Agreements with Employees and Independent Contractors

The employees of a software company are critical to the organization's success; they are usually even more important than the company's software programs. Without bright, effective employees, the company can hardly hope to prosper; it is often said that a software company's key assets go up and down in the elevator each day. In addition, a software company will often retain the services of independent contractors; they may be individuals, or they may be companies that have employees or that in turn hire other independent contractors. Independent contractors, who may have expertise in consulting or software programming among other skills, can be retained for many reasons, such as to assist with the development of a particular item of software that the software company wants to have developed quickly. Or a multimedia title developer might retain certain outside expertise to produce specific content, such as music or animation, or technology, such as navigation tool, for a particular multimedia product. Independent contractors come in very handy if the software company does not have adequate staff of its own to do a particular job, and in some cases a project is contracted out simply because the independent contractors have particular expertise that is useful or timely to the software company.

It should be noted that a software company using an independent contractor should indeed "contract out" the work to such entity. Otherwise, the software company could end up being considered the employer of the independent contractor's staff, if the software company supervised them so closely as to end up controlling their work to the same or a similar extent as that of its "real" employees. If this happens the software company could become liable for making employee income tax and related source deductions in respect of the contractor's staff; and if the company does not actually make the deductions, and the contractor's staff have spent all their fees and cannot pay Revenue Canada their proper taxes, then the software company may be liable for such amounts. This is always an issue deserving scrutiny when utilizing independent (or supposedly so) contractors.

While employees, and often independent contractors, are central to a software company's plans for success, they can also be a major source of leakage of the company's critical software and other information-based assets. There is significant mobility among employees of software companies. As for independent contractors, they invariably will go off to work for others, either after the particular project they are working on is finished, or sometimes even before, with the result that they may be performing services for two competing software companies at the same time. All this movement by employees and independent contractors presents software companies with the serious risk that their important proprietary rights will fall into the wrong hands. Obviously a software company must take certain steps to protect its interests, while at the same time being sensitive to the legitimate needs of employees and independent contractors. One part of the solution is even-handed, written proprietary rights protection agreements with employees and independent contractors that cover the following issues.

NONDISCLOSURE OR MISUSE OF PROPRIETARY INFORMATION

The employee and independent contractor will invariably be exposed to the software company's trade secrets and other confidential information, including software and related documentation. The proprietary rights protection agreement with the employee and independent contractor, therefore, should provide, at a minimum, that (1) the recipient will use the company's information only to perform the stipulated services for the company and for no other purpose; (2) the recipient will not copy or store in a database the company's information except as reasonably necessary to perform the recipient's services; (3) the recipient will not disclose the company's material to any third party, except with the consent of the company; and (4) access to this material by the independent contractor's employees (assuming the independent contractor is not an individual) or sub-contractors will be permitted only after these individuals sign additional proprietary rights protection agreements.

This last point is important because if the independent contractor is a corporation, and only it signs the agreement, it may be that the obligations of the corporate independent contractor will not adequately bind its employees or its sub-contractors. To eliminate this possibility, the employees and sub-contractors of the main independent contractor should personally be bound by the proprietary rights protection rules required by the software company, by signing an agreement virtually identical to that signed by the main contractor, at least insofar as protection of proprietary rights is concerned.

In the proprietary rights protection agreement the software company should describe the type of information subject to nondisclosure protections. This will include, of course, the software company's own trade secrets and other confidential information, such as technical and business data, new product plans, customer lists and personnel information, to name several key categories of information. The agreement should also go on, however, to list as proprietary information the trade secrets or confidential information owned by third parties, such as the company's customers and suppliers, which is in the possession of the company. For example, a software company will come to learn a great deal about a particular client's operations, financial condition, and other matters while developing certain types of software for the client. The client will be very anxious to ensure that this information is not disclosed to competitors of the client by the employees or independent contractors of the software company, and a nondisclosure requirement in the proprietary rights protection agreements with these parties will assist in this effort.

As noted in the previous paragraph, the nondisclosure provisions in the proprietary rights protection agreement should also cover certain materials provided to the software company by its suppliers. A key item in this regard is the software licensed by the company from other software developers. The problem with employees and independent contractors making illegal copies of such software is discussed at length in Chapter 7. To help combat this problem the proprietary rights protection agreement should make it very clear that the user of such material is not permitted to make extra copies of the third-party software used by the company unless appropriate permission is granted by the owner or distributor of the software (perhaps in the form of a "site licence" or "institution licence" or some other arrangement where the user can make multiple copies of the software on some volume-discount-price basis). This can be done by having the employee and independent contractor agree to abide by a set of computer/network protection rules that, among other things, would also include measures to be taken by staff to help reduce the likelihood of infection of the company's software by computer viruses.

Such a set of computer/network-protection rules could also cover some or all of the following matters:

- Users may use the computers and networks only for purposes directly related to the user's work with the company. Users shall not store or use games or entertainment software on the computers, nor shall users download from the networks into the computers any "freeware", "shareware" or any other software, nor shall users input any information or material into the computers that is unrelated to the user's work with the company.

- Only authorized copies of software may be used on the computers and users shall not operate on the computers software which has been copied illegally. Users shall not use the computers to copy illegally software. Users shall respect the software licence and network subscription agreements entered into by the company.

- Copies of computer software licensed to a user personally, and other computer software not licensed directly by the company, may only be used on the computers after approval for such use is obtained from the company. If approved, such software may be used and stored only on the personal computer assigned to the user who is the authorized user of such software.

- Appropriate virus protection software must be installed on each personal computer, and must be used whenever new software is being loaded onto a personal computer.

- A user may use the company's links to the networks only for purposes directly related to the user's work with the company, and no such access to the networks initiated from the company's computers shall be used for a personal or any other non-company purpose.

- If a user accesses the networks from the user's own computer from the user's home, the user shall not make any reference to the company in the course of such usage or to the fact that the user is associated with the company.

- Users shall not send sensitive information over the networks given that one risk of doing so is that a recipient may forward the information to numerous others.

- Users shall not transmit software or other copyright materials over the networks to third parties, nor shall users download such materials themselves, except without the prior approval of the company. Users shall not make or disseminate any defamatory, negligent or other similar statements on the networks.

- Users shall be responsible for using the computers and the networks in an effective, ethical and lawful manner. Users shall respect the rights and interests of others, as well as privacy and confidentiality.

- Users shall take all reasonable steps to protect the integrity and the security of the computers and the networks, including software and data. Users shall not access or disclose systems or data, nor shall they destroy or remove software or data, without authorization. Users shall not disclose confidential passwords, access codes, account numbers or other authorization assigned to them. Users shall not misrepresent themselves as another user, nor shall a user change another person's password without authorization.

Just as the software company does not want the employee or independent contractor to disclose in an unauthorized manner the proprietary information owned by or in the possession of the company, neither does the company want the employee or independent contractor to bring on to the company's premises, or otherwise use or disclose to the company's personnel, the confidential information of some other party, such as a competitor of the software company. In effect, the software company does not want to be tainted by the improper use of any information obtained by an employee from a former employer or by an independent contractor while on a previous consulting project. To this end a software company should include a provision in the proprietary rights protection agreement whereby the employees and independent contractors acknowledge that they will not make use of or disclose to the new company the trade secrets or other confidential information belonging to someone else. The agreement should also have employees and consultants agree that they will not knowingly infringe the proprietary rights of others as they create software for the company.

In a similar vein, the software company hiring an employee, or retaining the services of an independent contractor, should be extremely careful if the new person had previously worked for an organization that is the developer of a software product competitive with a product of the company. Particularly if the new person had a relatively senior position in the competitive organization, the company could well attract a lawsuit for the improper use of trade secrets or confidential information. This risk can be reduced if the new person is not immediately assigned to a project that competes directly with the former employer's project. The company might consider having the new person start in a different area of the company so that the former employer's fears are lessened somewhat, but in many circumstances this is not enough. The company proposing to hire a new employee, or retain the services of an independent contractor, must carefully weigh the possible consequences and risks of such a hiring attracting a legal claim by a third party. The risk of such a legal claim is heightened if the new employee is subject to a non-competition obligation in favour of the former

employer, and the former employer and the new employer are in fact competitors, given that a reasonable, well-drafted noncompetition clause is often
enforceable in many circumstances.

NONCOMPETITION AND
NONSOLICITATION OF CLIENTS

Many software companies believe that simply securing nondisclosure obligations in proprietary rights protection agreements with employees and independent contractors is not sufficient protection against improper disclosure of trade
secrets and other confidential information. For example, if an employee leaves to
join a competitor, how can the original company effectively monitor whether in
fact its proprietary information is being disclosed to the competitor? Or the company may be extremely worried about potential leakage of its confidential information where it has retained an independent contractor who is at the same time
performing services for a competitor.

To avoid such difficult situations, software companies will often require independent contractors, particularly consultants and software programmers, to
agree not to perform for a competitor of the company the same services in
respect of the competitor's competing products during the period that the independent contractor works for the software company and for a certain period
thereafter. As the aim is to protect only the reasonable interests of the software
company, the restriction, which should be set out in terms of its duration, the
geographic area for which it is effective, and the precise activities to which it
applies, should not be too broad or overreaching.

Particularly in the case of employees, it is important that the restriction be reasonable. As a general rule courts are rather unsympathetic to noncompetition
restrictions on employees, and judges have little hesitation in declaring unenforceable those that are overly restrictive in terms of temporal duration, geographic scope, or type of activity. Courts are, however, somewhat more receptive
to a restriction on an employee's soliciting of the customers of the former
employer, particularly where the restriction is limited to clients to which the
employee had formerly been assigned, and often a nonsolicitation-of-customers
clause is used in conjunction with a general noncompetition restriction. For
example, the general noncompetition obligation might restrict the former
employee from working in the same vertical software market in a certain geographic area for a period of six months, while the nonsolicitation-of-customers
clause might extend for a year. In either case, such provisions should be carefully
reviewed with legal counsel before they are agreed to; otherwise, the software
company may have a rude shock when a particular clause that it was heavily
relying on ultimately proves to be unenforceable in court.

It should also be noted, however, that employees, particularly those in senior positions, and even independent contractors in certain circumstances, in the absence of any written agreement with the software company, may still have general obligations under the law to protect the proprietary rights of a former employer and to temper prospective competitive behaviour. For example, certain senior officers (and sometimes more junior ones as well) owe a so-called fiduciary duty to a former employer not to pursue a business opportunity that the individual discovered while working for his or her former employer. This legal principle can be relevant where, say, a senior sales executive at one software company spends significant time and effort pursuing a certain client, and almost has the sale, but then switches jobs to a competing software company and soon after completes the deal on behalf of the new employer. Depending on the specific facts, a former employer faced with a similar situation may be able to successfully bring a claim against the sales executive and the new employer.

NONSOLICITATION OF EMPLOYEES

Many software companies and others in the software business are concerned that, when they enter into relationships with another participant in the industry, they will lose valuable employees to the other entity. For instance, independent contractors that are corporations are often very worried that their personnel may be hired by the software company for whom they are performing services. This can also be a two-way problem; the software company should be aware that some of its staff may be tempted to join the ranks of the independent contractor, particularly if it is a high-powered consulting organization. This issue also arises in the relationships between software companies and their clients.

To address these problems, participants in the software business often provide in their agreements that one party cannot solicit or even offer employment to the employees of the other party. Such a clause can be useful, but again it should not be an unreasonably broad prohibition on the employment options of the parties (or their employees). For example, if a small independent contractor is doing some work for a large software company, the no hiring restriction on the independent contractor might be limited to those employees of the software company who worked on the particular project with the independent contractor, rather than catching everyone in the organization, including those who had absolutely nothing to do with the independent contractor. Without finetuning the prohibition in this way, the software company may find it very difficult to persuade the independent contractor to agree to it or, ultimately, to convince a court to enforce it.

Another way of dealing with the movement of staff, rather than prohibiting the activity outright, (which may be impossible if a specific individual has his or her heart set on moving), is to institute a more positive and remunerative provision, which would stipulate that if one party hires another party's staff during the term of the agreement and for a certain period thereafter, then the hiring party will pay to the other party, as a form of employment-agency and training fee, an amount of money equal to some percentage of the individual's first-year salary with the new party. The benefit in this mechanism is that it allows employees to choose freely where they want to work, but it also recognizes to a certain degree the costs incurred in losing, and having to replace (often on extremely short notice), a valued staff member. In some cases of course, merely being reimbursed will be inadequate, and the outright prohibition referred to in the previous paragraph may be called for.

OWNERSHIP OF WORK PRODUCT

It is critical, particularly in the case of independent contractors, that the proprietary rights protection agreement of the software company stipulate in writing who is to own the copyright and other proprietary rights in the software and other materials developed by the independent contractor for the software company. Not dealing with this issue in writing can result in protracted and acrimonious legal proceedings.

The reason for this is that the *Copyright Act* states very clearly that, except in the case of employees, the author of a copyrightable literary work, which includes software and related documentation, is the first owner of the copyright in such work and that ownership in such a copyrighted work may be transferred only by means of a written agreement. Accordingly, except in unusual circumstances, if a software company hires an independent contractor to develop some software, and if the independent contractor never transfers, in writing, its ownership of the intellectual property rights in the software to the company, the independent contractor will likely end up owning the copyright in the software — even if the company paid the independent contractor a substantial sum of money to develop it. (There are exceptions to such a result, but they require very particular facts and generally present the software company with an uphill battle).

The scenario noted above, where the independent contractor ends up owning the intellectual property in specifically commissioned software developed by an independent contractor, occurs quite regularly and it can lead to serious problems for the software company. For example, a defect in the ownership of software developed by an independent contractor often comes to light when the software company wants to sell the copyright (and other intellectual property rights) in the software to a third party, and, not unreasonably, the third party wants some assurance that the software company actually owns all the rights in the software so the sale will be clear of any claims of others. Where the software company did not obtain a written transfer of ownership from the independent contractor such assurance generally cannot be given (unless, of course, the independent contractor is willing to sign such a document after the fact, and many may not, at least not unless they are paid an additional sum of money!). The absence of such assurance can often mean a decrease in the price the purchaser is willing to pay for the software (if the particular portion of software which is problematic is rather small) or even a cancellation of the purchase altogether (if the particular portion of software which is problematic is quite large).

This problem can be avoided very simply by having the independent contractor agree in writing that the software company will own all proprietary rights, including the copyright, patent rights, and trade secrets, in the works developed for the software company by the independent contractor. The proprietary rights protection agreement, which the independent contractor should sign before commencing the project, should contain such a provision. As well, at the end of the particular project, at the same time that the independent contractor is given the final payment for services rendered, the independent contractor should be required to sign a second document, which actually lists the works developed by the independent contractor, and which confirms that the independent contractor's ownership rights in these works have been transferred to the software company.

If the independent contractor is an entity other than an individual, then the software company should have each employee or sub-contractor of the independent contractor who works on the company's projects sign the appropriate agreements to transfer ownership rights of software and other materials to the company. It is not prudent to rely solely on the independent contractor to have these people sign, with the independent contractor, the relevant paperwork. The safest course for the software company is to secure signed agreements directly with each individual who works on the project.

The proprietary rights protection agreement should also include a provision whereby the individual who works on the software waives all so-called moral rights in the work. Moral rights are guaranteed by the *Copyright Act* to all authors and continue in favour of the author even after the author has sold the copyright in the work (unless these moral rights are given up or waived). Moral rights permit the author to object to a certain use of the work if it would reasonably be expected to diminish the reputation of the author. Such rights are seemingly more relevant to musical or traditional literary works; as Sookman notes in Chapter 5, as a result of the recent changes to the United Kingdom copyright statute, moral rights no longer extend to computer software in that jurisdiction. Thus, it is particularly important that multimedia title developers obtain waivers of moral rights from their employees and independent contractors in respect of the various copyright works such staff develop for the company.

In Canada the application of moral rights to computer software or related documentation is not inconceivable. Therefore, a waiver of moral rights in the software should be included in the document by which the independent contractor (and other individuals associated with it) assign their ownership rights in such works to the software company. A final word — and warning — in this regard: sometimes software companies attempt to address the moral rights issue by having the independent contractor transfer or assign to the company the moral rights, along with the ownership of the works. This is not the way to deal with moral rights, because the *Copyright Act* states clearly that moral rights cannot be transferred or assigned, they can only be waived. Thus the twofold rule for the work product of independent contractors is: ownership rights, including copyright, are to be transferred to the software company, and moral rights are to be waived.

The software company should also ensure that the proprietary rights protection agreements signed by employees convey ownership of work product to the company and that the employees waive their moral rights in the work product, as is discussed above in the context of independent contractors. It should be noted, however, that the *Copyright Act* provides that where an employee produces a copyrightable work (such as software and documentation) in the course of his or her employment the ownership of the copyright in such work rests with the employer. This is a different rule in Canada than that applicable to independent contractors (who own their copyrightable work product unless they transfer it in writing to the software company). Notwithstanding this legal rule for employees, it still makes good sense for software companies to have employees expressly confirm the transfer to the software company of their rights in any work product they develop in order that there be absolutely no question about who owns what. Moreover, the employee-employer ownership rule in the *Copyright Act* does not address the issue of moral rights, so a software company must have employees waive in writing their moral rights to any works produced by them. Thus, if employees have to sign such a waiver in any event, they may as well confirm in writing in the same document the software company's ownership of the software developed by them.

A proprietary rights protection agreement should always be signed, if at all possible, at the time the employee commences employment with the software company (or the independent contractor commences work with the software company). That is, the agreement should be presented to the employee *before* he or she begins employment, for example at the time the employment offer letter is provided to the prospective employee. The employment offer letter should also make it clear that the terms of the proprietary rights agreement will become terms of the employment relationship. Where this is not possible, such as when a company is introducing such an agreement into its workplace after several years of operation, the agreement should be put into place when the employee is given a pay raise or a promotion or some other form of benefit (e.g., a special one-time payment for signing the agreement) in order to help ensure the enforceability of the proprietary rights protection agreement. Similarly, it is a good idea to have the prospective employee/independent contractor obtain independent legal advice regarding the proprietary rights agreement, so that they cannot argue subsequently that they did not know what they were signing. If the prospective employee does not speak English fluently, such independent legal advice should be given in the prospective employee's native language so as to reduce the risk that the employee, upon his departure from the company, successfully argues that the agreement is unenforceable.

PART

III

Marketing Software

CHAPTER

9

The Software Business and Competition Law

Competition law impacts on how software companies develop, advertise, distribute, and price their products. The principal statute in Canada dealing with competition is the *Competition Act*. This federal law applies to all of Canada. The purpose of the *Competition Act*, as set out in the introduction to the legislation, is to maintain and encourage competition in Canada in order, among other things, to promote the efficiency and adaptability of the Canadian economy, to ensure that small and medium-sized businesses have an equitable opportunity to participate in the Canadian economy, and to provide consumers with competitive prices and product choices.

Competition law is serious business. Every year many companies in all sorts of industries are charged with and convicted of, or plead guilty to, criminal offences under the *Competition Act*. An investigation or other proceeding under the *Competition Act* may result in significant fines (and in some cases the imprisonment of company personnel as well), and may also require a tremendous amount of time and energy from senior officers. Accordingly, software companies, and others that distribute software and related products, must be sensitive to the rules governing behaviour in the marketplace contained in the *Competition Act*, or at least be sufficiently aware of competition law to know when to seek the advice of legal counsel competent in competition law matters.

By the same token, software suppliers should remember that the *Competition Act*, in addition to being used against them by competitors, customers, or the Competition Bureau (the government body charged with enforcing the *Competition Act*), can also be utilized by software suppliers to attain strategic commercial objectives when anti-competitive behaviour in the marketplace affects them adversely. Too often the business community views the *Competition Act* solely as a form of government regulation; in fact, the *Competition Act* can prove useful to participants in the high-technology community who are being treated unfairly by (perhaps much larger) suppliers, competitors, or even customers.

THE *COMPETITION ACT*

As noted above, the *Competition Act* provides for a number of criminal offences; those most relevant to software suppliers are discussed below. These criminal offences carry serious penalties, in most cases an unlimited monetary fine and/or imprisonment for a period of up to two and in some cases up to five years of the principals of the company who had a hand in the illegal activity. Additional costs associated with criminal offences include legal fees incurred to defend the charges and costs incurred to counteract the negative publicity generated in the media surrounding the charges, any subsequent trial and, especially, the conviction, if one is secured. Negative publicity can be very damaging, given that many people attach a certain social stigma to any criminal proceeding, even if the result is an acquittal. It should also be noted that the *Competition Act* permits a party who has suffered damages as a result of conduct that constitutes a violation of the Act's criminal provisions, to sue for and recover damages, as well as legal and related fees from the party engaged in the illegal conduct. Thus, a software supplier who contravenes the Act's criminal provisions may be confronted with two proceedings, one a criminal prosecution brought by the government to enforce the statute, and the other a civil lawsuit launched by a party to recover damages and losses sustained as a result of the criminal conduct.

In addition to criminal offences, the *Competition Act* contains "reviewable practices." These are particularly important to software suppliers in respect of the planning and implementation of product-distribution networks. Activity that constitutes a reviewable practice does not result in criminal prosecution proceedings, but rather may be scrutinized by the Competition Tribunal, a body composed of judges and nonjudge experts in the private sector. The Competition Tribunal was established in order to weigh the complex business and economic evidence surrounding reviewable practices. If a reviewable practice is found to lessen competition substantially, then the tribunal can make an order prohibiting the practice or otherwise alleviating its anti-competitive effects.

The Competition Bureau (before 1996 called the Bureau of Competition Policy) plays a critical role in respect of both the *Competition Act*'s criminal offences and reviewable practices. The Bureau's staff conducts the investigation surrounding the allegedly anti-competitive activity, and the Director of the Bureau decides whether to send a criminal case to prosecution or a reviewable practice before the Competition Tribunal. In many cases the Bureau will attempt to settle the matter before either type of proceeding is commenced. The Bureau strongly encourages businesses to come forward voluntarily before undertaking a potentially problematic activity in order to learn the Bureau's views regarding the possible anti-competitive impact of the activity. In this way an otherwise illegal arrangement might be avoided in advance so as to save everyone the cost and trouble of a subsequent investigation and a possible criminal or reviewable practice proceeding.

AGREEMENT TO LESSEN COMPETITION UNDULY

The *Competition Act* makes it a criminal offence for two or more parties to enter into a conspiracy, agreement, or arrangement that would lessen competition unduly. The classic and perhaps most obvious form of such an illegal conspiracy is price fixing; for example, the computer software retailers in a city agree to set common prices at which they would sell various software products. Agreements on price-related matters, such as terms of payment, discounts (i.e., if software suppliers were to agree not to discount from their published price lists, etc.), rebates, and allowances may also be illegal. The fixing of prices and associated matters are not the only types of activities that could be found to be conspiracies to lessen competition unduly. For instance, computer software retailers in an area might also violate this section of the *Competition Act* if they agreed with each other to divide up markets or customers in a certain way.

It is important to remember that a formal or written agreement among competitors is not necessary to constitute the conspiracy offence — an informal or tacit understanding with minimal communication between competitors may be enough. Indeed, competition law violations involving competitors are seldom established by direct, conclusive evidence. Usually, violations are established by circumstantial evidence that may arise in unexpected ways. It is not sufficient merely to comply with the law; it is also important to be seen to comply. Otherwise purely innocent conduct may be misconstrued because it assumes the appearance of a violation.

Not all agreements that lessen competition are illegal — only those that lessen competition "unduly." This term is not defined in the *Competition Act*. Courts have generally interpreted it in a quantitative fashion, that is, the parties to the conspiracy should represent something in the order of 50% or more of the market share for a particular product for the conspiracy to violate the Act. This percentage figure may vary, depending on the facts of each case, and in many cases a lower figure may be sufficient to secure a conviction. The safest approach for a software supplier, of course, is not to enter into any agreement or arrangement with competitors regarding pricing and other matters that may lessen competition.

It should be noted that the *Competition Act* does permit competitors to enter into certain types of agreements, as long as they do not directly or indirectly lessen competition unduly in respect of prices, quantity or quality of production, markets or customers, or channels or methods of distribution, or restrict any party from entering into or expanding their business. For software developers two types of exempted agreements are of particular interest: those relating to the defining of product standards and those involving cooperation in research and development. For example, in respect of the latter type of agreement, numerous public and private research consortia have been established over the past few years to foster the development of Canadian computer and related technologies. The *Competition Act* permits a company to participate in such an R&D group, but each participant should be careful to ensure that the group's activities do not stray beyond research and development into pricing, production, customer, or distribution matters.

In a similar vein, it is worth noting the risks associated with trade associations. There are many trade associations in the computer industry and they can perform many valuable functions such as public education and the presentation of industry positions to government. At the same time, however, they also provide occasions for software suppliers and other competitors in the computer business to meet with one another. As such, a company's representative in a trade association should ensure that matters such as prices, terms and conditions of sale, and future production and marketing plans are not discussed at trade-association gatherings, whether in the meetings or during informal contacts. As well, each member of a trade association should require that the association have formal procedures which are rigidly followed, including the preparation and circulation of written agendas and minutes of meetings.

One other type of agreement permitted among competitors by the *Competition Act* is a "specialization agreement" that has been approved by the Competition Tribunal. In such an agreement one company agrees to discontinue producing a certain product or service on condition that the other company agrees to discontinue producing another product or service. The parties may, and likely would, agree to buy exclusively from each other the products that are the subject of the agreement. An example of such an agreement in the software environment might be that one software developer agrees to discontinue development and production of its payroll software product to concentrate on accounting software, while the other software company discontinues its accounting software to concentrate its resources on payroll software, and then each company agrees to supply the other with the discontinued product (which they might continue to market under different brand names). The rationale for such an agreement would be to improve each company's economic efficiency and competitiveness, by a means other than a full-fledged merger or acquisition, by allowing each to concentrate its efforts on one product rather than spreading (usually severely limited) human and financial resources over two products.

A specialization agreement must be submitted to the Competition Tribunal for approval and registration, which will be forthcoming only if the tribunal finds that the agreement is likely to bring about gains in efficiency that will be greater than, and will offset, the effects of any prevention or lessening of competition caused by the agreement, and that the gains in efficiency would not be attained without the agreement. In considering the submission the Competition Tribunal must consider whether the prospective gains win result in a significant increase in the value of exports or a significant substitution of domestic goods or services for imported goods or services. If the tribunal approves the specialization agreement it is then registered for a period of time during which the *Competition Act*'s conspiracy provision does not apply to the specialization agreement. It should be noted that since the specialization agreement provision was added to the Act in 1986, no such agreement has been referred to the Competition Tribunal, and accordingly the tribunal has not yet had an opportunity to conduct its difficult task of balancing gains in efficiency against loss of competition in the context of any particular specialization agreement.

BID-RIGGING

Under the *Competition Act* it is a criminal offence for parties to agree to bid in a particular manner, or for one or more of such parties to agree not to bid, where the person calling for the bid does not know of such agreement. There need not be any effect on competition at all for the bid-rigging offence to be committed. The offence can be committed by, for example, two out of ten bidders colluding on their respective two bids (i.e., one bidder agrees to submit a very high (or low) bid to make the second bidder's price seem more attractive (or reasonable), and the bidders agree to reverse the roles on the next bid), even though they represented, collectively, only 20% of the bidders (and even though perhaps neither of the two bidders is ultimately awarded the contract).

The bid-rigging prohibition is relevant to virtually all software suppliers, given that purchasers of computing resources very often use the competitive bid mechanism. This is especially true of public procurements, inasmuch as govern-ments at all levels — federal, provincial, regional, and municipal — understand the significant cost savings and other benefits that generally flow from competi-tive tendering for the vast quantities of hardware, software, and related services purchased by public entities each year in Canada. On all such bids (and all kinds for the private sector as well) software suppliers must be scrupulous in not dis-cussing with other tenderers the terms of their bids, or even whether they are bidding on a particular project (unless the entity calling for tenders is made aware of such discussions at the time they take place, but always keeping in mind that such discussions between competitors may also raise problems under the conspiracy offence discussed above). The consequences of contravening this provision can be very serious indeed; for example, in a case a number of years ago several business forms suppliers were fined an aggregate of $2 million after they pleaded guilty to rigging bids to a provincial government.

PREDATORY PRICING

The conspiracy and bid-rigging provisions discussed above focus on the problem of a supplier being, or appearing to be, too cooperative with competitors. The law is also concerned with the other extreme of trying to destroy competitors or competition. In this regard, the *Competition Act* makes it a criminal offence for a supplier to engage in a policy of selling products or services at prices that are unreasonably low, or that are lower in one part of Canada as compared to other parts, if the intent, effect, or tendency of the policy is to lessen competition sub-stantially or to eliminate a competitor. The law is not entirely clear as to what is an "unreasonably low" price, but predatory pricing, as this practice is often called, probably includes a price that is at least below average variable cost.

ABUSE OF DOMINANT POSITION

Somewhat related to the criminal offence of predatory pricing is the reviewable practice of "abuse of dominant position." It is understandable that successful companies — those that demonstrate superior competitive performance — will grow. A company that has grown to the point, however, where, alone or together with several others, it dominates a category of business, it is obliged under the *Competition Act* not to engage in acts that could result in a substantial lessening of competition in a market; that is, such companies are required not to abuse their dominant positions.

    More specifically, where an entity substantially controls, alone or with others, a class of business throughout Canada or any area of Canada, and that entity engages in (or those entities engage in) anti-competitive acts such that competition is, or is likely to be, prevented or lessened substantially, the Competition Tribunal may order the entity (or entities) to stop the anti competitive behaviour. Anti-competitive acts include the following: use of fighting brands to discipline a competitor (i.e., a major company with a new competitor for a certain product may undercut the competitor's prices by introducing a lower-priced version of that product solely to drive out the new competitor; this is similar to the predatory pricing provision); preempting scarce facilities or resources required by a competitor in order to withhold those facilities or resources from the market; restricting the persons to whom a customer can sell; and adopting product specifications that are incompatible with products produced by another entity and are designed to impede that entity's flexibility to market its products. This last example of an anti-competitive act raises the (perhaps not so hypothetical) question of how a dominant computer-products manufacturer should go about effecting technical changes to its next generation of products so as not to have an adverse impact on other suppliers who produce compatible hardware or software, particularly where the previous technology has effectively become an industry standard.

In this regard it should be noted that the abuse of dominant position provision exempts as anti-competitive any act engaged in pursuant only to the exercise of any interest derived under the *Copyright Act* or the *Patent Act*. This is an interesting exemption because computer software is afforded express protection under the *Copyright Act*, and increasingly software is able to be patented under the *Patent Act*. As yet there has been no case law determining how this intellectual property exemption might be applied to various possible anti-competitive activities of software suppliers.

PRICE DISCRIMINATION

It is a criminal offence under the *Competition Act* to make a practice of giving a discount, rebate, allowance, or any other advantage to one customer that is not made available to all competitors of that customer in respect of sales of goods of like quantity or quality. This prohibition against "price discrimination" is particularly germane to suppliers, wholesalers, dealers, and other distributors of computer products in that it can affect the prices that an entity in the product distribution chain can charge to two purchasers who are competitors. Four key elements of the offence should be noted.

First, the offence covers only goods and not services. Thus, companies providing software consulting services, such as analysis, design, programming, testing, and support activities, could charge different hourly rates for such services to two purchasers who are competitors. As the section covers only goods, it may also be argued that it does not apply to software programs as these are usually considered to be intangibles. However, it would be wiser to assume that the provision captures at least standard off-the-shelf or prepackaged software programs, such as mass-marketed personal computer software products, as opposed to custom-developed software.

Second, price discrimination is illegal only where there is a practice of discriminating; thus, the offering of lower prices on a one-time basis to meet a competitive price, or for a store opening or an anniversary event would not constitute an offence.

Third, the offence of price discrimination applies only to sales to competing purchasers. Therefore, it is permissible to have different price structures for different customers provided they do not compete with one another. This might occur, for example, where a computer-products supplier has one exclusive dealer for Quebec, and another exclusive dealer for Ontario, and neither dealer is permitted to sell into the other's territory. By the same token, however, a supplier must be careful when determining whether two of its purchasers are competitors. For instance, one particular purchaser may be a dealer who sells only to end users, while another dealer, more properly termed a "distributor," may sell to dealers as well as to end users through a retail division. In such a case, the first dealer should be offered the same prices as the distributor for the same quantity of products because they both sell, to a greater or lesser extent, to end users and are therefore competitors (assuming they are able to sell in the same geographic area). Another way to deal with this is to have the supplier sell products to the distributor at two different prices, depending on which are being resold to dealers and which to end users, with the supplier being consistent in relation to other dealers in its pricing in respect of those products intended for resale to end users.

The fourth aspect of price discrimination is that the law requires that the same prices and discounts be made available only in respect of sales of like quantity; this means that the granting of quantity discounts is legitimate. Accordingly, where there is price discrimination, quantity is the crucial test. Cost-based considerations, such as those related to a supplier's production costs, are irrelevant. For many years, the Competition Bureau also took the view that price advantages offered for warehousing an article or for carrying a particular quantity of inventory are also not permissible, but in a recent guideline the Bureau has taken the position that functional discounts are permissible. No court has ever given a conclusive determination on this point. As for discount structures, these need not follow a series of gradual increases in volume, but may instead have sharp plateaus at various unit levels (or perhaps only at one), with the result that large purchasers may be disproportionately favoured over smaller ones (i.e., there may be a discount only for purchases of a certain volume of product, which would effectively deny discounts altogether to a purchaser of a small volume of goods). Of course, it is important that the discount structure be administered in a nondiscriminatory manner so that all buyers who are eligible to take advantage of it are permitted to do so.

There can sometimes be difficulties in determining what volume of purchases and what period of time (the period chosen must make reasonable commercial sense) are to be considered in calculating the relevant volume discount. Many discount plans use an annual period; plans with unusually long or short periods may be objectionable if they have the effect of defeating the intent of the price-discrimination provision. As well, dollar-value-based discount plans are usually acceptable where the supplier is selling one type of good, because in such a case the dollar-value discount generally reflects the relative volume of goods purchased, and certain discounts based on the increase in the number of units purchased over time may also be permissable.

PROMOTIONAL ALLOWANCE

The *Competition Act* requires that an allowance, discount, rebate, price concession, or other benefit offered to one customer for promotion, display, or advertising must be offered to all customers who compete with such customer. The allowances must be on a proportionate basis in relation to the value of sales to each customer. Thus, a customer who purchases twice as much by dollar value from a supplier as another customer must be offered a promotional allowance which is twice as much as that offered to the other customer. These allowances need not be offered at the same time to all like customers but must reach equivalent levels within a reasonable period of time.

It is worth setting out the differences between the criminal offence of price discrimination and the criminal offence prohibiting disproportionate promotional allowances; it should also be noted that sometimes it can be difficult to determine whether a particular discount is a price discount or a promotional discount, but it is critical to make this determination because the rules relative to the two are different. For a discount to be price discrimination it must be part of a practice; there is no need for a practice in the case of a promotional allowance, which must be given even for a one-time purchase. The price-discrimination provision allows for uneven discount structures, so long as they are consistently applied to all purchasers who are competitors; the promotional allowance must be in proportion to the value of sales, however small the sales. The price-discrimination provision requires that the discount or other benefit be "made available" to competing purchasers, which in effect means that only those purchasers likely to reach the relevant plateau of a discount structure need be informed of it; a promotional allowance must be "offered" to every competing purchaser.

RESALE PRICE MAINTENANCE

The *Competition Act* makes it illegal in Canada for a supplier of a product, or a licensor of a patent or copyright (such as a computer program), to attempt by threat, agreement, promise, or any like means to influence upward or discourage the reduction of the price at which any other person sells or advertises the supplier's product, or sub-licenses a computer program in the case of a software licence. This criminal prohibition on resale price maintenance precludes a software supplier, or anyone else in the distribution chain, from dictating what a dealer or someone else lower down in the distribution chain charges for the particular product or service.

It is not merely the practice of fixing resale prices that is prohibited, but any activity that has, directly or indirectly, the same or similar effect. For example, in one case a supplier permitted retailers to fix their own resale prices, but only those retailers that advertised their products at or above the supplier's suggested resale price became eligible for payments from the supplier under an advertising allowance program. The court found this practice to be the offence of resale price maintenance under the *Competition Act* because it had the effect of encouraging retailers not to sell their products below the supplier's stipulated resale price.

It should be noted, however, that a supplier can suggest a resale price, but if it does so it must make it clear that dealers and retailers are not bound to follow the suggested price and that they will in no way suffer in their business relationship with the supplier if they do not adhere to the suggested resale price. These two statements should be made to the dealer or retailer in writing so that there is no confusion as to the basis upon which the supplier is suggesting the resale price. In a similar vein, it is a criminal offence for a supplier (other than a retailer) to advertise the price at which a product may be sold by a retailer or someone else unless the advertisement states that the product may be sold at a lower price. One exception to these rules regarding suggested resale prices is that it is permissible for a supplier to affix or apply a price to a product or its package or container.

The resale-price-maintenance provision in the *Competition Act* can have a significant impact upon the distribution mechanism established by a computer-products supplier for its products. In some industries this provision leads suppliers, such as most encyclopedia publishers, to sell directly to the public in order that they can control the ultimate retail price paid for their wares. This is not feasible in much of the computer industry where a chain of some combination of distributors, dealers, and retailers is a necessary vehicle for getting computer products into the hands of end users. By the same token, particularly where a computer product requires extensive pre-sales advice and post-sales service, how can a computer-products supplier structure its distribution chain so that dealers that offer deep discounts on products, and who accordingly do not provide such services, do not erode the profit margins necessary for the full service dealers to provide the required attention to end users? Before answering this question, it is useful to illustrate by a case study how not to go about achieving this objective.

In this particular case, a computer products manufacturer pleaded guilty to resale price maintenance and was fined $200,000. The manufacturer committed the offence by inserting into its Canadian dealer agreements a requirement that dealers not advertise the relevant products for sale at a price lower than the manufacturer's suggested retail price. The court, in its sentencing decision, found that this clause violated the resale price maintenance prohibition in the *Competition Act*, even though the evidence showed that no dealer actually honoured the clause. In fining the manufacturer $200,000 for this violation (which amount was reduced to $100,000 on appeal), the court pointed out that the offence of resale price maintenance is committed even where there is no adverse impact on competition, and thus it did not matter whether dealers adhered to the illegal clause or not. Moreover, the court refused to take into account the manufacturer's stated rationale for the clause, namely, the desire to give dealers sufficient margins so that they could provide the pre-sale advice and after-sale service required by the complicated, new computer product that was the subject of the dealer agreements, and thereby avoid free-riding discounters who would tarnish the reputation of the new product.

Where computer product suppliers wish dealers to provide adequate sales and support services for a product that is technologically sophisticated or new, they should provide for such obligations directly, rather than trying to impose these standards indirectly through the resale price mechanism. For example, in most cases a dealer agreement could provide that the dealer will sell the relevant product only after providing face-to-face sales assistance and a certain amount of training. The agreement should also explain the need for such a clause, namely that lack of sales assistance and initial training could damage the reputation of the new or sophisticated product. At the same time, the agreement should clearly specify that the dealer can sell the product at any resale price. Another means to achieve the same end is to appoint exclusive dealers for certain geographic areas. Such a practice does not usually pose a problem under the *Competition Act*, though in certain instances it may raise an issue under the statute's "refusal to deal" and "market restrictions" provisions, which are discussed below.

REFUSAL TO DEAL (CRIMINAL OFFENCE)

Many computer-products suppliers are under the mistaken impression that the *Competition Act* requires them to sell products and services to every distributor, dealer, or end user (even a competitor of the supplier) that requests to be supplied. In fact, a supplier generally can refuse to supply someone, subject to several rules set out in the *Competition Act*.

Most importantly, a supplier cannot refuse to supply someone if the reason is the low pricing policy of that distributor or dealer: the *Competition Act* makes it a criminal offence to refuse to supply on this basis. This is so even if the supplier had never before done business with the prospective purchaser. This point is illustrated by the following common scenario in the computer industry. A supplier has an established network of dealers in Canada covering all the major markets. A new player appears requesting to become an authorized dealer. If it is the case that the dealer is an aggressive discounter, and the supplier does not wish to appoint the dealer because it will disrupt the current resale pricing structure, then a refusal to supply for such reasons will violate the *Competition Act*. On the other hand, if the supplier ignores the pricing reputation of the dealer, and instead refuses to supply the new dealer because of its poor creditworthiness, the quality of its workforce, its geographic location, or simply because it already has a sufficient number of dealers, then the supplier's refusal should not be objectionable under the criminal refusal-to-deal provision of the *Competition Act* (although it still may pose an issue under the reviewable practice section discussed below).

Sometimes a supplier's established dealers request the supplier to refuse to supply product to a new discounting dealer. In such a case, the supplier should point out to the established dealers that they themselves are committing a criminal offence under the *Competition Act* by attempting to induce the supplier to refuse to supply the discount dealer. As well, in certain circumstances an agreement between a supplier and its established dealers not to provide product to a new dealer may also constitute a violation of the Act's conspiracy provision discussed above, where such an arrangement, often called a "group boycott," lessens competition unduly.

The *Competition Act* makes exceptions to the general rule that a supplier cannot refuse to supply someone who has a low pricing policy in the following circumstances: when the discounter is using the supplier's products as loss-leaders (i.e., for the purpose of advertising rather than to make profit), when the discounter is engaging in misleading advertising in respect of the supplier's products, and when the discounter does not provide a level of service for the supplier's products that purchasers of such products might reasonably expect from a dealer. This last exemption may be particularly relevant to suppliers of computer products that require pre-sales assistance and after-sales service.

REFUSAL TO DEAL (REVIEWABLE PRACTICE)

One of the *Competition Act*'s reviewable practices is "refusal to deal." Under this provision, if a refused customer can show that it is substantially affected in its business because of its inability to obtain adequate supplies of a product due to insufficient competition among suppliers, this customer may be able to obtain an order from the Competition Tribunal requiring a supplier to provide it with product, provided the product is in ample supply and the customer is willing to meet the usual trade terms of the supplier. This provision may be of particular relevance to companies that provide maintenance and support services for computer products manufactured or supplied by others. For example, if such a third-party service provider were denied spare parts by the manufacturer of the product, and if the servicing of such products was and had been for some time a major portion of the service provider's business, then the service provider may be able to utilize this provision of the *Competition Act* to require the manufacturer to continue to provide it with spare parts.

EXCLUSIVE DEALING, MARKET RESTRICTION, AND TIED SELLING

The *Competition Act* defines the reviewable practices of "exclusive dealing," "market restriction," and "tied selling" more or less as follows:

> Exclusive dealing is the practice of requiring or inducing a customer to deal only or primarily in products of the supplier; market restriction is the practice of requiring a customer, as a condition of supplying him with the product, to sell a product only in a defined market area; and tied selling is the practice of requiring or inducing a customer as a condition of supplying him with one product (the "tying" product) to buy another of the supplier's products (the "tied" product).

These three practices are quite common in the computer industry. A hardware or software supplier will often require a distributor or dealer not to carry any products that compete with the supplier's products. When establishing a distribution system, a supplier may also require that dealers sell only in predetermined geographic areas. A supplier may also insist that in order to be supplied with a preferred product (the tying product, such as operating-system software), the dealer or end user must also purchase a less attractive product (the tied product, such as the hardware that works in conjunction with the operating-system software).

None of these activities is a criminal offence. Rather, they are reviewable practices, and the Competition Tribunal may make remedial orders in the event that any such practice results in a substantial lessening of competition. It should be noted, however, that the tribunal is not to make such an order where, in its opinion, exclusive dealing or market restriction is or will be engaged in only for a reasonable period of time in order to facilitate entry of a new supplier or of a new product into a market.

These latter provisions confirm the view that in many cases exclusive dealing and market restriction can be pro-competitive. In effect, the same activity may be either beneficial or detrimental to competition, depending largely on the market share of the supplier engaging in the activity. For example, a requirement by a software supplier with a small share of the market that an exclusive dealer of the supplier's new product not carry competitive products may be pro-competitive in that it causes the dealer to devote all his energies to the supplier's new product, thereby increasing the likelihood of effective inter-brand product competition (i.e., between the supplier's new product and the existing products of other suppliers). If, within a few years, the same product has captured 80% of the relevant market, the same exclusive arrangement may be anti-competitive if it has the effect of precluding intra-brand competition in the particular product (i.e., it would deny prospective purchasers the opportunity to acquire the very popular product from more than one source). This example illustrates why these provisions are reviewable practices rather than criminal offences: the precise effect on competition of any particular restriction can be gauged only after a detailed weighing of economic evidence by the Competition Tribunal. This example also illustrates that these practices must be constantly reviewed by a company engaging in them, given that an activity that the company believed was acceptable when it had a relatively small share of the market may become unacceptable if the company becomes an important player in its particular niche.

A final point worth noting with respect to tied selling is that the Competition Tribunal is directed not to make a remedial order where the tied selling is reasonable in terms of the technological relationship between or among the products to which it applies. For example, it may be reasonable for a computer products supplier, in the case of new or technologically sophisticated products, to require customers to purchase service contracts only from the supplier, at least until other service providers achieve levels of technical expertise where they can service the products equally well. A tied sale (the computer product being the tying product, the support service being the tied product) may thus be acceptable initially, but may be subject to challenge before the tribunal after several years. In other cases, such as where there is a functional connection between two technologically linked products (i.e., a software program and a related hardware component), the tied sale may be defensible for an indefinite period.

MERGERS

Under the *Competition Act*, the Competition Tribunal has the power to dissolve, or to order the disposal of assets in respect of, a merger that prevents or lessens competition substantially. A merger encompasses virtually every means by which companies might combine or by which one company might acquire control over or a significant interest in another company. This provision is of some relevance to the computer industry, given the large number of mergers between hardware, software, and computer-services firms in the last few years.

The reviewable practice merger provisions of the *Competition Act* are important not only to companies contemplating a merger, but also to businesses that feel they will be adversely affected by a merger of two or more of their suppliers, customers, or, especially, competitors. As mentioned above at the beginning of this chapter, companies in the computer industry should view competition law not only as a regulatory requirement that impacts on their operations. They should approach this law also as a vehicle to achieve strategic commercial objectives where appropriate. This latter dimension of competition law is illustrated in the first merger case involving the computerized reservation systems of Air Canada, Canadian Airlines, and American Airlines.

In 1987, Air Canada and Canadian Airlines decided to merge their respective computerized reservation systems (or CRS, as they are called) under the Gemini name. A CRS consists of a central computer which stores airline flight information as well as an increasingly diverse range of other travel-related data used to make reservations for hotels, car rentals, tours, etc. Travel agents are connected to the CRS by terminals on the agents' desks. As there is limited space on each agent's desk, an agent will generally use only one airline's CRS. The Gemini system, by allowing preferential access to the information of the two major Canadian carriers on only one terminal, would naturally be favoured by agents in Canada. American Airlines, together with the Competition Bureau, feared that the merger resulting in the Gemini system would adversely affect the presentation of American Airlines booking information and would not allow American Airlines' CRS to have equal access to the flight and ticket data of Air Canada and Canadian Airlines. Historically, each airline's CRS favours its own carrier's flight data in several subtle but important ways, which bias would have an increasingly anti-competitive impact, so argued the opponents of the merger, given that the Gemini system would be by far the dominant CRS in Canada.

After the commencement of a merger dissolution proceeding under the *Competition Act*, Air Canada, Canadian Airlines, the Bureau, and American Airlines agreed to settle the dispute by establishing rules relating to the operation of the Gemini CRS, including that the system would be reprogrammed in order not to portray flight booking and other information of any airline in a biased way, but rather to give nondiscriminatory treatment to the data of American Airlines and other carriers and to give all CRSs access to all booking information on the same basis. This result was quite useful to American Airlines and is one instance of how the *Competition Act* can be utilized to bring about pro-competitive results in the marketplace. Interestingly, a few years ago a decision of the Competition Tribunal was helpful in dissolving the Gemini partnership between Air Canada and Canadian Airlines in order to facilitate an important investment by American Airlines in Canadian Airlines, one which was conditional upon Canadian Airlines pulling out of the Gemini partnership and hooking up with the American Airlines CRS so that the American Airlines CRS could perform the "hosting" function for Canadian Airlines data, a service previously performed by the Gemini system.

MISLEADING ADVERTISING

The *Competition Act* makes it a criminal offence for a company to make a false or misleading representation to the public, or to make a claim to the public regarding a product (i.e., a claim about performance) that is not based on a proper or adequate test, or to make a warranty statement to the public that is misleading, or to misrepresent to the public the price at which products have been, are, or will be sold. Several points should be noted about these misleading advertising provisions.

First, the term "public" as used in this provision includes not only end-user customers of a supplier, but also retailers, dealers, and others in the distribution chain.

Second, the test for determining whether an advertisement or claim is false or misleading is the "average person general impression test." While an advertisement, for example, may be literally true, or may not be misleading to a person particularly knowledgeable about the related product or service, the key is whether, in the whole context of the advertisement, the average person would be misled.

Third, companies making statements about test results or guarantees about the performance or efficacy of a product should ensure that the underlying test is well designed and is in accordance with generally accepted scientific principles. Such test-related claims often cause problems because a poor methodology was employed in the test, or because the claim being made is inappropriate or unrelated to the actual test result.

The provisions for misleading advertising in the *Competition Act* are particularly relevant to computer companies. Given the intense competition in many areas of the computer industry, some suppliers are tempted to make claims about their products, such as actual performance standards or prospective delivery times for future products, which are not supported by hard scientific or other facts. Such statements risk subjecting the company to criminal prosecution under the Act, and hence every effort should be made to ensure that the company's communications with the public are accurate and not misleading. As noted in Chapter 11 under "Delivery," in one American case, a company was fined $275,000 for advertising as available a product that in fact was not ready for shipment to customers. This case illustrates, for Canadian companies as well, the dangers in making false or misleading representations about products or services.

ABUSE OF INTELLECTUAL PROPERTY RIGHTS

A final provision of the *Competition Act* worthy of mention in the context of the computer industry is the power of the Federal Court of Canada to make a remedial order in a situation where the exclusive rights conferred by a patent, trademark, or copyright have been used in a manner that prevents or lessens competition unduly. This provision, which is neither a criminal offence nor a reviewable practice, is aimed primarily at regulating a number of potentially anti-competitive, restrictive provisions in patent, trademark, or copyright licences, such as the requirement by a patent licensor that a licensee purchase from the licensor all the raw materials required to produce the patented product, an activity similar to tied selling.

Where such an act lessens competition unduly, the Federal Court may order one or more of the following remedies: declare the relevant licence agreement to be void, in whole or in part; prohibit the exercise of the objectionable provision in the licence agreement; order that licences be granted to other licensees on terms the court thinks fit; and order other acts to be done or omitted as the court sees fit so as to prevent future anti-competitive use of the patent or trade-mark. While these remedial provisions are very broad, this section of the *Competition Act* has been used very little. It may be used more in the future, however, now that patents are increasingly being issued for software programs.

COMPLIANCE WITH COMPETITION LAW

As mentioned above, failure to comply with the *Competition Act* can cause a company serious problems. Accordingly, companies should take steps to educate their sales and other staff regarding competition law. Many companies find it useful to distribute a short employee handbook to company personnel that outlines the major potential pitfalls confronting the company in this area of law. Some businesses hold periodic seminars with senior staff to help ensure that the company complies with the various facets of competition law. The importance of this type of education cannot be overstated. For example, notwithstanding that the conspiracy offence — an agreement among parties that lessens competition unduly — more or less in its present form has been part of Canadian law since 1889, every year companies continue to run afoul of this provision. Promoting awareness among staff is one key way in which to help ensure compliance with the law.

The following guidelines could usefully be made part of a company's employee education effort:

Competition Law Guidelines for Employees — Relations with Competitors

1. Do not enter into any agreement or understanding (whether written or oral, express or implied, formal or informal), with any competitor in regard to prices, terms or conditions of sale, quantity or quality of production, markets or customers, or channels or methods of distribution or supply.

2. Do not take part in any discussions with a competitor concerning prices, market conditions, future production or marketing plans, or any other matters affecting competition. Proposed activities and/or discussions with competitors regarding R&D joint ventures, trade associations, and the like should be reviewed in advance with legal counsel.

3. Do not provide to or accept from any competitor any information relating to competitive matters including price fists or future price changes. Information concerning prices or other activities may be obtained from customers, suppliers, and published sources; however, care should be taken to record the source of the information to avoid any inference that such information was obtained directly from competitors.

4. Obtain an agenda or program before any trade association meeting and, if any concerns are evident, submit it to legal counsel in advance. At any meeting where competitors are in attendance, confine your activities to the legitimate purpose for which you are present. If improper matters are discussed you should immediately insist that such discussions cease, and if they do not, you should leave the meeting. You should also request that your leaving be recorded in the minutes of the meeting if practical.

5. Under no circumstances should employees discuss requests for bids or tenders with any person outside the Company. Situations may arise in which the Company may be asked to bid against a customer of the Company and in such cases special care should be exercised to avoid any contact with your customers regarding the bid.

6. Do not engage in any pricing or other activity that is aimed at disciplining or eliminating a competitor. It is often difficult to distinguish between a legitimate, pro-competitive act and an illegal, anti-competitive one; if you are in doubt, consult legal counsel.

Competition Law Guidelines for Employees — Relations with Customers

1. Do not make discounts, rebates, or other advantages available to one customer unless they are also made available to the customer's competitors in respect of

sales of like quality and quantity. Proposed different discounts based on quantity, or functional discounts, should be reviewed with legal counsel.

2. Promotional allowances must be offered to all competing customers on a proportionate basis in relation to the value of sales to such customers.

3. Do not attempt by any means to influence the price at which a customer resells the products sold to him by the Company.

4. Do not refuse to sell to a customer because the customer is a discounter or engages in a policy of selling at low prices. Advise customers who complain about the discount pricing policies of their competitors for the products sold to them by the company that it would be contrary to law and to the policy of the Company to attempt in any way to control the resale prices of its customers.

5. Contact legal counsel before entering into any exclusive dealing, tied selling, or market restriction arrangement with a customer, or any patent or trademark licensing agreement that contains restrictive terms.

6. Ensure that all advertising and other marketing information of the Company made available to customers, distributors, and others is factually correct and not misleading. Ensure that testimonials are approved in writing, and that all statements regarding test results or guarantees of a product's performance are based on tests that are well designed and in accordance with generally accepted scientific principles.

INTERNATIONAL COMPETITION LAW

A final word about compliance with competition law should note that competition law is not restricted to Canada. The United States (where it is called "antitrust law"), most countries in Europe, and the European Union itself, as well as a number of other countries, have laws similar to the *Competition Act*. These competition laws of other countries in many ways reflect the same principles, and in some cases share very similar substantive provisions, as those found in Canada's *Competition Act*. There are, however, important procedural and substantive differences between the competition laws of different countries. Accordingly, whenever a Canadian computer company is establishing a distribution system or a more permanent direct presence in another country, particularly in the U.S. or Europe, it should obtain guidance as to the impact on the proposed arrangements of any local competition law.

10

Dealing with the Federal Government: Export Control and Government Contracting

Software companies and other suppliers of high-technology resources can come into contact with the federal government in many different ways. This chapter discusses several legal and policy aspects of two common types of dealings that these companies have with Ottawa. The first involves the export control regulatory regime administered by Ottawa; the second relates to the activity of selling computer products to the federal government. The intent of this chapter is to give an overview of the relevant legal rules and policies in each of these important areas. The chapter ends with a brief reminder of the federal access-to-information law (a subject discussed more fully in Chapter 7 under "Access-to-Information Laws"), which must be kept in mind whenever submitting information to the government in the context of export control or government-procurement dealings with Ottawa.

It is worth reminding readers that many of the laws, regulations, and policies discussed in this book change frequently; and readers should therefore always check to verify if the material presented here is up-to-date. While this caveat applies throughout the book, it is perhaps most applicable to the two principal subjects dealt with in this chapter, export control and government contracting. In addition to the myriad of laws and regulations in each of these areas, a great number of policies also affects each of them. And policies can, and constantly do, change very quickly. As a result, notwithstanding the attempt here to focus on general, more enduring principles, undoubtedly the material will age very quickly. Accordingly, after obtaining a general feel for the issues presented here, readers should always confirm matters with government officials or professional advisors.

CANADA'S EXPORT CONTROL REGIME

The Canadian government, primarily through the *Export and Import Permits Act* (EIPA), controls the export of munitions and a large number of strategic goods and technologies, including a wide range of computers and types of software. Such goods are listed on an Export Control List (ECL) which is set out in a regulation made under the EIPA. An exporter must obtain a permit from Foreign Affairs and International Trade Canada ("FAITC") in order to ship out of Canada goods on the ECL, subject to the general exception that all strategic products in the case of exports to the United States, do not require an individual export permit. As for destinations other than the United States, it is important to note that with respect to computers, the ECL only "embargoes" computers having a processing power of greater than 260 "Mtops". An "Mtop" is roughly equivalent to one Megahertz (MHz) of a pentium processor. Thus, only relatively high end computers are caught by the permit requirements under the ECL. It should be noted, however, that multiple personal computers with co-processors, or one computer having more than one processor operating in parallel, could easily exceed the 260 Mtops threshold. A computer that exceeds the ECL limit of 260 Mtops, but is below 500 Mtops, can nevertheless be exported without a specific permit, provided the destination is not one of a few countries which include, currently, Iran, Iraq and North Korea. As well, a computer not exceeding 1,500 Mtops can be exported without a specific permit if the destination is Japan, Australia, New Zealand, Turkey or one of 17 countries in Europe.

As for software, each controlled technology on the ECL includes an item for software to run or use the technology. Thus, if a technology is on the ECL it is safe to asume that the software designed for the development, production or use of such technology is also covered by the ECL . With respect to discreet, stand-alone software products, the ECL covers such products as the source code of operating systems software, software development tools and certain expert systems software, as well as certain types of encryption software. As a result, a Canadian software company should periodically review the ECL to see if any of its products, or sub-programs or modules embedded in its products — like encryption features — are on the ECL.

The Canadian government also controls the export of all goods (even goods not on the ECL) to countries on an Area Control List (ACL), which is set out in a regulation under the EIPA. An individual export permit is required for any Canadian export to a country appearing on the ACL, whether or not the good is listed on the ECL, subject to the general exception that certain nonstrategic goods listed in general export permits (also regulated under the EIPA) may be shipped to ACL countries without an individual permit. Under authority of the *United Nations Act*, Canada can also restrict the export of goods from Canada to any country against which the United Nations has imposed economic sanctions. Under this statute Canada implemented economic sanctions against Iraq when it invaded Kuwait in 1990.

It is an offence under the EIPA to export a good from Canada without an export permit where such an export permit is required. Under the EIPA a company may be fined and its employees may be fined or imprisoned or both if they are found to violate this law. Companies that contravene export control rules may also suffer serious harm to their business reputations and their relationships with suppliers, customers, and governments. For example, a number of years ago a Japanese company and a Norwegian engineering firm were found to have violated their respective national export control laws by selling highly sophisticated metal-milling technology to the former Soviet Union. This technology could have been used by the Russians to manufacture submarine propellers milled to such precision as to greatly reduce the noise generally produced by such propellers (Western sonar can track Russian submarines by the noise made by their propellers, and given this sale of Japanese and Norwegian technology, NATO's navies could find it more difficult to monitor Russia's submarines). The result of this illegal sale was the near passage in the United States Congress of legislation that would have banned consumer goods made by the Japanese company from the U.S. market — U.S. legislation was passed that prohibited this company and the Norwegian company from selling goods and services to the U.S. government! The Japanese company was also forbidden by the Japanese government to export to the Soviet Union and its then allies for a period of one year.

In most cases, obtaining an individual export permit from FAITC is a relatively routine procedure. It is always advisable, however, for exporters to give themselves reasonable lead time when making such an application and to send FAITC detailed specifications for the good to be exported, so that FAITC can quickly understand its functional and performance characteristics. The average application currently takes about two weeks to process, and can take much longer if the good is more sophisticated or if its destination is an ACL country or a country where a diversion to these countries is considered probable. Sometimes end-user certificates or international import certificates are also required and these also take a fair period of time to obtain from the end user's host government. In some cases, forward-looking exporters have gone to FAITC to discuss a product while it is still at the development stage so that certain design changes might be made that will more likely allow the product to receive an export permit. In a similar vein, an exporter that wishes to make sales of ECL goods at a foreign trade show would be wise to obtain prior approval for the export of such goods well before the date of the show. It should be noted that ECL goods requiring a specific export permit require such permits even if exported for trade shows, whether or not they are returned to Canada.

In order to expedite matters as much as possible, companies that export regularly, especially those in the high-technology sector, often assign at least one employee to gain familiarity with export-control rules and procedures. In any event, all employees should be educated sufficiently to realize that export control procedures apply to certain shipments out of Canada; even though the EIPA has existed since 1947, all too often Canadian business people learn of this important law for the first time when their goods are detained by Canada Customs for failure to comply with it.

SELECTED LEGAL AND POLICY ISSUES IN FEDERAL GOVERNMENT CONTRACTING

Government contracts, especially those for high-technology goods such as computers and software products, can be extremely complicated affairs. When a private-sector organization purchases a computer system, the decision-making calculus generally revolves around price and performance. While these two variables are not unimportant to governments, their purchases can be influenced by other criteria as well. For example, given the important role of the computer industry in the national economy, a major high-technology acquisition can be used by a government as a tool of industrial development policy if the supplier can be induced to obtain a certain portion of the value of the technology from within Canada. In some cases national security considerations may also be relevant in arguing for an acquisition strategy that favours domestic suppliers over foreign ones. And then there is simply the sentiment that Canadian taxpayers' dollars should be used by governments to benefit Canadian suppliers. In short, government procurements can be rife with hidden — and sometimes not-so-hidden — public policy agendas and objectives.

In an attempt to discipline the traditional tendencies of governments to favour their domestic suppliers in procurement matters, several international regimes have been developed which impact upon suppliers of high technology and other goods to the Canadian and a number of other governments. The discussion below considers the two most important of these from a Canadian perspective, namely, the WTO Government Procurement Agreement and the provisions regarding government procurement in the North American Free Trade Agreement (NAFTA). The following also discusses several Canadian government procurement policies that are outside the scope of the WTO and NAFTA systems.

THE WTO GOVERNMENT PROCUREMENT AGREEMENT

The WTO Government Procurement Agreement (GPA) was one of the significant achievements of the Uruguay Round of GATT negotiations. Canada was a signatory to the predecessor of the GPA, namely the GATT Government Procurement Code, since 1981, and currently most of Canada's major trading partners are signatories as well, including the United States, the European Union and Japan. The Agreement establishes a set of procedural rules designed to reduce discrimination against foreign suppliers to the governments who are signatories to the GPA. As such, the GPA presents foreign suppliers with greater access to the government procurement budget of Ottawa, which means more competition for Canadian suppliers, but it also provides Canadian suppliers with increased sales opportunities in foreign capitals. It should be noted that the GPA does not apply to the procurements of all federal governmental entities. Each country has its exceptions, such as the departments of Energy and Transport in the U.S. And with respect to entities that are covered, only contracts for goods worth SDR 130,000 (currently C$259,000) or more are caught by the GPA's rules ("Special Drawing Rights" — SDR — are units of account established by the International Monetary Fund). It should be noted that the GPA now applies to products and services; previously, the GATT Code only applied to goods.

If a procurement comes within the jurisdiction of the GPA, the government must follow a number of procedural and substantive rules set out within it. The call for proposals must be published a certain period of time, generally 40 days, before the closing date for bid responses. The government uses a publication entitled *Government Business Opportunities* for publishing proposed procurements covered by the GPA. The government also notifies the public of these calls for proposals by listing them on an electronic bulletin board. With respect to the tender documentation, the GPA requires that specifications not be biased, that they be based on performance rather than design criteria, and that international standards, rather than national technical regulations or national standards, be referenced. These rules are particularly important in the computer field inasmuch as a request for procurement proposal can easily be drafted unfairly to favour one supplier over another.

As for the substantive review of the bid, the Canadian government is prohibited by the GPA from applying a Canadian-content premium (which policy, applicable in non-WTO and non-NAFTA procurements, is discussed below) or any other mechanism that would discriminate against a foreign supplier. Rather, the award has to be based on criteria and essential requirements contained in the proposal documents. It should be noted that the GPA permits sole-source contracts — procurements that the government does not submit to competitive tendering — but only subject to the strict requirements that are stipulated in the GPA. Once a contract is awarded, the name of the winning bidder must be published (again, in the case of Canada, the publication is *Government Business Opportunities*), and additional information must be supplied to an unsuccessful bidder's government if so requested. These post-award procedures facilitate the monitoring of the GPA-based system and permit parties who wonder why their bids were unsuccessful to obtain relevant information quickly.

GOVERNMENT PROCUREMENT UNDER THE NORTH AMERICAN FREE TRADE AGREEMENT

The NAFTA's chapter on government procurement has broadened and deepened the obligations of Canada and the United States under the GPA in respect of "eligible goods" proposed for procurements having a value over US$25,000 (currently calculated to be C$34,300). Thus the NAFTA lowers the GPA's threshold for goods from C$239,000 to C$34,300, so that procurements of "eligible goods" valued between these two amounts by the Canadian and American federal departments and agencies caught by the GPA are subject to nondiscriminatory treatment. The NAFTA's threshold for service contracts is C$70,700.

In addition to opening up to increased competition many more federal government contracts in Ottawa, Mexico City and Washington, the NAFTA made useful improvements upon the GPA by requiring Canada and the U.S. to provide more information, both before and after the contract award, to prospective and unsuccessful bidders. It was this requirement that prompted the Canadian government to establish the publication *Government Business Opportunities*. As noted above, this source lists all the federal government's proposed procurements covered by the GPA and the NAFTA, as well as contracts actually awarded. Companies desiring to do business with the Canadian government should subscribe to this publication (as well as to the electronic bulletin board that lists calls for procurements in an electronic medium), just as those companies regularly selling to the U.S. government read the *Commerce Daily News*, the Washington publication that lists prospective and awarded U.S. federal government contracts. As well, companies should get themselves onto the "source lists" that Public Works and Government Services Canada (PWGSC) keeps of qualified bidders.

THE INTERNAL TRADE AGREEMENT

The Federal Government and the Provincial Governments are parties to the Agreement on Internal Trade (AIT). Chapter 5 of the AIT is patterned on the WTO's GPA and the NAFTA except that its purpose is to reduce discriminatory government procurement practices among the various governments within Canada. Under the AIT, the Federal Government and each Provincial Government has agreed not to discriminate against Canadian suppliers on the basis of their location within Canada in respect of contracts worth more than $25,000 (for goods) and $100,000 (for services).

The AIT also provides that governments limit the value of their preferences for Canadian content to 10%. For this purpose, a good qualifies as Canadian if it is produced entirely from Canadian materials, or it is a good produced in Canada that has undergone sufficient transformation in Canada to be considered Canadian goods under the relevant rules of origin. The AIT provides for a dispute resolution process that includes review panels at the provincial level, and resort to the Canadian International Trade Tribunal (discussed below) at the federal level.

THE CANADIAN INTERNATIONAL TRADE TRIBUNAL

The NAFTA was also important for having established in Canada a government bid-challenge mechanism for potential suppliers of eligible goods. At the heart of this new regime is the Canadian International Trade Tribunal (CITT), a body which is able to entertain complaints from disgruntled bidders on covered procurements for the designated government departments or agencies. The monetary threshold may be changed in the future, so it is always necessary for a disgruntled bidder on a government contract to check what the CITT's current monetary jurisdiction is. A Canadian supplier — or an American or Mexican or any other supplier for that matter — who is bidding to supply goods or services for a procurement, and who believes it is being treated in a manner contrary to the GPA and/or the NAFTA, may bring the matter to the CITT; if a bidder wishes to use the CITT mechanism it must lodge its complaint with the CITT within ten days of learning of the basis of its complaint. It should be emphasized that going to the CITT quickly — ideally before the government contract in question is awarded — is critical as, for all practical purposes, the potential usefulness of the CITT diminishes after a contract is awarded.

Once the CITT has received a complaint, it must move very quickly to ascertain the relevant facts and issue a recommendation. The whole process generally should take no longer than 90 days from beginning to end, and there is even the possibility that it will take as little as 45 days. In fact, one of the CITT's first cases took only a few days to settle. The relevant government department agreed to change its specifications for a high-technology procurement soon after it was contacted by the CITT in respect of a disgruntled bidder who felt that the tender specifications, as originally written, effectively precluded a bid by any but a single company. Based on the CITT's intervention, the relevant government department agreed to rewrite the specifications for the bid to make them more generic.

Where a problem is not resolved so quickly, the CITT is required to issue a report and, if relevant, recommendations for an appropriate remedy. Remedies might include that a new solicitation be issued, that new bids be sought, that the bids be reevaluated, that the contract be terminated, that an appropriate amount of compensation specified by the CITT be awarded to the complainant, or that the contract be awarded to the complainant. The governmental entity must consider the CITT's report and any recommendations and endeavour to implement the recommendations to the greatest extent possible. If the governmental entity does not intend to fully implement the recommendations, it must promptly notify the CITT of its reasons.

The CITT has considered a number of cases involving high-technology goods. In one case the lowest bidder for a procurement involving uninterruptible power supplies complained because it was not awarded the contract even though its bid was technically responsive. The CITT agreed with the complainant, and also found numerous irregularities in the tendering and bid-selection process, and accordingly awarded the complainant its costs and recommended that the government pay the complainant an amount equal to the profit it would have earned on the procurement.

The CITT's powers are, in the final analysis, recommendatory only (except with respect to the awarding of costs related to the complaint or the bid tender). Its reports, however, usually carry significant weight. And if the CITT's recommendation is not implemented, the complainant might also consider commencing a legal action where there has been a deficiency that would be actionable at law. While the CITT must dismiss any complaint that has been judged by a court, a court likely would not be prevented from entertaining a claim that was the subject of a review by the CITT.

The establishment of the CITT notwithstanding its current somewhat limited jurisdiction, constitutes a positive development for companies selling eligible goods to the Canadian government. The two cases noted above, and a number of others that have been before the CITT to date, show that, for those procurements that fall within its jurisdiction, the CITT is an efficient means of airing, and hopefully resolving (or obtaining limited remedies in respect of), any disputes relating to the federal government's procurement or contract-award procedures.

SOCIO-ECONOMIC FACTORS IN AWARDING CONTRACTS

In those procurements where the WTO's GPA and the NAFTA are inapplicable, the Canadian government is free to, and does, use government procurement to attempt to attain national industrial policy and other objectives. The government's intentions and practices to this end are intended to achieve the following: restricting solicitations to Canadian-based manufacturers provided sufficient competition exists; a Canadian-content premium policy; a contracting-out policy for science and technology to support Canadian industrial performers; a rationalization policy, which permits designated classes of imported products of multinationals to be treated as goods of Canadian origin in return for additional investment or activity in Canada; a policy of offset negotiations aimed at licensing, technology transfer, and sub-contracting arrangements on large offshore purchases; and an employment-equity policy, which establishes that firms employing more than one hundred people and doing business with the government will be required to implement employment equity.

The mechanism for implementing these diverse and often conflicting policy objectives is the so-called Procurement Review Committee (PRC). A PRC, which consists of the representatives of various government departments (such as Treasury Board, Finance, Industry, and PWGSC), reviews all major government procurement plans for soliciting proposals not subject to the WTO's GPA or the NAFTA in order to ensure that lasting economic benefits to Canada from the procurement are attained to the greatest extent possible.

In attempting to achieve economic benefits for Canada in a non-WTO/NAFTA procurement, a PRC will consider the degree of Canadian content proposed by the various bidders. Generally speaking, the Government will be looking for anywhere from 80% to 100% Canadian content, depending on the particular procurement. In this regard, the government considers as Canadian goods those that are wholly manufactured or originating in Canada. Products containing imported components can also be considered Canadian if they have undergone sufficient transformation as to satisfy the relevant rules of origin.

It should be noted that with respect to the procurement of computers, office equipment and photocopiers, only the products of companies that are MERIT Partners or CIRCLE companies under the government's MERIT and CIRCLE programs, or the predecessor to these programs, qualify as being Canadian goods. The MERIT program has as its objective to encourage international companies to grant their Canadian affiliate a "world product mandate," or at least a regional mandate (e.g., all the personal computers sold by a company in North America are made in a plant in Ottawa, Ontario). By establishing such a facility, or by other means (such as through R&D activity) developing in Canada, for a selected range of products, an autonomous capability for technological innovation as well as production, the international company can become a MERIT company. Additionally, and most importantly, the Canadian-content premium rules do not apply to any bids made by such companies on a procurement for computers, office equipment, or photocopiers; that is, all these products of the "rationalized" company, including those imported from abroad, are deemed to contain 100% Canadian content. There are currently 11 such rationalized companies in Canada: Sun Microsystems, IBM, DEC, Motorola, Unisys, AT&T Global Solutions, Xerox, Apple Canada, Olivetti Canada, Silicon Graphics Canada, and Hewlett-Packard.

Canadian-based firms, typically personal computer manufacturers, can qualify for the same treatment as MERIT firms through roughly similar criteria that emphasize total quality management, R&D and related high value-added activities. There are currently 11 CIRCLE firms: namely, Cemtech, Hewitt Rand Corporation, Mind Computer Products, Northern Micro, Patriot Computer Corp., Primax Data Products, Seanix Technology, Sidus Systems, STD Technology, VTech Computer Systems, and Hardware Canada Computing.

A high-technology company proposing to bid on a government tender must understand the PWGSC policies that apply to contracts falling outside of the WTO's GPA and NAFTA regimes. It is critical, for example, for a Canadian software company to know whether a proposed hardware partner on a joint government bid has been designated as a MERIT or CIRCLE company; if not, and if the hardware component of the contract is significant, the software supplier may well wish to find a hardware partner that is a MERIT or CIRCLE company. Similarly, if no rationalized hardware partner can be found, then it is important to understand the workings of the Canadian-content premium rules to be able to submit the most effective bid possible.

When looking for a partner to work with on joint government bids, it is advisable for the partners to enter into a written agreement — often called a "teaming agreement" — for each bid. This agreement would specify such matters as the specific responsibilities of each partner, the general method of dealing with the government (i.e., will one partner be the general contractor and the other a subcontractor, or will they be equals?), and the circumstances in which either partner can withdraw from the joint bid.

With respect to contracts, suppliers of computer products to the federal government are normally asked to sign the government's standard form purchase agreements. These agreements often fail to address some issues that are critical to the supplier, especially in respect of software products, and must therefore be reviewed in detail.

ACCESS TO INFORMATION ACT

The federal *Access to Information Act* and similar laws in Ontario, Quebec, and several other provinces can give third parties access to information submitted to the federal government by others. While this type of legislation is discussed at some length in Chapter 7 (under "Access-to-Information Laws"), it is worth reviewing several important aspects of the federal access-to-information regime because the material submitted to the DEA in respect of an export-permit application (including the application itself), and a proposal and other materials provided to the DSS or some other federal government department in response to a request for proposal for a prospective government procurement, will be subject to the federal *Access to Information Act*. A computer supplier providing the federal government with such information must be aware of the access-to-information laws because these laws raise the very real possibility that a third party, such as a competitor, may be able to gain access to such information that the supplier has deposited with the government.

Access-to-information legislation, however, does generally restrict the disclosure of trade secrets or confidential technical, scientific, and business information of a third party to someone requesting access under the relevant access-to-information law. To take the fullest advantage of these restrictions, and to help prevent the supplier's sensitive information falling into the hands of third parties by means of access-to-information laws, a computer supplier and its employees should carefully consider the procedures set out in Chapter 7 (under "Access-to-Information Laws") when contemplating providing the government with proprietary information.

11

Software Licence Agreements

A software company will almost always make copies of its software products available to customers under a licence agreement. The licence agreement allows the software company to impose certain restrictions on the customer's use of the software. Such restrictions would probably have little effect if the software company sold copies of its software. To understand why software is licensed rather than sold, consider the situation when a book publisher sells a copy of a book, which is the typical method of making available to consumers books and similar works such as magazines and newspapers.

When a customer buys a copy of a book in a bookstore, the customer, in addition to reading the book, can disclose it or even sell it to anyone else, and can make any other use of it, with the exception of making copies of all or substantial portions of it. This prohibition on copying, as discussed in Chapter 5, is contained in the *Copyright Act*, which provides that only the owner of the copyright in a copyrightable work, such as a book, can make copies of the work or authorize others to do so. When buying a book a customer does not buy the copyright in the book, the customer merely buys one copy of the work. Accordingly, the customer does not buy the right to make copies of the work, but there is nothing to prohibit the customer from lending to others the copy that was purchased or from making some other use of the copy that does not entail reproducing it.

A software company will normally want to limit more than the copying of its software, which is all it would be able to do if it sold copies of its software. Typically, it will also want to limit the use that can be made of the software, and it will also want to prohibit the disclosure and transfer of it. In order to impose these restrictions, the software company must retain ownership not only of the copyright in the software, but also of the copy of the software made available to the customer. Under the software licence agreement, therefore, the customer obtains no ownership right in the copy of the software, and no rights in the intellectual property comprising the software, but is merely given the right to use the copy of the software for a limited number of purposes.

The software licence agreement is also very important in order to limit the software company's potential liability to the customer. The software business can be a risky one, and the software licence agreement is the vehicle by which a software developer can shift to the customer some of the risks associated with software. This is done primarily through two key provisions, both of which are discussed at some length below. These provisions disclaim the software company's responsibilities for certain warranties and generally limit the software company's liability for certain kinds of possible damages.

It should be apparent from this brief discussion that the licence agreement is a very significant document from the perspective of the software company. It is also, however, a critical document for the customer, to whom the particular software may be, or become over time, extremely important. Accordingly, this chapter discusses the major provisions of the licence agreement from the perspective of both the software company and the customer. The days are long gone when customers would sign any agreement put in front of them, however lopsided it was in favour of the software company, and, frankly, this is all for the good because balanced, even-handed software licences make for better relationships between software companies and their customers.

This chapter, therefore, rather than describing what a software licence agreement heavily tilted in favour of the software company might look like, contemplates one that is fair to both sides. Indeed, in recognition of the fact that most customers today will not sign licence agreements that are grossly unfair to them, many software companies have made the wise decision to make their standard-form contracts quite even-handed by having them address the reasonable concerns of customers, particularly in the areas of delivery and acceptance testing (as discussed below). Such contracts prove to be very attractive marketing tools because they give prospective customers some confidence in the software company's products and abilities. A balanced standard-form agreement can also save the significant time and expense that was previously spent on negotiating the old one-sided licence agreement — which, after these negotiations, usually ended up looking a lot like the new even-handed agreement!

Before turning to the discussion of the key issues that should normally be addressed in a software licence agreement, it should be noted that not all of the following discussion is relevant to every software product. There may be some software products intended for the personal computer market that certain software companies are quite willing to sell copies of, as is the case with books or movies on video cassettes (which are increasingly being sold, whereas previously they were made available only on a rental basis, a rental being merely a short-term licence). In other words, for these particular software products it may be unnecessary to have a detailed (or indeed any) software licence addressing the provisions discussed below, though such a decision should be made only after careful consideration. Indeed, much of this type of software is marketed under the rather simple and short "shrinkwrap" licence discussed at the end of this chapter. For most software, however, particularly software of any size or complexity, many of the points raised below will be germane, though judgment most always be exercised when applying the points raised below to any particular software licensing situation.

It should also be noted that the contract provisions discussed in this chapter are presented in "chronological" order, that is, as the issues raised by these provisions are likely to be encountered during the course of installing a particular software program. This order is useful for highlighting the various aspects of a software project, but it is equally valuable for actual contract drafting, and software companies should strongly consider having their agreements organized in a similar manner. Such an approach will result in a quite user-friendly document that will be easy to work with rather than a disorganized hodge-podge of provisions in which it is hard for even the software company to understand how the various provisions all fit together. From the perspective of both the software company and the customer, there is much to commend a computer contract whose clauses appear in an organized, common-sense order.

SPECIFYING THE SOFTWARE

It seems almost too obvious a point to mention that the software product being licensed should be described or defined with some precision. In many cases this is not a problem, for the software company will have only one product, and perhaps even only one version of this product. In other cases, however, the software company will have multiple products, and they may each have several versions, and hence some specificity will be called for to avoid subsequent problems, particularly if the various products and versions all have different prices.

Another reason for requiring precision in describing deliverables is that, with so many buzzwords and jargon in the computer vocabulary, it is very easy for the software company and the customer to misunderstand one another as to what software is to be delivered under the licence agreement if it is described in only general, acronym-filled terms. Of course, all industries and professions — including the legal one — have their own vocabulary and jargon to a certain extent, but the degree to which the terminology in the software business, and the computer sector generally, can be misleading or confusing is attested in the following passage from an American judge's court decision some 25 years ago — but still relevant today — in a case dealing with a computer contract that gave rise to a lawsuit:

> Lawyers and courts need no longer feel ashamed or even sensitive about the charge, often made, that they confuse the issue by resort to legal "jargon," Law Latin or Norman French. By comparison, the misnomers and industrial shorthand of the computer world make the most esoteric legal writing seem as clear and lucid as the Ten Commandments or the Gettysburg Address; and to add to this Babel, the experts in the computer field, while using exactly the same words, uniformly disagree as to precisely what they mean.

For this reason, if there is ever any doubt in a software-licence agreement about the meaning of a technical term, then the term should be defined, preferably in relation to its function or purpose rather than by resorting to further buzzwords.

One issue that should be addressed clearly is whether the software will be provided in its object-code form, or in its source-code form, or in both. Software, in general, is written in one of several English-like, high-level computer languages, such as COBOL (Common Business-Oriented Language) or in more modern "object-oriented" programming environments. When written in such a language, the software is said to be in its source-code format. The source code sets out the logic flow of the software program and usually includes a programmer's narrative explanation of the various steps of the program. This makes the source code extremely valuable to the software company, and most software companies are extremely reluctant to make the source code available to customers, except under unusual circumstances, such as through the mechanism of the source-code escrow agreement described in the next chapter. Rather than provide source code, the software company normally provides the customer with the object-code version of the software, which is a translation of the source code into a format that is intended to be directly executed by the computer. In any event, if the customer is to receive source code this should be clearly set out in the licence agreement; and if the customer is to receive only object code, this should also be confirmed in the contract.

DELIVERY

Customers tend to have two major concerns about software: first, that the particular product be delivered to the customer by the specific date agreed upon by the customer and the software company; and second, that, when it arrives, it operate the way the software company said it would. This latter issue is usually addressed in a software licence agreement through an acceptance-test provision, as discussed below. As for the issue of timely delivery, customers are increasingly insisting that the software company commit to a specific date by which the software product will be delivered. This is usually coupled with a remedy, which provides that if the software is not delivered by such date, the customer will be reimbursed any deposit moneys that it paid, after which repayment it can terminate the software licence.

Of course, if the software company will be licensing an existing product that does not need to be modified for the customer, then meeting such a delivery requirement should not be difficult. Where, however, the program must be customized for the particular needs of the customer, and it is the customized program that must be delivered by a certain date, the software developer must take great care not to agree to too optimistic a final delivery date. Indeed, if the amount of customization work is significant, perhaps the project would be better characterized as a software-development exercise; and the software company should in such a case consider the issues discussed in the next chapter in the section on software development agreements.

The delivery issue also raises the problem of "brochureware" or "vapourware," terms coined to describe the practice of certain irresponsible computer companies in announcing unreasonably optimistic dates for the availability of new products. In an increasingly competitive vendor environment this practice is perhaps understandable, but it is also extremely dangerous. Apart from losing credibility with actual and potential customers when the previously announced release date is not met, the practice can also amount to illegal misleading advertising (the misleading advertising provisions in Canada's *Competition Act* are discussed in Chapter 9). In one American case a company that makes software for personal computers was fined $275,000 when it advertised as available a product that in fact was not ready for shipment to customers. To avoid such lawsuits, software companies must either be responsible in their announcements of planned release dates for new products or new versions of existing products, or they should refrain from announcing specific future release dates altogether.

INSTALLATION

While some software can be installed on the relevant computer hardware without too much difficulty, most software installations require some effort as well as a certain amount of education or training of the customer's personnel. Significant effort may also be required in converting the customer's data on its previous computer system (or it may even be in manual form) to the new software. To avoid misunderstandings, the licence agreement should specify who is responsible for performing these and related activities. If they are to be the responsibility of the software company, the agreement should set out the basis on which the company will be paid for its efforts. If these activities are included in the licence fee, this should be mentioned explicitly, and if they are to be performed by various staff members of the software company at certain hourly rates, these rates should be clearly set out in the agreement, perhaps in a separate schedule attached to the contract.

Particularly in respect of larger software-implementation projects, it may be appropriate to set out in the contract certain project-management provisions. These might include requiring each party to appoint a project coordinator. Such an arrangement can be useful for the software company because it then will have only one individual to deal with when receiving the customer's instructions, or consents, instead of having to concern itself with the actual management or approvals structure in effect in the customer's organization. In a similar vein, the agreement should describe those activities and responsibilities that will be borne by the customer, or perhaps by an agent of the customer — but in any event, not by the software company. This might include such critical matters as ensuring that the customer obtains delivery of all relevant hardware and operating-system software that will be needed for the proper functioning of the particular application program of the software company.

ACCEPTANCE TESTING

Customers are increasingly demanding that the licence agreement contain a provision that permits the customer to test the software product against some predetermined criteria to ensure that it operates as the software company said it would. Usually associated with this acceptance-testing provision is a remedy that allows the customer to terminate the licence agreement, and to have a refund of any licence fees paid, if the acceptance test is not passed successfully within a certain time period. At first blush these provisions seem to work to the benefit of only the customer. In fact, an acceptance-test clause can be useful to a software company also, because a successful acceptance test significantly reduces the ability of the customer to repudiate the software at a subsequent date on the grounds of some alleged shortcoming of the product.

While a customer's demand for an acceptance test is not unreasonable, it is unfair if the benchmark for the successful passage of the test is that the software operate to the satisfaction of the customer, or some other criterion that is equally subjective to the customer. Rather, to be fair to the software company, the test should be based on objectively ascertainable criteria, such as whether or not the software operates in all material respects in accordance with its related documentation or with certain specifications that are set out in a schedule to the contract. In this way, both the customer and the software company know in advance precisely what the software must be capable of in order to be acceptable.

To illustrate this point further, a customer often has the requirement that the software operate with a certain response time; that is, after depressing the last keystroke for a certain on-line enquiry, the relevant screen will appear in so many seconds. Accordingly, the response-time performance of a software program will often be part of an acceptance test. If it is, a software company should strongly resist the relevant benchmark for the response-time test being something as ambiguous as the relevant "industry standard," which is really an admission by the customer (and the software company) that it is (and they are) too lazy (or perhaps too busy with others matters) to think through properly what the actual response-time requirements for the software should be. The danger, of course, in a phrase such as "industry standard" is that there is likely no such thing as an industry standard, or at least not one that can be stated with any precision. Or, more ominously, what happens when the customer and the software company have different understandings of what is the relevant industry standard?

To attempt to avoid these types of problems, the precise response-time requirements should be set out in the agreement, by stipulating, for example, that for a certain type of on-line inquiry, the response time for a certain percentage of inquiries over a particular period of time shall be no greater than a specified number of seconds. As well, the technical parameters and assumptions relevant to the response time figure should be set out in the contract with some precision (i.e., an exact hardware configuration should be provided, etc.). Crafting such a test criterion requires both parties to do their homework, and this means investing some time and effort, but the result will be a far more meaningful and useful acceptance test — one that both the customer and the software company will have confidence in.

It is often sensible for a software company to provide in the software licence agreement that if the software company does not receive notice from the customer of any errors in the software by the last day of the acceptance-test period, then the customer shall be deemed to have accepted the software on such date. Many customers do not like this provision, but frankly it is quite a reasonable one. It forces customers to take the acceptance test process seriously and to make the software company aware of problems in a timely manner. In other words, customers are given the opportunity of an acceptance test; if they don't use it, they lose it.

When a customer does bring errors to the attention of the software company during the acceptance test, the latter should be given some period of time to correct the problems. If need be, the software company should have the right to require that the acceptance test be run once more, or perhaps even a couple more times, before the customer can claim that the software company is in default under the agreement. In short, customers should not be permitted to walk away from a software licence arrangement merely upon a pretext or a lame excuse. In this regard, however, software companies should know that, while court cases dealing with disputes over the adequacy of software products have decided that a customer must give the software company some time to fix minor problems in the programs, courts tend not to extend this rule to the point where the software company is permitted to reprogram wholesale problems with the software. A bit of finetuning or ironing-out of relatively small glitches is one thing; a major overhaul is something else again, and courts have very little sympathy for the latter when confronted with a claim by the user that the software does not work, particularly where the software company made clear statements in advance about the availability and features of its software product.

PAYMENT

The contract should be very clear as to how much, and when, the customer has to pay the software company for the software and services provided under the contract. Unless both parties are in Canada, it is wise to specify the currency in which the amounts are to be paid. If one party is in Canada and the other in the U.S., which of the two countries' dollar will be used? The contract should also provide that if the customer is late in paying amounts due, the software company will be entitled to charge interest on the unpaid balance until paid in full. As for the interest rate, something more than "Prime plus 2%" is called for (Prime plus 6%, for example), because the interest rate should not simply be another cheap source of financing; it should actively discourage the customer from not paying in full.

An interesting approach to payment is the one that requires nothing to be paid to the software company until certain benefits or advantages attributable to the software are being experienced by the customer. Software companies, and other suppliers — in particular system integrators — have to be extremely careful with such an approach. It is necessary to specify, and possibly in great detail, the elements on which the benefit will be paid. Ideally the criteria should be quite "objective" and easily determinable, leaving no room for doubt as to whether the supplier has met its obligations.

LICENCE GRANT —
RESTRICTIONS ON USE

The software licence should contain a clear statement that the software company owns all rights in the software, including all intellectual property rights, such as copyright. As its name implies, however, the licence agreement will contain a provision that grants the customer the right to use the software company's software product. As noted at the beginning of this chapter, one of the reasons that software companies licence, rather than sell, copies of software is so that they can control with some precision the actual use made of the software. Thus, many software licences provide that the customer can use the software to process only the customer's own internal data. By this restriction, the software company is attempting to protect its commercial market. Without this limitation, the customer could establish itself, for example, as a service bureau to process the data of a number of other organizations, while the software company would receive no financial return from this additional exploitation of its product. Of course, software companies regularly permit service bureaus to use software, but the licence fee paid by a service bureau generally far exceeds the usual one-time fee paid by the typical regular customer; in addition, a service bureau might also pay to the software company a percentage of the fees generated by its use of the software company's program.

A customer might request that it be entitled to process not only its internal data, but also that of its subsidiaries, and perhaps even its affiliates, such as sister companies owned by the same company or person that owns the customer company. A software company that agrees to this request, often in return for some increase in the licence fee, should be careful to specify whether the right extends only to companies that are affiliates on the date the licence is granted, or whether it encompasses all affiliates acquired in the future (which, in some cases, can ultimately mean a large number of companies). The term "affiliate" should also be carefully defined so that the net is not cast too broadly. A common practice is to use the definition of affiliate found in Ontario's business corporations statute (or any similar laws in other provinces or in other jurisdictions outside of Canada), which links as affiliates certain corporations that are directly, indirectly, vertically, or horizontally connected by majority shareholdings sufficient to elect the majority of the board of directors of the relevant companies. This may be contrasted with the term "associate" in the same Ontario statute, which links together entities that are connected, directly or indirectly, by a 10% share-ownership relationship. The definition of "affiliate" should be reviewed carefully before being used, so that both the software company and the user of the software clearly understand which entities in the corporate group are indeed affiliates and which are not. In short, any extension of the right to process data beyond that of the customer must be carefully circumscribed so that the customer is not able to make greater use of the software than was anticipated by the software company.

Another restriction on use often imposed by software companies is that the copy of the licensed software must be operated on only a certain unit of hardware located at the customer's premises. In many cases today this type of restriction is probably too onerous and can usefully be replaced by a provision that merely requires the software to be used on the customer's premises located in a certain place. Indeed, some software companies now go so far as to allow the customer to use the single copy of software anywhere within the customer's organization in Canada so long as it is always used on the regular premises of the customer. Particular care should be given to the use and copying restrictions when licensing software for a network of personal computers or in what is called a "client-server" environment; one approach might be to limit the number of simultaneously authorized users of the network. These sorts of options offer flexibility to the user while, in most cases, still adequately protecting the interests of the software company. Of course, there may still be situations where a restriction to use the software on a certain machine will be required, such as where the software company is also selling the related hardware and it desires the customer in the future to buy additional hardware only from the software company (such a restriction should be reviewed by both parties to ensure that it does not present a problem under the applicable competition laws).

Yet another restriction on the use of software by a customer relates to whether the customer will have the right to modify the software itself rather than rely solely on the software company to make any required modifications. In this regard it is worth noting again the point regarding modifications discussed in Chapter 5, namely, that the *Copyright Act* permits owners of a copy of software the right to make modifications to it for limited purposes. This provision, however, is relevant to a minuscule number of software users only, because it applies solely to owners of a copy of software and, as mentioned previously in this chapter, copies of software are invariably licensed and not sold. Accordingly, the licence agreement should address expressly the question of customer-developed modifications. If the software company does not intend the customer to have the right to modify the software, the licence agreement should say so in no uncertain terms. By the same token, if the customer is to have such modification rights, then the agreement should also address who is to own these modifications. (Preferably the software company should own the modifications, particularly if they will incorporate any elements of the software company's software; for a fuller discussion of this question, see Chapter 12 under "Software Development Agreements.")

RESTRICTIONS ON TRANSFER

In an effort to further protect its potential market, in the licence agreement a software company will invariably prohibit its customer from transferring the licensed copy of the software to another potential user of it. The reason for this is relatively straightforward. If the software company licensed a certain computer program to one customer for, say, $50,000 on the basis that it would be used to process 50,000 transactions per month, the software company would not want the software transferred to another user who might be processing 100,000 transactions per month, inasmuch as the software company might have charged this latter user $100,000 for the same software. Accordingly, the software licence will usually prohibit the customer from transferring the software.

The software company may occasionally agree to certain exceptions to this rule. For example, it may in some cases be appropriate to permit the software to be transferred to an affiliate of the customer, particularly if elsewhere in the agreement the customer already has the right to process the data of its affiliates (in addition to its own internal data). In a similar vein, it may be reasonable to allow the assignment of certain types of software to anyone who purchases from the customer the hardware on which the customer had operated the software. In many situations, however, such an assignment right may not be sensible from the point of view of the software company, and when it is allowed certain further restrictions are usually reasonably required by the software company. For example, if a software company that licenses to insurance companies a program that administers life insurance policies were to permit such an assignment, it would be reasonable for the software company to stipulate that the recipient of the software from the initial licensee shall not process more policies with the software than were being processed by it immediately prior to the assignment of the licence.

RESTRICTIONS ON DISCLOSURE

A key objective for the licence agreement, from the software company's perspective, is to have the customer agree, in writing, that it will not allow third parties to have access to the licensed software. This is a critical requirement for the software company because if there are trade secrets in the software (and usually there are), then securing such a nondisclosure promise and related undertakings from the customer is perhaps the only effective way to preserve the required secrecy for the trade secrets. Without such a restriction, what may be the key elements of the program, namely, the concepts and ideas embodied in it, would no longer be able to be adequately protected by the software company. As noted in Chapter 5, patent protection for such aspects of the software may not be available, or if it is it may be quite expensive to obtain. And while copyright would still be effective without the nondisclosure provisions in the licence agreement, it will not likely provide protection to a number of the key attributes of the software that the software company is keen to protect. Accordingly, the restrictions on disclosure in the licence agreement are critical to the software company, and in some cases the provision should go so far as to prohibit the customer itself from decompiling, disassembling, or in any way reverse engineering the object code of the software, that is, taking it apart to see in detail what makes it tick.

Having the customer who is a corporation or some other form of nonindividual organization agree to nondisclosure provisions may not be enough. Particularly if the source code is provided to the customer, it is sensible for the software company to have each employee or independent contractor of the customer who will have access to the software company's proprietary materials also sign a short proprietary rights protection agreement directly with the software company. This document would come in very handy if, for example, an employee of the customer decided to try to walk away with (literally or even just figuratively), say, the trade secrets in the software and the software company wanted to take quick remedial action against such a threatening transgression, which it would have to do if it wished to maintain its trade secret rights in the program.

RESTRICTIONS ON COPYING

In the licence agreement a software company will invariably prohibit the customer from making multiple production (and even other) copies of the software product. The rationale for this restriction is twofold. First, as with the restriction on use discussed above, the software company wants to maximize its economic return on its products by precluding a customer from making and installing production copies of the product on two (or more) of its machines, all for a single licence fee. If the customer's volume of transactions or hardware configuration requires additional production copies of the program, the software company will want the customer to pay an extra amount for them.

The second reason for limiting copying is similar to the rationale for the nondisclosure prohibition discussed above, namely, that the software company wishes to control the number of copies of its software in circulation in order to protect its proprietary rights. The more copies there are in circulation, the greater the possibility that the program will be used, or further copied, by an unauthorized third party who has not signed or otherwise agreed to any licence or other kind of protective agreement with the software company. In addition to the foregone revenue this represents to the software company, it also raises the danger that its critical trade secrets and other proprietary rights will be made available to its actual and potential competitors.

The restrictions on copying in a licence agreement effective in Canada are a second layer of protection in that the *Copyright Act*, as discussed in Chapter 5, also prohibits the copying of software. In other words, the restrictions on the use, transfer, and disclosure of software products discussed above can only be implemented by means of having customers enter into software licence agreements, while the restriction on copying in the licence agreement bolsters and complements the restriction on copying in the *Copyright Act*. Indeed, the restriction on copying in licence agreements was probably more important some years ago when it was unclear whether software was protectible under the *Copyright Act*. It is, nevertheless, useful to continue the restriction on copying in the licence agreement inasmuch as this gives the software company a second front of attack on customers who make unauthorized copies of software. In addition to its claims under the *Copyright Act*, the software company would also have a breach-of-contract claim for damages if the customer violated the agreement's prohibition on making copies.

It is useful for a software company to have the double protection afforded by the *Copyright Act*'s anti-copying provisions in Canada (and by similar laws in many other countries) as well as those in its software licence agreement because, frankly, there is an awful lot of illegal copying of software occurring in Canada and all over the world. Some software-industry participants estimate that for each copy of software licensed in an authorized manner, an illegal copy will be made. The result is a huge revenue loss for software companies. Not surprisingly, several associations have sprung up in Canada and elsewhere to combat software piracy as well as the practice of "noncommercial piracy," where staff at companies and other organizations make illegal copies (which is the essence of piracy) not for commercial resale but rather solely for personal use or for use elsewhere in the company or organization. The organization established in Canada to combat this activity, the Canadian Alliance Against Software Theft (CAAST), is composed of several Canadian subsidiaries of American software companies. CAAST estimates that the use of unauthorized software cost software companies in Canada about $316 million in 1993. All software companies in Canada can help combat the unauthorized copying of software by, among other means, bringing the activities of CAAST to the attention of their customers so that they can in turn educate their staff in the legal use of computer software.

It should be noted that not all countries have copyright statutes or other intellectual property rights laws or procedural protections similar to those found in Canada. If a Canadian software company is planning to license software to a customer located outside of Canada therefore, the company should review what legal protection for software exists in the particular foreign jurisdiction, and if it is inadequate, the company should consider augmenting its contractual protections with that customer.

Taking legal action to enforce the anti-copying provisions of a licence agreement or the *Copyright Act* is, of course, only one way for a software company to combat the significant problem of illegal copying of its software products. The software company may want to consider establishing generally, or at least for its biggest actual or potential customers, volume-discount programs in which the prices paid for software licences drop as the number of copies licensed increases. Such a program would give the customer a financial incentive to ensure that its employees do not violate the software company's proprietary rights. Similarly, creative licensing solutions might be usefully explored when supplying software to educational institutions, given that, generally speaking, students have a tarnished reputation, sometimes deserved, sometimes not, regarding compliance with copying restrictions.

A second approach to the problem of illegal copying is for the software company to implement some technical device in the software to eliminate or greatly reduce the risk that the product will be copied in an unauthorized manner. For example, the term of the licence could be only one year long, renewable each year directly with the software company, perhaps by paying a nominal fee. Upon renewal the authorized user would be given a device that would allow the software to operate for another year, while those users who are not authorized to use the software will not have the new device issued to them. Without this device, which may be simply a new password, the software will simply cease to operate on a certain date.

A software company must exercise great care when employing such devices. As noted in Chapter 6 (under "The *Criminal Code* and Computer Viruses"), such a device that actually destroys the customer's data, or makes it impossible or even just difficult for the customer to access its data, may be problematic under the *Criminal Code*'s section that prohibits anyone from destroying or interfering with someone else's data. Apart from the possible criminal law consequences of such a device, its use, especially where the adverse consequences of the use of the device far outweigh the original harm caused by the illegal copying, may also cause the customer to bring a lawsuit against the software company for damages, the customer's argument being, among other things, "that the punishment did not fit the crime" (i.e., the damage caused to the user was disproportionate to the damage caused to the software company). Accordingly, it is generally not advisable for a software company to use such a device to combat illegal copying of software. If it is used, however, it should be designed not to destroy or otherwise interfere with the customer's data. As well, clear written notice should be given to customers that the software contains such a device in order to deter unauthorized copying of the program in the first place, as well as to put users of illegal copies on notice that their software will become disabled within a certain period of time, unless they obtain, and pay for, a proper licence from the software company in the interim. Such a notice should be displayed prominently on the packaging of the software, in the related documentation, and on at least the first screen of the program itself. In short, the software company that utilizes such a device should take great pains to notify users — whether authorized or not — about the device, its consequences to users, and how the adverse consequences can be avoided, namely, by paying the required licence fee and entering into an appropriate licence agreement in a timely manner with the software company.

While the main purpose of the copying provisions in the licence agreement is to prevent the making of unauthorized copies of the software product, many agreements also usefully address what copies a customer is able to make. Customers, not unreasonably, will insist that they be given the right to make one or a few copies of the software for backup or archival purposes, which copies could then be used to produce a new production copy of the program if the original production copy is destroyed or lost because of a computer malfunction or some operator error. This right to make backup copies should be expressly dealt with in the licence agreement because the section in the *Copyright Act* that permits an owner of a copy of a software program to make one backup copy of it applies only to owners of copies of software and not to mere licensees. Therefore, as was mentioned in Chapter 5, this section is of little use to most customers because copies of software are almost invariably licensed rather than sold. When addressing the issue of backup copies, the licence agreement should make it clear that all the nondisclosure and other protective provisions of the agreement that relate to the single production copy apply equally to any backup copies.

WARRANTIES AND WARRANTY DISCLAIMERS

"Warranty" is a legal term meaning "promise." The user of a computer product will invariably require the software company to make certain promises — or warranties — about the software company's product. A number of these requests for warranties are quite reasonable and normally will be given by the software company, usually after some negotiation. By the same token, it is not sensible for a software company to give certain other warranties, especially those warranties (and conditions) that are implied by Canadian sale-of-goods legislation, and therefore software companies are justified in requiring the customer to agree that they will not apply as between the two of them. And it should be remembered that in Canada it is not just implied warranties, but implied conditions as well, that must be disclaimed by the software company. This point is often overlooked by, for example, Canadian subsidiaries of American parents that use their parents' standard-form software licences, which disclaim only implied warranties because under United States sale-of-goods law there are no implied conditions.

A standard warranty requested by customers is that the software company owns the particular software product being licensed to the customer, including all the intellectual property rights in it (i.e., the copyright in the software program), or that at least the software company has the authority to grant the software licence to the customer. The latter situation would be relevant where the software company is distributing another party's software. In either case the software company should be prepared to state that it is the owner of the relevant software, or has the applicable right to distribute it to the customer. In this regard the software company should be careful to ensure that it has the necessary distribution rights to any software components of third parties that are embedded in its own software. It is sometimes easy for a software company to forget that its product contains sub-routines or constituent elements that, for example, were licensed only for development purposes. In such a case, a further distribution licence will also have to be acquired before copies of the software company's product can be licensed to customers.

The customer will want some guarantee that, if a third party comes forward with a claim that the software product infringes an intellectual property right owned by the third party, the software company will protect the customer from the financial and other consequences of such a claim. It is extremely common practice for a software company to meet this concern by providing the customer with a proprietary rights indemnity, which provides that the software company will pay for any damages or costs awarded by a court against the customer because of a claim that the software company's product violates the intellectual property of another person.

From the software company's perspective, such a proprietary rights provision should clearly require the customer to report promptly any such third-party claim. The provision should also permit the software company to have full and exclusive carriage of the claim so that it is directly involved in, and directing the legal defence of the software company for, the resulting lawsuit and any relevant settlement negotiations. And as for the prospective solutions to any such claim, the software company, in its licence agreement with the customer, should have the ability to take at least one of the three following actions in the event the product becomes the subject of an infringement claim (or if the software company believes it will so become): (1) make technical modifications to the software to render it noninfringing, or replace it altogether; (2) procure for the customer the right to continue using the software in question; and (3) terminate the licence agreement and the customer's right to use the software. This last option is often made subject to the software company's refunding a portion of the original licence fee to the customer — typically the whole licence fee less a certain percentage of such fee for each month that the customer has used the software.

As these proprietary rights indemnities are given so commonly, it is easy for a software company to forget to conduct the necessary due diligence before giving such an indemnity. A key requirement is to ensure that the software company in fact owns all the rights in the software product (unless it is merely distributing it for another party, in which case the software company's proprietary rights indemnity to customers should be no broader than the similar indemnity given by the owner of the software to the distributor software company). This means having all of its employees, and especially its independent contractors, sign proprietary rights agreements that unequivocally transfer ownership of the product to the software company, as discussed in Chapters 7 and 8. It also means periodically reviewing the software to ensure that none of these employees or independent contractors has violated the intellectual property rights of any other person when developing the software. From a trade-secret and copyright perspective, this review would involve ascertaining, among other things, whether any such individuals had access to a third party's software having the same design or function.

With respect to an indemnity for patent rights, the software company will have to search the records of the patent offices of the relevant jurisdictions to ascertain whether any patent has been issued that may curtail the ability of the software company to license the use of the software. This search would have to be updated regularly in order to review new patents issued by the various patent offices. This is an expensive exercise, and will become more so as an increasing number of patents are issued for software, a trend discussed in Chapter 5. Accordingly, some software companies have made the decision not to offer a proprietary rights indemnity in respect of patent rights. Many customers will resist such an approach, arguing that it is far more reasonable, efficient, and cost effective for a software company to bear the risk of patent-rights infringement, and the cost of the relevant patent searches, than for a customer to do so.

As discussed earlier in this chapter under "Delivery" and "Acceptance Testing," a software company should be willing to make some promises as to when the customer can expect delivery of the software product and as to the ability of the software, once it arrives, to operate in all material respects in accordance with its related documentation or with certain mutually agreed-upon specifications. It was recommended above that the proving ground for this latter warranty be an even-handed acceptance test in which the objective criteria of the warranty can be proven by the software company, or be shown by the customer to be lacking, in which case the software company will be given a period of time to rectify the problems. After acceptance another warranty is often applicable, namely, that the software continue to operate as it did to pass the acceptance test for a certain period of time, typically between 30 and 90 days — though sometimes longer. During this "warranty period" the software company would normally undertake to provide error-correction services at no cost to the customer.

Apart from these express warranties, the software company should be careful to disclaim any other warranties or conditions that may be effective (if they were not displaced by the licence agreement). Two implied warranties and conditions provided by sale-of-goods legislation across Canada are of particular relevance. These are the implied warranties and conditions of "merchantable quality" and "fitness for a particular purpose." The former means that the goods sold will be fit for the ordinary purpose for which they are sold, that is, they will operate properly and generally be of good condition. The latter means that where the customer is relying on the seller's skill and judgment to select or furnish certain goods, and where the seller has reason to know the particular purpose for which the goods are required, the seller is responsible for ensuring that the goods are fit for that purpose.

It should be mentioned that, depending on the facts of a particular case, these (and other) implied warranties and conditions may simply not apply to a situation where a software company is supplying custom software development services and no more, as these provisions cover only sales of "goods," which tend to mean physical, tangible personal property (like hardware). Courts, nevertheless, have often applied these provisions to certain types of software, particularly in cases where the supplier was selling a whole system comprised of software and hardware. In any event, even when a software licence agreement does not contemplate a companion contract for the sale of goods, it should contain a provision disclaiming these and all other implied warranties or conditions. Excluding these implied terms is permissible, except in the context of consumer sales, provided the exclusion is clear (it is therefore useful to type it in bold capital letters), and is always reasonable because it sends a clear signal to the customer that the software company will be held responsible for ensuring only that level of performance that was clearly stipulated in the agreement between the parties, such as a performance criteria schedule that is the subject of a fair acceptance test.

This can be contrasted with the much more ambiguous standard inherent in the "fitness for a particular purpose" implied warranty and condition, which in effect would require the software company to do the customer's homework in ensuring that the particular software product meets all the specific needs of the customer, a task that few software companies can ever hope to perform with complete success. Indeed, some software companies expressly provide in their agreements that they do not warrant that the software will meet the particular needs of the customer. In short, the warranty disclaimer imposes a useful discipline on the customer to conduct its own research as to what its detailed requirements are and whether the software company's product will meet these needs, it being the responsibility of the software company to ensure only that the software works as promised. It should be noted that most customers understand this division of labour, and therefore the warranty disclaimer tends not to be a very contentious provision in the software licence agreement.

LIMITATION OF LIABILITY

Another provision used by software companies to shift some of the risk of software to customers is the limitation-of-liability clause. This provision generally stipulates that under no circumstances, even in the case of negligence by the software company, will the software company be responsible for consequential and related damages suffered by the customer as a result of the poor performance of the software. An example of consequential damages would be lost profits. Therefore, if, to use a hypothetical situation, a customer's inventory-control software were to malfunction such that it could not meet a tight production schedule for one of its clients, and as a result it lost the ongoing supply contract for this client and the healthy profit margins associated with it, the customer (subject to, among other things, fundamental breach discussed below) could not recover these lost profits from the software company if a limitation-of-liability clause precluding their recovery were in effect between them.

The limitation-of-liability provision will typically also limit the amount of direct damages a software company will be liable for. Direct damages would be items such as a customer's additional labour or services costs to fix a particular software malfunction or to continue operating its business while the software is inoperable. As with the total exclusion of consequential (and special and incidental) damages, the rationale for this limitation on direct damages is that for a limited economic return for the supply of a software product, the software company cannot reasonably be expected to assume an unlimited liability exposure in the event the software malfunctions. A related argument is that the software company may have little or no knowledge of, and no control over, what the customer will be doing with its software product, and whether these activities will be particularly risky or risk free. Thus, limitation-of-liability provisions have the effect of making the customer take responsibility for ensuring that it has, among other things, adequate backup procedures and recovery plans. Indeed, if the particular software application is an extremely critical one, the customer may be led to implement a second, redundant system that can immediately be put into production if the main system goes down. Given these considerations, most customers do not object to most limitation-of-liability provisions.

Objections are raised, however, if the limitation-of-liability provision contains a complete exclusion of direct damages (as it does for consequential damages). This would mean that the software company is not responsible for any amount of damage suffered by the customer as a result of problems with the software. Except in unusual situations, such as Beta site licence arrangements discussed below, such a wholesale exclusion of damages is probably unreasonable. A typical compromise is to limit the direct damages to the amount of the licence fee for the software product paid by the customer to the software company. It can also be unreasonable to have the limitation-of-liability provision apply to the proprietary rights indemnity, inasmuch as the amount of risk posed by third-party infringement claims is generally within the control of the software company, and not the customer. Similarly, it is common for the limitation-of-liability provision not to affect recovery from the software company where it or its employees, as a result of negligence or wilful wrongdoing, cause physical injury or property damage to the customer's employees or premises, respectively, as again these actions are within the control of the software company (and should be covered by insurance). Finally, damages resulting from an unauthorized disclosure of the customer's confidential information by the software company usually are also not subject to a limitation of liability, particularly if no such limitation of liability would apply in the event the customer disclosed the software company's confidential material in an unauthorized manner.

It is increasingly common for customers to require that the contract's limitation-of-liability provision be made mutual, so that its benefits would apply to the customer as well as to the supplier. Such a request is usually acceptable to the software company, provided care is taken to exclude from the limitation any claim related to a breach by the customer of the agreement's confidentiality provisions or its licence terms, or for the customer's failure to pay any amounts when due under the agreement.

FUNDAMENTAL BREACH

It is very important, for the reasons discussed above, for a software company to include a warranty disclaimer and a limitation-of-liability provision in its licence (and other) agreements with customers. It is equally important, however, for a software company to understand that these clauses may be unenforceable in certain circumstances. Of particular relevance is the legal rule known as "fundamental breach," which holds that where a party to a contract has so failed to perform its obligations that the other party really has not received anything even approximating what it bargained for, and has therefore been deprived of the essential benefits it intended to receive, the defaulting party will not be entitled to rely on provisions in the contract that attempt to exclude or minimize its liability. This rule is ignored by software companies at their peril.

The rule of fundamental breach often comes into play when a software company is unable to deliver a specific software product that it had promised to a customer. For example, assume the customer has ordered a software product to be custom-developed, or has ordered a standard program that requires significant modification. In either case, if the delivered product is able to perform most of its required functions, including several deemed critical by the customer, but has some shortcomings that cause damage to the customer (e.g., the customer has to expend additional amounts to operate or fix the software), the warranty disclaimer and limitation-of-liability provisions in the contract should operate to shield the software company from exposure beyond the previously agreed limits. If, however, the product is woefully sub-standard, for example, or if it cannot be made to operate in any meaningful way, or particularly if it is not even delivered in the first place because the software company simply was unable to design or program it, then the rule of fundamental breach may operate to invalidate the provisions of the agreement that attempt to limit the liability of the software company. The software company would then be liable under general contract-law rules for all damages that reasonably could have been seen as resulting from the default of the software company. In other words, a software company should not rely blindly on the warranty disclaimer and the limitation-of-liability clause to extricate itself from a situation in which its standard of conduct falls significantly below that which the customer contracted for. Such provisions are useful, but they should not be seen as substitutes for adequate performance of contractual obligations.

The limitation-of-liability clause may also become unenforceable in other circumstances, such as if the software company were to make negligent, or even fraudulent, misrepresentations about a particular software product during the marketing phase of the product. Accordingly, software companies should carefully supervise the marketing practices used by their sales people, and their marketing statements, to ensure that any representations of their products are reasonable and responsible in all respects.

ARBITRATION

Many computer companies and customers provide in their software licence agreements that any disputes between them that cannot be settled amicably will be submitted to an arbitrator, or a panel of three arbitrators, where each party appoints one arbitrator and these two choose the neutral arbitrator, with a decision requiring at least a majority of the panel. Arbitration is a method for settling legal disputes that takes place outside the court system. There are several good reasons for choosing arbitration over the regular court system in the context of computer contracts.

First, because the parties can appoint the arbitrator(s), they can choose someone with particular technical or business expertise in the matter which is the subject of the dispute. For example, a highly regarded computer consultant might be chosen to settle a dispute over whether a certain software program has passed its acceptance test. In such a situation, a likely second advantage would be that the arbitrator, in addition to bringing superior technical expertise to bear on the problem, would probably be able to furnish a quicker decision than would normally result from the regular court system, given that in many Canadian cities today a lawsuit can take two years to come to trial. A further benefit of arbitration is that the software company and the customer can keep their dispute private, inasmuch as the material presented to the arbitrator need not be made public and the arbitration hearing itself can be held behind closed doors. This is in contrast to the regular judicial process where, generally speaking, the papers filed with the court are available to, and the court proceedings are open to, the public.

Arbitration is not, of course, a panacea. The parties have to pay for the fees and expenses of the arbitrator(s) and for the costs of any meeting rooms; the government pays for the judge and the courtroom for a regular court case. As well, while arbitrators may have technical expertise in computers, they probably do not have the same experience as judges in conducting hearings, weighing evidence, assessing the credibility of witnesses, and writing decisions; this means that the legal procedures that protect the parties to a lawsuit may not be as carefully followed in an arbitration. As well, arbitrators are often unable to make a tough decision; hence many arbitration decisions merely find a compromise between the parties' more extreme positions. For all these reasons, some software companies consciously refuse to employ the arbitration alternative, preferring instead the regular court system, or, more commonly, the threat of resort to the judicial system in order to bring about a consensual resolution to the dispute.

Notwithstanding the concerns with arbritration (which can be mitigated somewhat by appointing an arbitrator who has both legal training and experience in the computer industry), the benefits of arbitration have led many parties to use it in computer contracts (including software licences and especially in software development agreements) as a mechanism for resolving certain types of disputes, such as whether an acceptance test has been passed. At the same time, however, a software company should always reserve the right to use the courts, and particularly the judicial system's ability to grant interim relief, such as the interlocutory injunction and the Anton Piller order discussed at the end of Chapter 5, in cases where the customer or its employees and independent contractors seem to be abusing the software company's intellectual property rights or the licensing provisions of the contract.

It is worth noting that some software companies take seemingly aggressive self-help measures when they believe their customers are in breach of legal obligations. In a recent case, for example, a software developer, by remote access, reportedly disabled its software, which was being implemented on a customer's computer, because of a contract dispute, thereby causing the customer serious damages. This action prompted the customer to bring a lawsuit against the software developer on, among other grounds, the basis that the disabling of the software was an unreasonable measure, given the disproportionate damage it caused to the customer. One lesson from this case is that software companies should always consult with legal counsel before taking measures to enforce contractual or other obligations against customers.

SHRINKWRAP LICENCES

The above discussion concerning the protective provisions in a licence agreement in favour of the software company, as well as the provisions intended to limit the software company's liability, make it clear that a software company should strive to ensure that the licence agreement entered into by a customer is an enforceable document. To this end, it is always advisable to have a senior officer of the customer sign the licence agreement to ensure the customer's unequivocal agreement to be bound by its terms.

For certain software, however, such as mass-marketed software for the personal computer, it is often considered cumbersome or impractical to have the customer sign a licence agreement. Rather, a licence "statement" is included in the package containing the software and documentation. This licence typically contains the various provisions discussed above regarding the restrictions on the use, transfer, disclosure, and copying of the software, as well as clauses disclaiming any warranties or conditions and limiting the software company's liability. This licence also stipulates that the customer denotes its acceptance of the licence terms and conditions either by breaking open the package containing the software and/or by commencing to use the software. Such licences are often referred to as "shrinkwrap licences" because in many cases they are (and always should be) displayed to the prospective customer through the plastic wrapping surrounding the box containing the software. Moreover, in some cases the licence states that the prospective customer should read the licence statement even before paying for the software, and if the customer does not agree to be bound by the licence it should then not purchase it, or if it already has been purchased, it should be returned to the retailer who will provide the customer with a refund. This is a useful provision and should be included in all shrinkwrap licences.

There has always been some doubt as to the enforceability of shrinkwrap licences. Indeed, in a case in Alberta a judge held such a licence to be ineffective because it was not prominently displayed to the prospective customer at the time of purchase of the software, but rather was tucked away in the binder containing the documentation for the software, and therefore would likely have been seen for the first time only after the customer commenced using the software. Similarly, in several American cases such shrinkwrap licences have been found unenforceable. In a recent American appellate court decision a judge found otherwise; nonetheless, it is fair to say that in Canada the enforceability of these licence statements remains quite problematic. Accordingly, to help ensure the effectiveness of these sorts of licences, a software company should package its mass-marketed software in such a way that the licence agreement is clearly readable in its entirety at the retail point of purchase so that a customer can decide whether or not it wishes to agree to the terms before paying for the software. It is also a good idea to have any exclusion clauses, such as those relating to warranty disclaimer and limitation of liability, printed in bold, capital letters in a further effort to bring them to the attention of the prospective customer.

Notwithstanding these measures, there will still continue to be a degree of uncertainty as to the effectiveness of shrinkwrap licences in Canada until such time as a court in this country clearly upholds one. This may not be a big problem for certain types of software, given that even if the shrinkwrap licence were found to be unenforceable, the user of the software still could not make unauthorized, multiple production copies of the software to sell to others or even to use itself, as this right would remain with the software company. By the same token, however, if the shrinkwrap licence is not effective, the software company could not enforce its restrictions on use, transfer, or disclosure, and perhaps most importantly, the software company would not have the benefit of the agreement's warranty disclaimer and limitation of liability provisions. Accordingly, a software company marketing a program that could cause serious loss to a customer if it malfunctioned should not use a shrinkwrap licence, but rather should always have customers sign a licence agreement in order to be able to argue that the customer clearly agreed with the contract's limitation-of-liability mechanism for apportioning risk inherent in the use of the software.

EVALUATION LICENCES

Prospective customers will sometimes ask a software company if they can review a particular software product before deciding to purchase a licence for it. Such a "test drive" may be sensible from a marketing perspective, and some software companies permit prospective customers to have access to their software for a limited period of time on such an evaluation basis. Unfortunately, many software companies, when providing a prospective customer with a copy of their software for evaluation purposes, have the prospect sign a licence agreement only if, and after, it has decided to acquire a regular licence for it. This is a mistake.

What the software company should do is have the prospective customer sign a licence agreement at the time it takes delivery of the evaluation copy of the software. This contract will in all respects be the same as the software company's regular licence agreement, but it will address several additional points. First, it will have a specific date by which the software must be returned to the software company, unless by such date the customer indicates in writing that it has decided to take a standard licence and has paid the regular licence fee. As well, the evaluation licence agreement might provide that during the evaluation period the prospective customer cannot use the software to process data in a live, production mode; in other words, the scope of the licence is limited to evaluating the software. Apart from these additional provisions, the software company will want the regular restrictions on use, transfer, disclosure, and copying of the software, and the warranty disclaimer and limitation-of-liability provisions, to apply from the very moment a prospective customer first comes into possession of the software product. Thus, a software company should ensure that its software is never made available to anyone, even on an evaluation basis, without an appropriate licence agreement first being in place. Similarly, prospective customers should be required to sign proprietary rights protection agreements even before they receive a copy of the software, if the software company's marketing materials contain trade secrets or confidential information.

BETA-TEST LICENCES

Just as prospective customers sometimes wish to evaluate a software company's product, so too might a software company approach several existing customers to have them evaluate a new product that has been developed by the software company. Such an arrangement, commonly referred to as a "Beta test," is usually a standard phase in the development and testing of a new software product; the term "Beta test" can be contrasted with the prior "Alpha test," which is conducted internally by the software company. The Beta test is beneficial to the software company because it provides useful information necessary to fine-tune the software and to iron out any residual problems in it, while the customer conducting the Beta test appreciates the opportunity to get an early look at the software before most other prospective users.

A software company should make its software available for a Beta test only after the customer agrees to sign a Beta-test licence agreement. As with the evaluation licence agreement discussed above, the Beta-test licence will in many respects resemble the software company's standard software licence agreement, but it will be modified to deal with a number of additional issues. First, as part of its attempt to limit its liability, the software company should require, as with the evaluation licence noted above, that the customer not use the software to process its data in a live, production mode during the Beta test. As well, the Beta-test licence agreement should clearly stipulate, and the customer should acknowledge, that the software is still in a development stage, and that as such it could be full of errors, and that it is therefore provided "as is," without any warranties whatsoever. Indeed, the software company will want the customer to provide it with detailed reports of any problems with the software, often in a predetermined format, as receiving this feedback is probably the primary rationale for the software company entering into the Beta-test arrangement. In effect, as with the evaluation licence, no software product of the software company should be made available to a Beta-test site without the recipient first signing an appropriate licence for such purpose.

This chapter has covered certain key issues that are regularly addressed in a software licence. There are a number of other matters, some of which can be quite important in certain circumstances, that are not discussed here. Accordingly, each software company should have legal counsel experienced in computer-law matters draft its software licences. It is also a good idea to review these agreements periodically with legal counsel to ensure that they reflect any new changes in the law or computer-industry practice.

12

Other Agreements with Customers: Support, Software Development, Source-Code Escrow

In addition to the software licence agreement, the software company will usually enter into one or more other agreements with the customer. It is very common for the parties to conclude a support agreement under which the software company will perform certain specified services to keep the licensed software up-to-date and operating in good condition. If the software company is being asked to develop some new software for the customer, a software development agreement will be called for. And if the software company licenses only the object-code version of the particular software product to a customer, the customer may require the software company to deposit the source code for the product with a neutral, third-party escrow agent pursuant to an escrow agreement, under which the customer would be given access to the source code under certain conditions. This chapter discusses the major issues involved in these three types of agreements. Again, as with the previous chapter, the discussion takes a balanced approach between the interests of the software company and the customer.

SUPPORT AGREEMENTS

It is a fact of life that no software is error free. Regardless of how well software is designed or written, it will almost always contain some defects — or bugs, as these problems are called in computer jargon. While theoretically it may be possible to make perfect software, the cost of doing so would be prohibitive. It is for this reason that virtually all software companies offer their customers certain support services, the main one being to provide error-correction services whenever the customer experiences a bug in the software.

While it is unrealistic for customers to expect software not to have any errors in it, it is equally unreasonable for software companies to release to customers prematurely a software product that has, in addition to minor errors, major design and operational flaws that would have been detected through usual pre-release testing. In other words, software companies should be able to expect customers to put up with certain small problems on the understanding that they will be corrected under the support agreement; what software companies should not expect is that a customer will countenance the software company's complete redesigning or rewriting of the program as part of the error-correction services provided under the support agreement.

In addition to error-correction services, most software companies, as part of support, will provide to customers new releases of the licensed software. In today's highly competitive vendor environment, the software company that stands still, or merely rests on its past successes, is quickly overtaken by someone with a superior product. It is therefore the usual practice in the software business to add new features and improved performance to software products and to keep the new developments flowing to the customer under the support agreement.

A key consideration in a support agreement, from the perspective of both the software company and the customer, is to define with precision the nature of the services to be provided by the former to the latter. With respect to error correction, for example, a software company must usually reject a customer's request that the software company ensure that any error, or even just those that cause a major problem, will be corrected within a certain period of time (usually measured in hours, rather than days). Except in extremely rare circumstances, this type of request is unreasonable, given that it is virtually impossible to predict how long it will take to fix a certain software problem. In certain hardware environments, such as personal computers, maintenance performance levels can sometimes be specifically enumerated in terms of requiring full problem resolution in so many hours because the problematic part can merely be replaced. It is not so simple or straightforward for software, and the most that the vast majority of software companies can agree to is only to be able to start the error-correction service within a certain number of hours of a customer's call — they cannot usually guarantee in advance how long the job will take.

With respect to the provision of new releases, again the software company should be vigilant against promising too much. The support agreement should stipulate that the software company will make available to the customer, as part of support services, only those new releases that the software company generally makes available as part of support services. While this phrasing sounds a little circuitous, its intent is to permit the software company to release a new product as just that, and to be able to charge existing customers an additional licence fee for it (if they wish to use it), rather than having to provide absolutely every new product to the existing customer base under the much less remunerative support fee, even though the new product may have little to do with the previously licensed software. In short, the software company must use some discretion in classifying and marketing its products, and it should be careful to avoid entering into support obligations that greatly fetter its freedom.

This raises the important point that the support agreement should state clearly what is not included as a support obligation. For example, in respect of error correction, the agreement should stipulate that custom software development is outside the scope of support services, and if it is requested by the customer and the software company decides to provide it, it will be subject to additional charges. The same point should be made for any education or training services provided in addition to any mentioned in the software licence agreement.

With respect to the issue of what might not be included as support services, it is quite common for a software company to stipulate that the basic error-correction service — the one paid for by the regular support fee — does not cover services necessitated by any modifications made to the software by the customer. Indeed, some software companies insist on being able to terminate support services if modifications are made to the software by anyone other than the software company. Such a provision addresses the software company's concern that as soon as a third party, or even the customer, begins to make modifications to the software that are not approved in advance by the software company, the software, even perhaps its unmodified portions, will likely become more difficult to support for the staff of the software company, who are used to dealing with only their own handiwork.

Some software companies will require customers to implement all new releases of the software so that their staff have to work on only one version of the software. Some customers object to such a provision because they wish to have the flexibility of staying with a previous version of the software if, for example, they have become very comfortable with it and if they are not interested in utilizing the new features contained in the latest version. In such a case the solution is often to have the software company agree to provide error-correction services for the old software, but on a time-and-materials basis rather than under the regular support fee.

A final point worth noting is that the warranty disclaimers and limitations-of-liability provisions discussed in Chapter 11 should be included in support agreements also. Indeed, what this requirement often means to software companies is that, rather than having separate support agreements, they merely include the operative support provisions relating to error correction, new releases, exclusions from support services, etc., in the licence agreement, or perhaps attach these support provisions as a schedule to the licence agreement, with the schedule and the licence agreement clearly indicating that the support services are made available on the basis of the other terms of the licence agreement. Combining the support and licence agreements in this way can significantly reduce the amount of paperwork that the software company presents to customers — a result that should be welcomed by both parties.

SOFTWARE DEVELOPMENT AGREEMENTS

Probably the riskiest of all relationships between a software company and a customer is the one involving the development of custom software by the former for the latter. So many things can go wrong in a custom software development project. The customer can misunderstand its own needs, and even if it understands them it can convey them inaccurately to the software company. As a result, the custom software may be inadequate for the required task. Or the program may be designed or programmed under time constraints that do not permit all of its bugs to be ironed out, resulting in frequent malfunctioning. Given these and other risks with custom software, software companies are well advised to encourage customers, as far as is reasonably possible, to utilize the standard products of the software company, even if this means making some modifications in the customer's business procedures. In other words, it may be easier, and less expensive, to change a certain method or practice in the operations of the customer than to modify the software, or to develop some from scratch, to accommodate such unusual business methods or practices.

Indeed, at least one software company strongly discourages customers from requesting custom changes to its standard software by expressly bringing to light the potentially extensive costs involved in maintaining custom software (in addition to the expense of creating it in the first place). This software company, in its standard-form software licence agreement, states that while the software company will perform custom modifications to its basic software, the customer should realize the following:

1. The software company will provide support for the custom software only on a time-and-materials basis because the standard maintenance fees cover only the standard base software.

2. The software company's telephone hotline service cannot answer questions concerning the modifications because the staff performing this service are knowledgeable about the base software only; a telephone request regarding modifications would be routed to that customer's account manager, who would deal with the request on a time-and-materials basis. Again, this service is not included in the general support fee, while telephone support for the base software is.

3. It is the customer's responsibility to provide documentation and training for the custom software; the software company provides these for the base package only.

4. The expense of refitting the custom software to new releases of the base software will be borne by the customer. "Fix tapes," which contain software corrections to reported problems and minor enhancements between new releases, cannot be implemented automatically in situations where the base package has been modified; these fixes have to be entered manually, again at the customer's additional expense.

5. Finally, this software company admits that the performance of the base software may be affected negatively by the custom changes.

While not all software companies are as forthright about their concerns with custom modifications, at least with major ones, in most cases some or all of these additional costs and inconveniences arise when changes or additions are made to standard software.

If, after all due consideration, it is decided that custom software is really the only solution to a particular problem, then the software company should ensure that the scope of the project is clearly set out in a document, often called the "functional specifications," which describes in detail what the custom software is to do. This is a critical document because it will be the basis for the further steps in the project, such as the development of a second specification, often called the "system design specifications," which describes how the custom software will perform the tasks described in the functional specifications. The functional specifications will also likely have a major impact on the actual coding of the software and will probably serve as a key benchmark for determining whether the acceptance test for the custom software is passed. It is therefore important to attach to the software development agreement a detailed schedule containing the functional specifications.

It is only with a satisfactory functional specifications document that has been approved by the customer (as would be the case when it is attached as a schedule to the software development contract) that the software company should consider undertaking a custom software development project for a fixed price. Without such a document defining the scope of the project, how can a software company know with any confidence how much it will ultimately cost? Where such a document is not available, the software company and the customer should seriously consider entering into a time-and-materials consulting contract to develop the functional specifications rather than rushing into a fixed price contract, the first deliverable of which would be this document.

Even where the functional specifications form part of the contract from the outset, there should be in every software development agreement a provision that sets out the process by which changes can be made to the functional specifications, if any are requested by the customer. An effective process would entail the customer's delivering a written request to the software company (for example, the customer decides after signing the contract that it also wants the custom inventory control software to include a daily reporting feature which was not previously contemplated). The software company must then respond to this request within a certain period, stating the cost (including additional support fees, if any) of the additional feature, its impact on the project's implementation schedule, and its impact (if any) on the performance of the software overall. After receiving this reply, the customer must decide whether the various aspects of the modification are acceptable, and if they are, then the contract would provide that, upon acceptance of the change, the other parts of the agreement affected by the change will be deemed to be modified accordingly. The objective of such a procedure is to provide for a disciplined yet flexible system for changing the scope of a software development project in mid-stream, an activity that can be very dangerous if it is not thought through and documented properly.

It should be noted that the foregoing discussion is premised on the existence of what is often called the "cascading" approach to software development; that is, different stages of the software — from functional specifications to design specifications, software coding, delivery, testing and acceptance — follow one another in an orderly, "cascading" (i.e., linear) progression, and that it is therefore enough to set up contract "control check points" at each of these stages to ensure customer sign-off and supplier performance. This model of software development is still very much in use.

Such a linear approach, however, is not found in many newer computer programming environments. Instead, the process of creating software is more iterative, or spiral-like; that is, a particular module of the overall system may be at the prototyping and test stage, while other modules are not yet designed, and still other modules are at various stages in between. In such an environment, software suppliers should be extremely leery about agreeing to fixed price contracts, since the complete scope of the project and the commensurate effort required of the supplier frequently cannot be determined in advance. This is particularly true where the customer is looking for a unique technological solution, one which has never been built before.

In these situations it sometimes makes great sense to break up the overall project into smaller constituent elements, and allow the customer to review its decision to move forward with the project at various intervals, if it discovers certain cost estimates are being significantly exceeded. As well, in these large, complex projects it is imperative that the software developer enumerate clearly the type and amount of resources the customer will be required to devote to the project, particularly in terms of user representatives from the various departments or areas that will ultimately deploy the software. Increasingly, in these large-scale software development exercises the relationship between supplier and user is almost that of partners or joint venturers, as opposed to the traditional "active supplier" and "passive user" model.

A key issue that often arises in custom software development projects is which party, the software company or the customer, should own the intellectual property rights (including copyright) in the custom software. To the software company, the answer to this question is very clear — it must own it, because if it does not, it cannot amortize the cost of the development effort over other users of the software, and therefore the customer will be charged a much higher fee for the custom development work. Moreover, if a single customer owns any custom-developed software, the software company may find it quite difficult to quickly bring competitive software to another customer or the marketplace generally, given that the developer will not be able to reuse the copyrights and trade secrets that form part of the initial custom work. This could result in the software company foregoing significant business opportunities.

Of course, while insisting on retaining ownership of the intellectual property rights in any custom software, the software company should be ready to respond to the reasonable concerns of the customer regarding custom software. These are essentially twofold. First, and this is usually the major concern, the customer does not want to see the particular custom software made available to its competitors, at least for a long enough period so that it can derive the maximum competitive edge from the custom software. Second, the customer feels that the software company should not be able to reap the economic rewards of marketing the custom software to others if the customer paid the lion's share of the development costs.

Except in rare circumstances, a software company should not address these issues by giving the customer ownership of the intellectual property rights in the custom software. Rather, to meet the concern about competitors of the customer being given access to the custom software, the software company could provide the customer with an exclusivity undertaking whereby, for a period of some months — but generally not exceeding one year — the software company would not make the custom software available to the competitors of the customer. This marketing restriction should be limited to the country or other geographic area in which the customer actively conducts business, so that the software company can market the new software in other countries from the outset. To address the second concern of the customer, the software developer might agree that after this exclusivity period, if the software company does make the custom software available to a third party, the developer will reimburse the customer, out of the licence fees received by the developer for the custom software, a certain percentage of the customer's development fees, perhaps as a credit against ongoing support fees. In short, without acquiring ownership of the custom software, the customer nevertheless achieves its goals, and the software developer is also satisfied.

SOURCE-CODE ESCROW AGREEMENTS

In Chapter 11 it was mentioned that most software companies make available to customers only the object-code versions of their software, rather than the source code, which contains a detailed description of how the software is structured and organized. This is so because software companies want to minimize the disclosure of their extremely valuable trade secrets and other proprietary information, of which the source code is a prime repository. By the same token, however, customers who license the object code of software want some assurance that, if the software company goes bankrupt or otherwise ceases to support the product, the customer will be able to have access to its source code in order to continue to correct any errors in the software used by the customer, or to be able to modify it.

In order to meet these dual objectives, the software company and the customer often enter into a source-code escrow agreement with a neutral third party, the escrow agent, whereby the software company agrees to deposit the source code with the escrow agent. Under the agreement, the software company agrees that upon the occurrence of certain events, such as the inability of the software company to provide error-correction services to the customer within a certain period of time after being requested to do so, the customer shall be entitled to receive a copy of the source code from the escrow agent and to use it on a licensed basis for the sole purpose of supporting the object-code version of the program. The escrow agreement serves the security needs of the customer by assuring that it has access to the source code if the software company is unable to provide appropriate, agreed-upon service to the customer. At the same time, it meets the need of the software company by keeping the source code out of the possession of the customer until such time as the software company is in default of its contractual obligations to deliver support services.

The source-code escrow agreement will normally deal with the following three issues, which are of some concern to customers, and often these issues are inadequately dealt with in the standard escrow agreements developed by software companies. Rather than spend a lot of time negotiating these points, it is probably wise to simply have them dealt with appropriately in the standard form agreement. First, the definition of "source code" in the agreement should be defined in terms of function rather than by reference to jargon. That is, what is deposited with the escrow agent should include whatever source code and other documentation (including third party tools or utilities if appropriate, unless they are readily commercially available) the software company itself would use to provide support services for the customer's version of the software. The agreement should also stipulate that whenever the customer is provided with a new release, or a major update, of the software, the corresponding source code (and related materials, if any) will be deposited with the escrow agent at the same time. This updating exercise is very important to the customer inasmuch as without it the whole escrow exercise could become useless very quickly if the materials deposited in escrow did not always correspond to the software being used by the customer.

A third issue involves verification of the source code. It is reasonable for the customer to request the right to periodically review what is held by the escrow agent to ensure that it in fact corresponds to the software being used by the customer. A typical procedure would operate as follows. The customer gives notice to the escrow agent and the software company that it wishes to verify the source code. At a mutually agreed-upon time, a representative of the escrow agent delivers the source code materials to the premises of the customer, where a representative of the software company is also in attendance. Under the supervision of this representative, and likely with this person's assistance, the customer then proceeds to compile the source code on its computer system and to take the other steps deemed necessary to verify the source code. Upon completion of this procedure, the representative of the software company ensures that all elements of the source code are deleted from the customer's computer; the source code materials are then returned to the premises of the escrow agent.

The choice of escrow agent can be important. Some software companies use their law firms or accountants to act as escrow agents. These are not good choices because they invariably put these providers of professional services to the software company in an untenable conflict of interest situation. This is particularly the case where the software company, for example, wishes to dispute a customer's claim that it is entitled to the source code. If the software company's lawyer is holding the source code as an escrow agent, it will likely be precluded from acting for the software company in respect of such a claim — this is, therefore, also a strong reason for lawyers to refuse to accept appointments as escrow agents when asked to do so! A more neutral choice for escrow agent is one of the number of specialty companies in both Canada and the U.S. which focuses on providing source code escrow services.

Some customers demand that they be their own escrow agent by requesting that the source code be held not by a third party, but by a department within the customer's organization unrelated to the group using the software company's product. For example, where the customer has a large data-processing division, the in-house legal counsel for the customer might be designated to hold the source code under a so-called source-code access agreement; in fact, it is not an "escrow" agreement as there is no neutral third party to serve as the disinterested repository of the source code. The software company should point out how dangerous such an arrangement is, from the point of view of the customer, given that it is rife with conflicts of interest, and some software companies may feel so strongly about the dangers inherent in such an arrangement that they simply refuse to agree to it.

Many software companies, however, particularly some smaller ones, may not be in a position to walk away from a potential customer for this reason, however reluctant they may be to have the customer serve, in effect, as its own escrow agent. In such a case, the software company should ensure that the source-code access agreement contains a provision requiring the recipient to keep a detailed log of all access made to the source code, and the software company should be fully indemnified for any loss that may arise from premature or unauthorized access to the source code. In addition, the software company may require that the source-code access agreement, and the main software licence agreement, stipulate that unauthorized access to the source code by the customer shall entitle the software company to terminate the licence for the underlying software, irrespective of whether any quantifiable harm has been suffered by the software company. This is one of the few practical means by which the software company can deter the customer from prematurely accessing the source code.

This chapter has offered a general discussion of some key issues involved in support, software development, and source-code escrow agreements. Software companies should retain legal counsel experienced in computer-law matters when drafting or negotiating their own versions of these contracts.

13

Agreements with Distributors

$\mathbf{A}$ software company can supply its products to end users directly or through a third party. A mature, financially healthy software company may decide to distribute its products itself in all markets, domestic and foreign, in order to control all aspects of the marketing of the products, including the prices at which they are licensed to end users. Similarly, if the software product is a complicated one implemented in, say, a mainframe environment, and therefore requires significant pre-sales advice and post-sales customization and service, the software company may decide that it does not wish to permit any other party to be involved in the marketing or installation of the product for fear that end users will receive inadequate service, with the reputation of the product thereby becoming tarnished.

In many other situations, however, the appointment of distributors to promote, market, and service a software company's products makes eminent good sense. The product may require little or no maintenance once it is installed, or if it requires support, the distributor may be able to provide routine support relatively easily, with the software company perhaps acting as a backup for any really difficult problems. More importantly, the software company may have no other choice but to appoint distributors in certain territories if the product is to be marketed there at all.

For example, assume a Canadian software company has just completed the development of a powerful product intended to be used by banks and other financial institutions. The product is starting to find a number of licensees in Canada and to spark serious interest in the United States. The software company believes that it can handle directly from its base in Canada all marketing and service for North America. This is no simple task, and already the financial and human resources of the company are being stretched to the limit. Its product, however, is proving to be quite a success, and several financial institutions located in Europe have asked to evaluate the product. The software company is presented with a difficult choice. Does it attempt to establish a branch office or subsidiary in Europe, or should it explore the possibility of having someone already in the software business in Europe distribute the product in that part of the world?

In fact, the decision may be made for the software company by the simple reality that it just cannot afford, at this stage of its development, to tackle the European market directly. At the same time, however, it wants its new product distributed as widely and as quickly as possible before competitors come on the scene with products aimed at the same market. In short, to take advantage of the product's narrow marketing window of opportunity — given that most versions of a software product have quite a short shelf life — the software company decides it will have someone in Europe act as its distributor.

The desire to license a software product into foreign countries, or even more distant parts of a software company's own country, when the software company is unable to do so directly is not the only reason for appointing distributors. The particular software product may be able to be used in a number of quite different environments, and the software company may decide to appoint distributors for one or more specific vertical markets. For example, a distributor with its own software products that services the retail sector may be given distribution rights to a product that complements its own, but only for purposes of marketing it to end users in the retailing industry. In this way the software company hopes to achieve faster penetration of the overall market than if it tried to license the product directly to all potential customers.

The appointment of a distributor should be preceded by careful planning and review on the part of the software company. The distributor will be granted numerous rights, often on an exclusive basis, in respect of the particular software product (or products) for a certain territory or a vertical market. If the relationship is successful, both sides should benefit handsomely. If, however, the distributor does not live up to the software company's expectations, or vice versa, the software company can get into serious trouble as it may be difficult (and sometimes impossible) to switch distributors on short notice. Accordingly, the issues discussed in this chapter should be carefully scrutinized by the parties contemplating entering into a software-distribution relationship, with the assistance of legal counsel, and then addressed in a written distribution agreement.

DESCRIPTION OF DISTRIBUTED PRODUCTS

The distribution agreement should describe with precision the product (or products) for which the distributor will receive the various marketing rights. This seems like a straightforward task, but there can be complicating nuances. For example, it should be clarified whether the distributor is entitled to distribute the source code for the computer program, or just its object-code version (this distinction is explained in Chapter 11). It may also be appropriate to stipulate what hardware environment the software product is intended for or perhaps restricted to if, for instance, the software company wants the distributor to market the product only to certain types of customers.

The distribution agreement should also address whether the distributor is entitled to market subsequent versions or releases of the software product. Some agreements even provide the distributor with an option to obtain the marketing rights to new products of the software company that are related to or perhaps functionally interconnected with the initial product being distributed. This is usually done by granting the distributor a "right of first refusal" whereby it can match the offer proposed by any other potential distributor for the particular follow-on product. By contrast, some agreements that grant marketing rights to multiple products may provide that the software company can delete a product from the agreement if the software company itself decides to discontinue developing, licensing, or supporting the product. In essence, there are many issues relevant to describing the particular products (and possibly future products) that will be the subject of the distribution agreement; the parties have to make sure that these issues are reviewed thoroughly, and then the agreements on these points should be accurately recorded in the distribution agreement.

If the software company's product contains third party software — for example, it requires a specific database program in order to operate — then the issue arises as to whose responsibility it is to procure the relevant licence for each copy of the database program. At least three scenarios are possible: the software company acquires the rights to embed a copy of the database program in each copy of the application program; the distributor is expressly given the responsibility of obtaining copies of the underlying database software; or the distributor in turn requires the end users to do this. Each approach has its advantages and disadvantages; the key is to make sure the distribution agreement clearly articulates which approach is chosen, so that the parties to the agreement understand who is responsible for what activity.

DEFINING THE TERRITORY

Distribution rights are usually granted for a certain geographic area. While some agreements permit the distributor to market the product throughout the world, most of them grant rights for only some specified smaller area, such as one or more countries, or perhaps a certain region within a larger country. When rights are granted for some specific area, it is extremely important to define precisely the boundaries of the distributor's territory. For instance, if a Canadian software company were dividing up the continental United States among five different U.S. distributors for a particular product, it should not define the various territories in terms such as "Northeastern U.S." (or "New England") and "Midwestern U.S."; rather, the specific states belonging to each distributor's territory should be enumerated in each respective agreement.

Another example of this point arises when Canadian software companies are granting rights to the Asian market. Often a distributor will be granted the marketing rights to all of Asia, and the territory will be defined as such, namely, "Asia." This can lead to misunderstandings because one person's understanding of where Asia begins and ends may be different from another's. For instance, is Australia included in Asia? To remove any doubt, the names of the actual countries intended to be included in the territory should be listed. Or better still, a map could be attached to the distribution agreement that shows clearly the relevant territory by outlining it in coloured ink. This has an advantage over listing the countries because it is easy to miss a country or two in certain parts of the world when compiling such a list. The approach of outlining countries on a map also provides greater certainty for the future if any country in the distributor's territory changes its name, a relatively frequent occurrence in Asia, for example, over the past few decades. These considerations — and the suggestion of indicating the relevant territory by outlining it on a map — are also germane to other parts of the world, such as the Caribbean.

In determining whether to permit a distributor to market a product in a certain country, the software company should ascertain whether there is adequate intellectual property protection for the software in the intended country. A number of countries, such as the United States, Australia, the United Kingdom, and most other OECD countries provide, like Canada, substantive protection for software under their copyright and trade-secret laws (and in some cases Patent laws as well). Many of these countries also provide, like Canada, adequate procedural protection by permitting the owners of intellectual property rights to obtain, among other things, interim injunctions and similar remedies under certain circumstances where intellectual property rights are being infringed.

Many countries, however, do not provide these substantive and/or procedural protections, and in these cases the software company has to seriously consider whether it is willing to run the attendant risk of having its software marketed in such a jurisdiction. Fortunately, a number of countries with currently substandard levels of legal protection for software are working at improving their laws in this regard. Thus, a distribution agreement might provide that while the territory initially comprises just a few countries in, say, Asia (or the area outlined as "Asia" on a map attached to the agreement), certain other countries in the region may be added to the distributor's territory at the request of the distributor, but only after the software company receives an opinion from legal counsel in the proposed country to the effect that suitable substantive and procedural protection exists for software in such country.

DEGREE OF EXCLUSIVITY

It is extremely important to address in the distribution agreement what degree of exclusivity, if any, the distributor is to be given in respect of the marketing of the particular product. Many other matters that define the relationship between the software company and the distributor will be determined by the degree of exclusivity granted to the distributor. For example, if the distributor is granted "exclusive" distribution rights such that no other entity, not even the software company, can market the product in the distributor's territory, then the distributor should be inclined to devote greater financial and human resources to the marketing of the product because it does not have to worry about other distributors free-riding on its marketing efforts (e.g., one nonexclusive distributor's sale is "stolen" by another distributor because of the latter's lower price, even though all the preliminary advertising and sales work was performed by the former distributor). Similarly, an exclusive distributor should be more willing to establish a service and support capability if it knows that it will be able to recoup these expenses more readily by capturing all the sales of the product in the distributor's territory.

While these performance factors on the part of an exclusive distributor are equally attractive to a software company, an exclusive appointment also means that the software company must choose its exclusive distributor with great care, for if the distributor turns out to be less capable than anticipated, the software company cannot merely immediately appoint another distributor or commence marketing directly. Thus, a mutually beneficial trade-off is usually arrived at whereby the distributor is granted exclusive rights, but these rights can be terminated before the end of the normal term of the agreement if the distributor does not meet certain performance milestones, the primary one being the obligation to pay a certain amount of royalties to the software company during each successive specified period (say, during each 12-month period of the agreement). In essence, the distributor is given exclusive rights for the particular market while it is doing well, but, if it falters, the software company can establish a new distribution arrangement or a direct sales strategy for the relevant territory.

Some distributors request a provision to the effect that if there is a shortfall in royalties for a particular period, the distributor can simply pay the amount of the shortfall as a lump-sum cash payment if it wishes to keep alive its exclusive distribution rights. Many software companies will agree to such a "top-up" clause, although some only on the basis that the top-up payment cannot exceed a certain amount. This is done to ensure that the top-up does not come to replace the overriding requirement for the distributor to actually license a sufficient number of copies of the products of the software company, and thereby build a customer base that the software company will likely eventually profit from directly (as well as indirectly while the customers are being serviced by the distributor).

A distributor will often also request that the distribution agreement provide that if the distributor does not meet the annual (or other periodic) royalty payment requirement, it will lose its status merely as the exclusive distributor, but will retain a nonexclusive distribution right for the product. While this might seem a reasonable request at first blush, on reflection its adverse impact on the software company becomes apparent. If the software company allows its original distributor to remain in the territory on a nonexclusive basis, the software company forfeits the option of appointing a new distributor on an exclusive basis, something that may be required to attract a top-notch distributor. Accordingly, a software company should be extremely cautious about granting nonexclusive distribution rights at any time because such a grant may severely restrict the company's future distribution options.

TERM OF AGREEMENT

An issue similar to the one noted immediately above arises with respect to the term of the distribution agreement. Generally speaking, the distributor will request a longer term, perhaps five or more years, so that it can have sufficient time to recoup its investment in the marketing of the product. This is particularly likely if the distributor will be required to expend significant financial or human resources customizing the product for the particular territory for which it is granted distribution rights, as is often the case. By contrast, the software company will usually want a shorter term, often only one year, so that if it is not satisfied with the distributor for any reason it can bring the relationship to an end simply by not renewing the distribution agreement.

The middle ground often arrived at between distributors and software companies is to provide for a longer term, perhaps three to five years, coupled with a provision that stipulates that if certain performance criteria are not maintained during each year of the contract, such as certain predetermined minimum royalty payments not being achieved annually, then the software company can cause the early termination of the agreement. With such an arrangement the distribution agreement is effectively a one-year contract capable of being renewed for several successive one-year periods at the option of the distributor if it maintains certain performance levels.

OBLIGATIONS OF THE SOFTWARE COMPANY

The distribution agreement should spell out clearly the obligations of both the software company and the distributor. With respect to the former, the most important provisions will be the ones already mentioned in this chapter, namely, that the software company grant certain marketing rights to the distributor for certain products, including related trade-marks (if appropriate), on either an exclusive or a nonexclusive basis for a specified period of time in a stipulated geographic territory and/or industry-based market segment. There are other obligations, however, that a distributor will often require a software company to perform during the relationship, two of which are worth mentioning.

A critical question involves software support and other maintenance requirements. Who is to perform these tasks for end users, the software company, the distributor, or both to some degree? Or, put another way, which of these two will sign the support and maintenance agreement with end users? There are many different ways a division of labour can be arrived at on this issue, and much will depend on the nature of the product and the level of sophistication of the distributor and/or the expected end users. For instance, in situations involving many of the more complex software products that operate on, say, large mainframe computers, the distributor (assuming it has the required technical staff) will look upon support and maintenance revenues as an extremely lucrative revenue source, in which case the role of the software company may be confined to intermittent backup of the distributor on particularly difficult problems.

In other cases the distributor may wish to have nothing or very little to do with support, particularly in the case of certain software for personal computers, in which case the software company might be solely responsible for correcting defects experienced by end users. As with most other aspects of the distributor relationship, there is no "industry standard" for such matters; the objective, rather, is to come to an understanding in the distribution agreement that makes sense to both sides — and that will be attractive to the end users of the product. Indeed, in some cases the support function will be shared, with the distributor providing software error-correction services to its customers, but at the same time passing on to them new releases of the software product developed by the software company.

One obligation that the distributor invariably will require of the software company is a proprietary rights indemnity very similar, if not virtually identical, to the one described in Chapter 11 (under "Warranty and Warranty Disclaimers") in respect of end-user licenses. In other words, the distributor will wish to have the software company indemnify the distributor (and its end-user licensees) for costs and damages awarded by a court that may arise from a third party's claiming to be the rightful owner of the intellectual property in the particular software product that it is distributing; most of the comments noted in Chapter 11 in respect of proprietary rights indemnity provisions apply equally to this indemnity for a distributor.

OBLIGATIONS OF THE DISTRIBUTOR

The distribution agreement will require the distributor to undertake a number of obligations. A key one is the payment of royalties, and this is such a critical item that it is dealt with separately in the next section. Apart from royalties, the other major issue to address in the distribution agreement is to determine what level of promotional, advertising, and marketing activity will be required of the distributor.

In this regard, many distribution agreements contain a provision that stipulates that the distributor will use "best efforts," or "reasonable efforts" (sometimes the confusing amalgam of "reasonable best efforts" is used, improperly it might be added), to market the software company's product. While the first two of these three phrases serve a limited purpose, it is far preferable to set out objectively ascertainable criteria for determining when a distributor is living up to the expectations of the software company. This might involve specifying that the distributor must employ or expend certain resources in its marketing effort, such as a certain number of staff or a certain amount of money or a combination of the two. This approach, however, has the disadvantage of requiring the software company to engage in some detailed monitoring of the distributor's business practices, an activity that is probably as bothersome or even onerous to the software company as it is offensive to the distributor (which believes that it should be able to run its operation as it pleases as long as it meets the annual royalty quotas).

Accordingly, many software companies set performance levels in two ways. First, the mechanism of a minimum royalty required to be paid by the distributor for each stated period (usually of 12 months duration), as noted above, is used to indicate the financial target that the distributor must meet if it wishes to continue to exercise distribution rights for the particular product. How the distributor meets this target is the business of the distributor. This criterion has the benefit of being simple and easy to measure: either the software company has received the stipulated amount of royalties or it has not.

The second means to ensure performance is a provision that prohibits the distributor from developing or marketing any software that is competitive with the software company's product during the term of the distribution agreement. Such a requirement, which may not be appropriate in all cases (say, where the distributor is marketing relatively straightforward software applications for personal computers, as opposed to highly complex mainframe software), has the effect of ensuring that the distributor does not divide its attention, in respect of a particular geographic or industry-based market, among products that compete with one another. This alone may not guarantee that the distributor meets the royalty minimums required of it, but it will ensure that any failure on this score is not due to the distributor's being distracted by a competing product. Before such an exclusivity clause is implemented, however, the software company should review the various sections of the *Competition Act* that may apply to it (see Chapter 9, particularly the section entitled "Exclusive Dealing, Market Restriction, and Tied Selling"), but in most cases such a provision will not be anti-competitive, unless the software company controls a significant share of the relevant market; indeed, in most cases such a prohibition on carrying competing products is generally pro-competitive in that a new software product will be more likely to be introduced successfully into the market with the full, unflagging support of its distributor.

The restriction on a distributor's carrying a competitive product, particularly in the context of a complex mainframe product, can also be important from the perspective of protecting the proprietary rights of the software company. This raises a major problem that is quite common between software companies and their distributors, namely, that soon after the end of the term of the distribution agreement, and sometimes even sooner where the distributor is not prohibited from handling a competing product, the distributor appears in the marketplace with "its own" product and commences to compete against the product for which it was formerly a distributor.

Some software companies try to guard against this by extracting an undertaking from the distributor not to market a competitive product for a certain period of time after the termination of the distribution agreement. Such a provision is rarely accepted by distributors. It is much more common to secure an acknowledgement by the distributor that it will acquire no intellectual property rights in the software company's product. Armed with such a provision, if the distributor's new product infringes, for example, the copyright of the software company, the latter will be able to bring an intellectual property claim against the former. It should be understood, however, that there may be numerous aspects of the software company's program that are not protected by copyright, trade-secret law, or otherwise. A software company should therefore recognize that, except in unusual situations where the distributor is willing to abide by quite extraordinary restrictions, there is always the risk that the distributor will gain a certain head start in competing against the software company after the termination of the distribution agreement. By the same token, distributors also have to realize that if they market another company's software product, it may be very difficult for them to develop a program to serve the same function that they can call their own (i.e., that does not infringe the other company's intellectual property rights), but employing a "clean-room" approach to software development (discussed in Chapter 5 under "Creation of Competitive Software") may assist in this regard.

In order to protect its intellectual property rights to the fullest extent possible, it may be appropriate for the software company to require that the employees and independent contractors of the distributor also sign proprietary rights protection agreements directly with the software company, particularly if these individuals are to be given access to the source code of the software company's product. In a similar vein, the software company will want to ensure that the distributor implements adequate proprietary rights protection with the end users to whom the distributor sub-licenses the product. This is generally done by having the distributor agree, in the distribution agreement, that before it gives any such end user access to the product, it will have the end user (and its staff if necessary) execute a licence agreement that has been approved by the software company.

A prudent approach in this regard, from the perspective of the software company, is to actually attach to the distribution agreement a copy of the approved end-user agreement so there is no question what it must contain. The distributor would then be required to obtain the approval of the software company if it wished to make any changes to certain sections of the end-user agreement. These sections would include the nondisclosure provisions, for sure, but they should also include the provisions of the agreement that disclaim certain warranties and that limit the liability of the licensor of the software and its supplier (namely, the software company). A variation on this approach is to set out in the distribution agreement the several such provisions that must be included in every end-user agreement entered into by the distributor. In short, the software company must provide for some means by which it ensures that the distributor licenses the product under appropriate contractual arrangements.

This is important not only in order to attempt to shield the software company from liability arising from the customers of the distributor. The other reason for ensuring that adequate contracts are signed by the distributor with its customers is that the software company, upon a default of the distributor, or upon the expiry of the distribution agreement, may be required to (or may wish to even if it does not have to) assume the licence agreements, and possibly the maintenance agreements, entered into by the distributor. Thus, it makes sense for the software company to take steps to control, to a certain degree, the form and especially the content of these agreements.

ROYALTIES

A key obligation on the part of the distributor will of course be to pay royalties to the software company in consideration for the right to distribute the software company's products. The royalty is usually some percentage of the licence fees received by the distributor from end users in respect of the product. Or the royalty can be a set dollar amount for each licence for the product granted by the distributor to end users. It is often useful to provide for a royalty structure that includes both of these mechanisms, namely, that the royalty will be the greater of (a) a certain percentage of the license fees received by the distributor and (b) a specific dollar amount. This approach offers the best protection to a software company, for a number of reasons.

The percentage-based first prong of the dual formula royalty structure ensures that the software company will share in any increase in the prices charged by the distributor for the product over time. By the same token, however, if the percentage royalty is the only remuneration formula, then the distributor may try to take advantage of the software company by setting the licence fee for the software company's product very low, and making up the difference in the installation, support, or other nonlicence fees charged to the customer which the distributor does not have to share with the software company. Or the distributor may use the software company's product as a "loss-leader," marketing it at a relatively low price as long as the customer acquires a licence to one or more other products of the distributor, at perhaps inflated prices, with such other products again producing no revenue for the software company. For these reasons it is a good idea to build a minimum royalty amount into the royalty structure, which is the purpose served by the set dollar amount. With such a minimum the distributor can still determine its own prices for licences as it sees fit, but even if they are set quite low the software company will still receive a reasonable minimum royalty rather than what might be an unreasonably low amount if the software company were to receive only a percentage of the distributor's licence fees.

In this regard it is also worth repeating a very important point first made in Chapter 9 regarding Canada's *Competition Act*. It is a criminal offence for a software company to dictate what the distributor will charge as licence fees for the software company's product. This rule in the *Competition Act* is very vigorously enforced and companies often run afoul of it. The most that a software company can do is to suggest a resale price, but if it does so it must make it clear to the distributor, preferably in writing in the distribution agreement, that there will be no untoward impact on the parties' business relations if the distributor does not follow the suggested prices. Indeed, the inability to set a distributor's minimum resale prices leads some software developers not to use distributors but rather to employ representatives, an option discussed at the end of this chapter. For a further discussion of this critical provision in the *Competition Act*, see "Resale Price Maintenance" in Chapter 9.

Three other points are worth mentioning about royalties. First, in respect of the rate for the percentage royalty, it can be said that there really is no industry standard for what this rate should be. The portion that the software company should receive of the licence fees payable to the distributor by end users of the product (it may range from less than 10% to more than 50%) depends on a whole host of factors, including the amount of support the software company will be expected to provide to the distributor, the degree of customization, if any, of the software product that must be undertaken by the distributor in order that the product can be used in another jurisdiction (e.g., if employee-payroll software must be changed to comply with local tax laws), and the general reputation and popularity (if any of each) enjoyed by the product (i.e., how hard a sell will it be!). Indeed, rather than try to pluck an "industry standard" out of the air, the royalty rate (and the minimum set dollar amount per licence) should be the result of careful consideration by the software company and the distributor as to their respective reasonable expectations for the product in the particular marketplace.

A further issue that has to be tackled when crafting the royalty mechanism is to determine when the relevant royalty becomes due and payable, and to a lesser extent, how frequently it should be remitted. On this latter issue, the software company will invariably want more frequent payment periods, perhaps even monthly, while the distributor will ask for longer intervals, perhaps yearly. A reasonable trade-off is to have the royalties remitted once every three or six months.

With respect to payment due dates, the question is whether the software company or the distributor should have to bear the cost associated with a customer of the distributor not paying the required licence fees in a timely manner. Put another way, assuming the distributor is obliged to remit royalties once every six months, on the royalty payment date should the distributor remit royalties only on licence fees actually received to that date, or on all the amounts required to be paid eventually under a licence agreement signed prior to the royalty remittance date, even if the customer has not paid some portion of its licence fees? One argument favouring the latter approach is that if the distributor has a problem in collecting payment from a customer, it should remain the distributor's problem because the distributor is generally best placed to limit or indeed eliminate the problem; in short, this approach institutes a discipline on the distributor to implement the software products quickly and to monitor closely payments due from customers. On the other hand, it may be that a distributor simply cannot pay the required royalty until it is paid by its own customers. Not surprisingly, this issue usually results in lively negotiation between software companies and distributors. Regardless of how this issue is resolved, however, from the perspective of cash flow during the term of the distribution agreement, it should be made clear that if there is a provision requiring the distributor to make a certain minimum amount of royalty payments by a certain date, this requires full payment to the software company of the stated minimum amount and the fact that the distributor may not have received its respective payments from its customers should be of no concern to the software company.

Whatever the precise royalty arrangements, the distribution agreement should require the distributor to keep accurate books and records regarding all aspects of the accrual and remittance of royalties. In addition, the software company will want the right to audit directly, or through a representative, these materials to satisfy itself that the proper royalties are being paid under the distribution arrangement. Some agreements also provide that if such a review reveals a shortfall in payments of more than, say, 5%, then the distributor will pay for the cost of the audit.

TERMINATION

Although it might seem to be a rather negative exercise, when entering into their relationship the software company and the distributor should each carefully consider on what grounds either may terminate the distribution agreement and what the consequences will be upon such a termination, or even on a simple expiry of the agreement. All too often not enough thought is given to these issues. This is unfortunate, because most distribution arrangements do come to an end, often much sooner than the parties initially anticipated, and if the steps to be taken by both parties upon the termination have not been planned for with some care, then all sorts of problems can result.

Turning first to the events that can trigger an early termination of the distribution agreement, the remedy of termination by the software company for failure of the distributor to pay certain minimum royalties has already been discussed above. Other events should also give either party the right to bring the relationship to an early end. Most typically, if one party commits a breach of a material term of the agreement, and if such failure is not cured within a certain period, say, 30 or 60 days, then the other party should have the option to terminate the agreement. It should also be noted that the software company will often insist that the cure period will not apply to certain defaults, such as may be contemplated in the context of the unauthorized disclosure of the software company's critical software assets (and particularly source code, if it is provided to the distributor).

If one party contests the other's assertion that an event calling for termination has occurred, then, assuming they cannot settle the matter amicably on their own and in the absence of an agreement to arbitrate disputes, the parties will in all likelihood be involved in a court proceeding. This may be quite unfortunate because a lawsuit can be an extremely expensive and slow process. It is also a public one. The documents filed by both sides, in which they typically hang out lots of each other's dirty laundry, are available for all to see. Both sides may wish to avoid such a public airing of their problems. If the software company and the distributor are based in different countries, which is often the case, they may also have a concern about the impartiality of the courts in each other's jurisdiction.

In an effort to avoid these perceived problems in the regular court system, many distribution agreements provide that any disputes — except perhaps for those relating to intellectual property and licensing matters where a party may want to retain its option of going to court in an expedited manner — will be resolved by arbitration. Arbitration is essentially a private court procedure, as detailed in Chapter 11 (under "Arbitration") in the context of licence agreements between software companies and their customers. All the advantages of arbitration noted there apply in the relationship between a software company and a distributor. Suppose for instance that the two parties disagree as to the amount of royalties properly due under their agreement for a certain period. Through arbitration a financial expert, perhaps a chartered accountant with experience in the software business, can be called upon to review the facts quickly and make a decision before the relatively minor disagreement festers and grows into a major problem. This can all be done privately, in an effort to reduce the likelihood of the distributor's customers or the software company's competitors ever getting wind of the dispute.

In addition to addressing the substantive and procedural aspects of termination, the distribution agreement should also set out clearly and in some detail what is to happen upon a termination or expiry of the distribution relationship. Of course, the distributor should have to cease to promote, advertise, license, or otherwise market the software company's product (or products). By contrast, however, the distributor will want the licences that it granted to end users for those products to continue for at least the terms set out in the licences (which may be perpetual-term licences), notwithstanding the cessation of the marketing rights of the distributor. This raises a further important issue, namely, who will provide on-going support to these customers after the termination of the distribution agreement? If the software company was providing support prior to the termination, then it would simply continue to do so afterwards. If, on the other hand, the distributor was responsible for support, then it may be appropriate for the distributor to continue to provide these services even after it ceases to have marketing rights; in short, it can continue to service the customer base it built up prior to the termination, but it cannot expand this customer base afterwards.

If the distributor has the right to provide continuing support to the customers it has at the time its marketing rights come to an end, it will likely need to have ongoing access to certain materials of the software company, likely even the source code for the product, to provide this support. For this reason, much of the distribution agreement, especially those provisions dealing with the protection and nondisclosure of the software company's intellectual property assets, will also have to continue after the termination of the distributor's marketing rights. While this can all be provided for in the distribution agreement, the software company should retain the right to deny this continuing support option to the distributor if in fact the relationship is being terminated for a violation of any of the proprietary rights protection provisions in the distribution agreement. In such a case the likely outcome will be that the software company assumes the support obligations of the distributor, which possibility in turn highlights the importance of requiring the software company to approve the form of such agreements before they are signed by the distributor's customers, as noted above.

INTERNATIONAL CONSIDERATIONS

It has already been mentioned that a major rationale for using a distributor in a foreign country is so that a software company's product can be brought to the market quickly in such country. And while the benefits of using foreign distributors can be great, the pitfalls can be equally significant. This chapter has already discussed several aspects of international distribution arrangements. A few additional ones, however, are also worth noting because Canadian software companies are so active in foreign markets.

It was noted above that a software company must review the local law of each prospective country it desires to do business in to ensure that adequate substantive and procedural intellectual property protection is available for the software company's products. In a similar vein, the software company must also ascertain, by retaining reputable local legal counsel to give advice on these matters, whether the distribution agreement is binding upon the distributor. This would entail reviewing, among other things, whether the termination provisions in the contract would be enforceable as they are written. For example, the software company will want to know whether the local law of the foreign country contains any rules that, say, require the software company to pay a certain amount of money to a distributor whose agreement is terminated, regardless of how the termination occurred, or whose agreement merely expires. The company will also want to know whether the warranty disclaimer and limitation-of-liability provisions in its distribution agreement (and in its standard license agreement, for that matter) are enforceable in the foreign jurisdiction.

As well, the local competition law, if any, will have to be checked to ensure that all of the particular marketing arrangements between the software company and the distributor, such as that the distributor cannot carry competing products during the term of the agreement, are legal and binding. In this regard it is important to note that while the competition laws of most OECD countries who have such laws share many principles and objectives, there are many differences and nuances between them as well. In effect, a software company cannot assume that just because a certain business practice is permitted in Canada, it is treated in the same way everywhere else.

Some countries have foreign exchange rules that may hamper, or in some cases even block altogether, the payment of a licence fee and/or other revenues from the distributor in the foreign jurisdiction to the Canadian software company. Often these countries with exchange controls (and others, as well) will also have a requirement that the distribution agreement must be approved by a certain governmental authority, ostensibly to ensure that its terms and conditions are not unfavourable to the distributor. If such approval is required, the software company will want a clear provision in the distribution agreement to the effect that the agreement itself is conditional, and no rights are granted thereunder, until (and only if) the requisite government approval is granted. Obviously a Canadian software company will want to know how these foreign exchange and government approval processes work before it appoints a distributor for the relevant territory; indeed, if the rules are too onerous the software company may decline appointing a distributor for the particular country altogether.

REPRESENTATION AGREEMENTS

As noted at the beginning of this chapter, a software company that does not have the financial or human resources to properly market its products directly (through a branch office or a subsidiary) in a certain territory, may nonetheless make the decision not to appoint a distributor for the territory for fear of losing control over numerous aspects of the marketing and implementation of the products. Such a software company might consider, as a compromise solution, appointing a "representative" in the territory, whose duties would, in several important respects, be quite different from that of a distributor.

Generally speaking, a representative would merely promote, on behalf of the software company, the product in the relevant territory and perhaps offer demonstrations of it if it is a relatively simple-to-operate product. If a prospective customer, however, were interested in obtaining a licence for the product, the representative would merely pass along the prospect to the software company. The software company would deal directly with the prospect on matters such as pricing and other business terms, and the prospect, if it acquired a licence, would sign the relevant agreement directly with the software company. Support and other services would flow directly from the software company to the end-user customer.

A major attraction of a representative arrangement in jurisdictions, like Canada, that prohibit a software company from setting the resale prices of its distributors, is that the software company has complete control over the pricing of its products to end users. The representative's only connection to pricing is that the representative receives a commission in respect of each software product licensed to an end user for which the representative provided marketing and other representation services. Otherwise, the software company keeps a tight rein on all the financial aspects of the licensing and support of its products.

In other respects many of the same issues discussed above in the context of the distributor apply equally to a representative. For example, it must be decided whether the representative will enjoy an exclusive status, or whether the software company will have the right to appoint other representatives (or distributors). The territory and obligations of the representative also should be defined with precision as noted above. And the software company should review local laws effective wherever the representative will be resident to ensure that no unusual provisions exist granting significant rights to the representative upon termination or expiry of the agreement.

DISTRIBUTING MULTIMEDIA PRODUCTS

Virtually all of the issues discussed earlier in this chapter apply to the distribution of multimedia products. But a number of additional issues need to be addressed in a distribution agreement for multimedia products that are not as germane for a more traditional software product. Several of these are discussed below.

- *Credits* The developer of the multimedia title may wish to ensure that it, and its creative personnel, are given specific credit in the material acompanying the CD-ROM or other media containing the title. This could include credits provided in the early screens of the product itself. Given the more "artistic" nature of many multimedia products, compared to their traditional software counterparts, issues like credits (and modifications, discussed below) tend to be much more contentious for multimedia title developers than mainline software developers.

- *Modifications.* The multimedia title developer may be very hesitant to permit the distributor to make any changes to the product, for creative and aesthetic reasons. On the other hand, the distributor, or publisher, may need the flexibility to alter the multimedia product for a local market. Often a sensible compromise is to permit the distributor to modify the title, but only after the first right to make the changes has been offered to, but refused by, the title developer.

- *Free copies.* The distributor or publisher is often the manufacturer of the commercial copies of the CD-ROMs, and their related jewel cases, for the multimedia titles. So it is not surprising that the title developer will wish to receive a good number of free copies of the product once it is published.

- *On-line rights.* It is important in a multimedia product deal to scope out with some precision what electronic or other rights are being given to the distributor. The core right would be to distribute the product in CD-ROM form. But what about rights to distribute the title over the INTERNET or other networks or through on-line service providers? Some title developers wish to retain these rights, at least for the time being, because it is not yet clear how products will be exploited on the INTERNET, and consequently, how to structure the attendant royalty mechanisms. Title developers are well advised to grant any such rights only for short terms, to permit subsequent revision if the technology or economics changes — and they invariably will.

- *Merchandising.* In a similar vein, the title developer has to determine if the particular multimedia product lends itself to one or more merchandising opportunities, which can include anything from clothes to boardgames. If so, these rights likely should be retained by the developer, who will then be in a position to grant them to someone that may be better placed than the distributor to exploit these aspects of the product. Equally, book, movie and similar rights are often carved out from the CD-ROM distribution deal.

- *Pooling.* Where the title developer is preparing two or more titles, perhaps in the same series, all of which will be distributed by the same publisher, and all of which will have advance royalties paid on them, the developer should resist "pooling" (or as it's sometimes called, "cross-collaterization"), the accounting practice applied by many distributors whereby royalties earned on any title are applied against all advances previously paid to the developer in respect of all of its titles, thereby reducing the distributor's risk if one or two titles sell very poorly. Title developers, of course, prefer not to "pool" so that they can begin to see money flow from each title much sooner after the title has recouped its own distribution advance.

The material presented in this chapter has given an overview of the main points to consider in distribution agreements. These are important contracts, and parties contemplating entering into them must obtain competent legal advice so that all the relevant issues can be identified and dealt with appropriately.

NOTES

Chapter 1

page 4   "This type of corporation ... can be established in Canada under federal law ..." *Canada Business Corporations Act*, R.S.C. 1985, c. C-44, as amended.

page 5   "Under Ontario's *Business Corporations Act* ..."*Business Corporations Act* (Ontario), R.S.O. 1990, c. B.16, as amended.

page 5   "Under the federal *Income Tax Act* ..." *Income Tax Act*, R.S.C. 1985, c. 1 (5th Supp.), as amended.

page 8   "Once a corporation is incorporated, it must put its full corporate name ..." *Business Names Act*, R.S.O. 1990, c. B.17, as amended.

page 15   "... the relevant provincial law governing partnerships ..."In Ontario, the *Partnerships Act*, R.S.O. 1990, c. P.5.

page 17   "... the *Copyright Act* ..." *Copyright Act*, R.S.C. 1985, c. C-42, as amended.

page 17   "... provincial personal property security registry system." In Ontario, the *Personal Property Security Act*, R.S.O. 1990, c. P.10, as amended.

Chapter 2

page 37   "... regulations under the *Income Tax Act* ..." *Income Tax Act*, R.S.C. 1985, c. 1 (5th Supp.), as amended.

page 39   "The income tax regulations define 'experimental development' ..." Part XXIX of the Regulations to the *Income Tax Act*, Income Tax Regulations, C.R.C. 945, as amended.

Chapter 3

page 59   The substance of Chapter 3, Raising Money for Growing Software Companies, by Linda Willis, appeared in an earlier version in *Business Basics for Software Developers* (Software Ontario, 1989). It is used here with the kind permission of Software Ontario.

page 79   "The Ontario Small Business Development Corporation (SBDC) program ..." *The Small Business Development Corporations Act*, R.S.O. 1990, c. S.12, as amended.

page 80   *The Small Business Loans Act* (SBLA) is a federal government initiative ..." *The Small Business Loans Act*, R.S.C. 1985, c. S-11, as amended.

Chapter 4

page 97   "This is so because the *Copyright Act* ..." *Copyright Act*, R.S.C. 1985, c. C-42, as amended.

page 98   "Another danger area worth noting briefly about strategic partnerships relates to the *Competition Act* ..." *Competition Act*, R.S. 1985, c. C-34, as amended.

page 99   *Edward H. Hanis* v. *The University of Western Ontario et al*, March 17, 1995 (Ont. Gen. Div.) (unreported).

Chapter 5

page 105   "Recently, one of the judges of the Supreme Court of Canada ..." *International Corona Resources Ltd.* v. *Lac Minerals Ltd.* (1989), 44 B.L.R. 1 (S.C.C.).

page 110   "Copyright law is governed by the *Copyright Act.* ..." *Copyright Act*, R.S.C. 1985, c. C-42.

page 111   "... a decision of the Federal Court of Canada in the *Apple* case ..." *Apple Computer Inc.* v. *Mackintosh Computers Inc.* (1986), 28 D.L.R. (4th) 178 (Fed. T.D.); varied (1987), 44 D.L.R. (4th) 74 (Fed. C.A.); affirmed, 30 C.P.R. (3d) 257 (S.C.C.).

page 112   "However, the Federal Court of Canada in two cases ..." *IBM Corp.* v. *Ordinateurs Spirales Inc.* (1984), 2 C.I.P.R. 56 (Fed. T.D.) and *Apple Computer Inc.* v. *Mackintosh Computers*, noted above.

page 113   "... a controversial decision of the United States Supreme Court ..." *Feist Publications Inc.* v. *Rural Telephone Services Co.*, 111 S. Ct. 1282.

page 114   "A leading case in this area in the United States ..." *Computer Associates International Inc.* v. *Altai Inc.*, 23 U.S.P.Q. (2d) 1241 (2nd Cir. 1992).

page 114   "In two of the Canadian cases ..." *Matrox Electronic Systems Ltd.* v. *Gaudreau*, [1993] R.J.Q. 2449 (C.S.); *Delrina Corp.* v. *Triolet Systems Inc.* (1993), 47 C.P.R. (3d) 1 (Ont. Gen. Div.).

page 114   "In a third case, a British Columbia court ..." *Prism Hospital Software Inc.* v. *Hospital Medical Records Institute* (1994), 57 C.P.R. (3d) 129 (B.C.S.C.).

page 114   "This test was recently summarized by an American appellate court ..." *Gates Rubber Co.* v. *Bando American Inc.*, 28 U.S.P.Q. 2d 1503 (10th Cir. 1993).

page 115   "Lotus Development Corporation sued ..." *Lotus Development Corporation* v. *Paperback Software International et al*, 15 U.S.P.Q. 2d 1577, (D. Mass. 1990); *Lotus Development Corporation* v. *Mosaic Software, Inc.* (Civ. No. 87-74-K, D. Mass.); *Apple Computer, Inc.* v. *Microsoft Corporation*, 709 F. Supp. 925 (N.D.Cal.1989), *Apple Computer, Inc.* v. *Microsoft Corporation*, Vol. 9, No. 6. Comp. Law. Rep. 1043, motion to reconsider dismissed Oct. 9, 1989, (N.D.Cal.1989); *Xerox Corporation* v. *Apple Computer, Inc.*, C.I.L.R. 11155, (N.D.Cal.1990); *Lotus Development Corporation* v. *Borland International Inc.* (Civ. No. 90-11662-k, D. Mass.).

page 116   "... a decision of an appellate court in *Lotus* v. *Borland* ..." *Lotus Development Corporation* v. *Borland International Inc.*, 34 U.S.P.Q. (2d) 1014 (1st Cir. 1995).

page 118   "Several American courts have, ..." *Sega Enterprises Ltd.* v. *Accolade Inc.*, 24 U.S.P.Q. 2d 1561 (9th Cir. 1992); *Atari Games Corp.* and *Tengen Inc.* v. *Nintendo of America Inc.*, 24 U.S.P.Q. 2d 1015 (Fed. Cir. 1992).

page 119   "For instance, in the *Solartronix* case ..." *Systèmes Informatises Solartronix C. Gegep de Jonquire* (1988), 22 C.I.P.R. 101 (Que. S.C.).

page 119   "In the United States *NEC* case ..." *NEC* v. *Intel Corp.*, 10 U.S.P.Q. (2d) 1177 (N.D. Cal. 1989).

page 119   "The June, 1988, amendments to the *Copyright Act* specifically exempted the following from infringement of copyright ..." *Copyright Act*, paragraph 27(2)(l).

page 120   "... the 1988 amendments to the *Copyright Act* created the following exemption from infringement ..." *Copyright Act*, paragraph 27(2)(m).

page 122   "... Canada's *Industrial Design Act*." *Industrial Design Act*, R.S.C. 1985, c. I-19.

page 123   "... under Canada's *Trade-Marks Act* ..." *Trade-Marks Act*, R.S.C. 1985, T-13, Section 2.

page 124   "The *Patent Act* ..." *Patent Act*, R.S.C. 1985, c. P-4, as amended.

page 126   "... the *Schlumberger* case." *Schlumberger Can. Ltd.* v. *Commr. of Patents* (1981), 56 C.P.R. (2d) 204 (Fed. C.A.).

page 127   "... on June 28, 1990, royal assent was given to the *Integrated Circuit Topography Act* ..." *Integrated Circuit Topography Act*, S.C. 1990, c. C.37.

page 129   "... the *Anton Piller* case ..." *Anton Piller K.G.* v. *Manufacturing Processes Ltd.*, [1976] 1 All E.R. 779 (C.A.).

page 129   "The Federal Court of Canada has set out ..." *Turbo Resources Limited* v. *Petro-Canada Inc.* (1989), 91 N.R. 341 (F.C.A.).

page 130   "The subjects discussed in this chapter have been comprehensively treated in other works. ..." See Sookman, B, *Sookman Computer Law* (Carswell 1989); Sherman, C., *Computer Software Protection Law* (The Bureau of National Affairs, Inc., 1989, 1990); Bender, D., *Computer Law: Software Protection* (Matthew Bender, 1991).

Chapter 6

page 132   "... the federal *Criminal Code.* ..." *Criminal Code*, R.S.C. 1985, c. C-46.

page 132   "... the *McLaughlin* case, ..." *R. v. McLaughlin*, (1980) 113 Dominion Law Reports (3d) 386.

page 133   "... the *Turner* decision." *R. v. Turner*, (1984) Canadian Criminal Cases (3d) 430.

page 134   "... several years ago *Time* magazine devoted a cover story to the issue." *Time*, September 28, 1988.

page 135   "... a recent *Globe & Mail* story ..." "Threatening Call Rattles TSE" *The Globe & Mail*, August 21, 1992.

page 136   "... the *Stewart* case ..." *R. v. Stewart*, [1988] 1 Supreme Court Reports 963.

page 136   "Commentators within the legal and high-technology communities have criticized the *Stewart* decision ..." See, for instance, Potter, "Theft of a Secret: The Information Age Overtakes the Supreme Court of Canada — R. v. Stewart," (1988) 3 *Review of International Business Law* 115.

page 137   "... the *Leahy* case ..." *R. v. Leahy*, (1988) 21 C.P.R. (3d)

page 138   "... in a recent Canadian criminal case ..." *R. v. Pecciarich* (1995), 22 O.R. (3d) 748; [1995] O.J. No. 2238, July 20, 1995.

Chapter 7

page 143   "In a recent case ..." *Vermont Microsystems, Inc. v. Autodesk, Inc.* and *Otto G. Berkes*, 5 CCH Computer Cases ¶47,210 (1994), (Dist. Vermont).

page 148   "The following case ..." *Dickerman Associates, Inc. v. Tiverton Bottled Gas Co.*, CILR 12, January 1987.

page 151   "... there is federal legislation and similar laws in Ontario, Quebec, and the other provinces ..." *Access to Information Act (Canada)*, R.S.C. 1985, c. A-1, as amended; *Freedom of Information and Protection of Privacy Act*, 1987 (Ontario), S.O. 1987, c. 25.

Chapter 9

page 169   "... the *Competition Act." Competition Act*, R.S. 1985, c. C-34, as amended.

page 174   "... several business forms suppliers ..." *The Queen* v. *R. L. Crain et al*, (1988) 2.2 C.P.R. (2d) 462.

page 178   "... in one case a supplier permitted retailers to fix their own resale prices ..." *Regina* v. *A & M Records of Canada Ltd.*, (1980) 51 C.P.R. (2d) 225.

page 179   "In this particular case, a computer products manufacturer ..." *R.* v. *Epson (Canada) Ltd.*, (1987) 19 C.P.R. (3d) 195.

page 179   "... (which amount was reduced to $100,000 on appeal) ..." *R.* v. *Epson (Canada) Ltd.*, Ontario Court of Appeal, June 15, 1990.

page 183   "... merger case involving the computerized reservation system of Air Canada, Canadian Airlines, and American Airlines." *The Director of Investigation and Research* v. *Air Canada et al*, (1989) 44 B.L.R. 154.

Chapter 10

page 190   "... the *Export and Import Permits Act ..." Export and Import Permits Act*, R.S. 1985, c. E-19, as amended.

page 190   "... Export Control List (ECL) which is set out in a regulation ..." Export Control List. SOR/89-202, as amended.

page 191   "... Area Control List (ACL), which is set out in a regulation ..." Area Control List. SOR/81-543, as amended.

page 191   "Under authority of the *United Nations Act ..." United Nations Act*, R.S.C. 1985, c. U-2.

page 196   "... one of the CITT's first cases took only a few days to settle." *Tektronics Canada Inc.*, File No. B89PRF66W9-021-0003.

page 196   "In one case the lowest bidder ..." *Cardinal Industrial Electronics Ltd.*, File No. D89PRF6608-021-0005.

Chapter 11

page 204   "... an American judge's court decision some 25 years ago ..." *Honeywell Inc.* v. *Lithonia Lighting Inc.*, 317 F. Supp 406 (N.D. Ga. 1970).

page 205   "In one American case ..." *United States* v. *Commodore Business Machines Inc.*, (1990) 2 CCH Computer Case ¶46,281.

page 223   "... in a case in Alberta ..." *North American System Shops Ltd.* v. *King*, (1989) 68 Alta. L.R. (2d) 145 (Alta. Q.B.).

page 223   "In a recent American appellate court decision ..." *PROCD* v. *Zeidenberg*, June 20, 1996 (7th Cir.).

INDEX